Mulder, It's Me

GILLIAN
ANDERSON

Mulder, It's Me

GILLIAN ANDERSON

AN X-HAUSTIVE X-POSÉ OF THE WOMAN WHO IS SPECIAL AGENT DANA SCULLY

GIL ADAMSON
AND
DAWN CONNOLLY

ECW PRESS

Materials reprinted from previously published sources are
reproduced with the permission of the copyright owners:
Jon Casimir, Cynthia Schmidt, CBC Radio,
Autumn Tysko, Mary Ann Wilson.

Photographs are reproduced with the permission of Cindy Stable
(for the Convention photos), T. Charles Erickson (for the off-Broadway
photos), Shooting Star (for the episode guide photos, and the
interview shots), Famous Pictures for the photos at the
Screen Actor's Guild and the première of *Children at Play*
(both photos by Hubert Boesl) and at the Golden Globe
Awards (photo by Rob Howard), and Ponopresse (for the rest
of the colour photos by Armando Gallo, Stuart Davis, Bruce
Malone, and Dave Hogan, cover photo, and back cover photo).

CANADIAN CATALOGUING IN PUBLICATION DATA

Adamson, Gillian
Mulder, It's Me : an x-haustive x-pose of the
woman who is special agent Dana Scully

ISBN 1-55022-316-X

1. Anderson, Gillian. 2. Television actors and
actresses — United States — Biography.
3. X-files (Television program).
I. Connolly, Dawn   II. Title.

PN1992.4.A52A32 1997   791.45'028'092   C97-931338-4

Printed by Kromar Printing, Winnipeg, Manitoba.

Distributed in Canada by General Distribution Services,
30 Lesmill Road, Don Mills, Ontario M3B 2T6.

Distributed in the United States by Login Publishers Consortium,
1436 West Randolph Street, Chicago, Illinois, U.S.A. 60607.

Published by ECW PRESS,
2120 Queen Street East, Suite 200,
Toronto, Ontario M4E 1E2.

http://www.ecw.ca/press

PRINTED AND BOUND IN CANADA

TABLE OF CONTENTS

FOREWORD

This book is an attempt to gather some of the many interviews and articles written about Gillian Anderson and put them into an order and context which will shed light on some of the details of her upbringing, her early work, and her recent successes. All quotes are drawn from radio, television, and print sources as listed in the Sources. We hope that fans of Dana Scully and the actress who portrays her will find some fun between these pages and we hope that even the most ardent fans may find a few things they haven't seen before.

Pictures, interviews, and articles on *The X-Files* and on Anderson herself dominate television and fans' sites on the Internet. But, as not all fans of the show have access to the World Wide Web, we hope that this book will give fans a taste of the wealth of information available online and in print. For those fans who are beginning their online searches we have included a section of bookmarks: a list of some of the best places to get you started.

Finally we offer an episode guide to *The X-Files*, complete to the end of season four.

GILLIAN

ANDERSON

BIOGRAPHY

INTRODUCTION

On Sunday, January 19, 1997 in Los Angeles, California, the best and the brightest of Hollywood's film and television industry gathered to be honored at the 54th Annual Golden Globe Awards, held by the Hollywood Foreign Press Association. Gillian Anderson's private life had just been thrown into the media spotlight hours before, when a British tabloid broke the news of her separation from her husband of three years, Clyde Klotz. Wearing a pale sequined gown that emphasized her fragile beauty, she walked the gauntlet of paparazzi and reporters, down the red carpet, and into the Beverly Hilton Hotel. Her escort this night was her costar David Duchovny. The pair walked hand in hand in a show of mutual support that reflected their on-screen personas.

Inside, it wasn't long before the nominees for best actress in a dramatic television program were being read: "And the Golden Globe goes to . . . Gillian Anderson, for *The X-Files*."

As Anderson rose, Duchovny stood up, applauding. She leaned across and kissed him, and then made her way through the crowd of her peers to the podium:

"I want to thank my daughter, Piper. I want to thank the writers John Shiban, Frank Spotnitz, Vince Gilligan, Howard Gordon, the directors Rob Bowman, Kim Manners, Bob Goodwin: executive producer.

"Most of all I would like to thank the mother of all creators, Chris Carter, for having the foresight and sensibility to create, to introduce into our lives a character: a woman who is strong, intelligent, equal opportunity, employed. And she has had a profound impact on women, young and not so young, around the world because of those positive characteristics, and I thank you for that. And many other people do too, I'm sure. Thank you for allowing me to have the opportunity to spend this time with her and for being a component of this amazing, magical, historical odyssey that you have created. Thank you."

With these words Gillian Anderson summed up the odyssey of her own life's journey: a journey which had taken her in four short years from life as a struggling actor waiting on tables, to a television star of international stature; a journey which had taken her from an angry teen, dressed in punk regalia, to a world-class beauty, known across the globe and across the Internet. But it was with these words that she put into perspective the real contribution her work has made in bringing to life the character of Dana Scully, a modern role model of integrity and intelligence.

ONE

JUST GROWING UP

Gillian Leigh Anderson's life began on August 9, 1968 in St. Mary's Hospital, Cook County, Chicago. She was born to Rosemary and Edward Anderson, the first child in a family that would eventually grow to five.

For now, though, she was an only child and enjoyed the complete love and attention of her parents. The trio's early years would be somewhat nomadic. At the age of six months she was living with her family at her grandfather's home in Puerto Rico (grand-dad was employed by the Air Force). Her parents saved as much money as they could and in 1970 the family packed their bags again and moved to London, England, so that Gillian's father could continue his education.

Edward wanted to pursue a career in film production and was accepted into the London Film School. Life is never easy with a new baby. Trying to make ends meet as a student with a new family didn't make things easier and Gillian's dad has said of the decision, "We had hardly any money and they were quite tough times for the family." But they stuck it out and, in 1972, Edward graduated from the two-year course and began the search for work in the competitive job market of the British film industry.

The family moved several times, living in Clapton Common, Tivoli Rd, Harringay. They settled in Crouch End in north London for a time, where, at the age of five, Gillian began her schooling in Coleridge Junior School. By this time Gillian had spent most of her life in London but she had picked up her parents' American accent and she stood out from her classmates every time she opened her mouth to speak. Her classmates teased and taunted her and she was bullied in the schoolyard. But she quickly learned how to fight back in the yard and how to blend in in the classroom. She practised the north London accent until it became her own.

Later Gillian described herself as "independent and bossy," but it didn't stop her from being beaten up by the friends of a boy she'd stood up, or getting into a fight with a boy who'd taken her out on a date.

In school she showed a decided interest in science, and biology in particular. Digging up earth worms in the backyard, she performed her first "autopsies." "I loved to cut them up," she recalls. "All in the name of science, of course." She was a confident child, by all accounts, earning good grades and with a steady circle of "mates."

"I would have to say my childhood years were fairly normal. I knew my father was doing the type of work that not many people were doing. My parents were always fairly liberal so I guess I was given a certain degree of freedom that a lot of children did not have. And I guess you could say I was a bit of a tomboy, getting into things that the boys would do."

Her love of science would follow her into high school, later, in the States, and she thought for a time she would find her career there. "I was interested in marine biology, geology — all those 'ologies."

But for now, as a young girl, she got into the usual mischief: kissing her first boy, Adam, and learning how to swear. "I was very into swearing as a child. I remember asking my mom what fuck meant, what fucking was, and I can't remember on my life what her response was. I remember hearing it in the playground when I was eight, off a kid who was 12. He fancied me and I fancied him but I was scared to death because his affection was like grown-up affection — he may have even done the fuck word. And I had no idea what it meant."

Even now, as an adult, Anderson's favorite swear word is a British expression. "Fuck me. It's really satisfying saying it. *Fuck me*! It's my favorite swear word. I say it a lot, really quickly, like 'fuckme!' " she told a reporter, laughing.

In 1979, Gillian was a happy 11-year-old with a settled home life, lots of friends, and the memories of being an outsider well behind her. But by 1979 the British economy was less than booming and Edward and Rosemary decided to move back to the United States. "My husband just couldn't get work in the film business in London," Rosemary later recalled. "The market was depressed at the time." Edward found a job in Grand Rapids, Michigan, and the family packed up for the last time and headed west across the Atlantic. Her father secured work as a cameraman, working mainly in the areas of industrial training films and commercials and later became involved in post-production. He currently has his own tape post-production company. Rosemary works as a computer programmer.

In Grand Rapids, Gillian was enrolled at Fountain Elementary School to complete her primary education. To her horror she found herself the outsider again. Her British accent now alienated her from the American children. So the process of "fitting in" began once more. "I may well have picked up a vibe and taken it back to America because I was very British, with a very heavy accent. Coming from London to a small town there was something exotic about me in an unworthy way. I think I relied on that to give me self-esteem in a new environment."

She grew adept at switching between accents to suit the occasion and the company. Her mother recalls, "Her classmates all thought she talked funny because she didn't have an American accent. Gillian had to learn to speak like an American for the first time in her life, just to fit in. She did extremely well in school considering the upheaval. The teachers said that she was two years more advanced than her classmates. She worked very hard to fit in. Another problem was spelling. American English has dozens of words that are spelt slightly differently from how they are in England and she had to learn to make that adjustment."

In fact it was Gillian's facility for accents that later made her a favorite with drama teachers casting school plays in which an English accent was required.

"In the beginning her English accent came in handy. She got her start partly because she learned to turn it on and off at will," Rosemary remembers.

Although Gillian did make the adjustment to this new life, she was less than happy. She had left exciting London behind and by contrast Grand Rapids hardly measured up. Her mother continues, "The contrast was just incredible. Grand Rapids is a sleepy prairie town and the kids were totally out of it as far as Gillian was concerned. Plus she missed all the friends she had grown up with in London."

Rosemary says Gillian "hid her unhappiness" and never complained, but her frustration was evident in other ways. Practical jokes and classroom stunts brought her to the attention of more than her fellow pupils and the teachers. "I was in the principal's office every other day [for] stealing papers, throwing paper airplanes." She even planted pigs' eyes in the desk drawer of a teacher. She remembers being "withdrawn" and "unpopular" at school. "I was always off in my own little world or being sent to the principal's office for talking back."

As an adult she now observes, "There is only one thing that I regret and it is something that I can make up for eventually when I have the time. I didn't pay as much attention in school as I would have liked to. I was a daydreamer, and there is a lot of history and geography and science I missed out on because I was in my head. And I regret that."

The Andersons' ties to England had not been completely severed. They kept a flat, or apartment, in Harringay for holidays which they retain to this day. And on alternate summer breaks Gillian was allowed to travel back and visit friends. What she saw on the north London streets were the first signs of the punk movement: kids in army gear, mohawk haircuts in purple and blue — an external, angry expression of alienated youth.

In the British punks, Gillian saw a reflection of her own inner desire for rebellion. And she returned home to Grand Rapids with the first of her outward symbols of these feelings. "One summer when I was 12 or 13 I went back [to London] and was suddenly taken by the punks." She returned with a nose-ring on the left side of her nose. "I fainted when it was inserted. My father was furious about it," she said. "I would walk sideways around my dad so he wouldn't see it." She eventually stopped wearing it when the fashion spread to the U.S. "I finally took it out because people in Grand Rapids were starting to get nose rings and I decided it was passé. So I've got the tweezers up my nose and it won't come out because it's grown into the side of my nose. It was horrible! I remember standing in front of the mirror just about ready to puke trying to get at this thing."

Body piercing and even tattoos still figure in Anderson's life. A recent photograph in *Us* magazine shows her with a belly-button ring, a gift from a friend. In her second interview for the U.K. magazine FHM she spoke of her first tattoo. "Well, I got it in a very innocent place. On my inner right ankle. I got it done in Tahiti, the birthplace of tattooing. It's like a tribal design — maybe two inches long and an inch wide. Part of me didn't want to have it done because tattoos are so common now — which is why I got rid of my nose-ring — but there's this real bonding thing with people who have tattoos." The design features two Polynesian-style tortoises. "I wanted something that represented peace of mind."

Big changes were on the way for the entire family. Shortly after the return to the States, her brother Aaron was born and about a year later Gillian's sister Zoe completed the family. Gillian went from being an only child to being a young teen with parents whose attention was split between Gillian and a new baby. Puberty, with all its natural stages of rebellion, combined with her sense of alienation from family and the life she had left behind in London. She embraced the punk dress and punk lifestyle and began a period of intense rebellion. "There was a whole summer . . . when I wore sweaters and jeans and an olive-drab Army jacket, and it was almost as if I'd trained my body not to sweat," she recalls. "We'd walk down the street and give the finger to [whoever stared at] us. We'd go hear bands and smash against each other and jump off the stage. It was cool to get hurt. I needed to express my anger, because I had a lot of it — and still do. I was never very good at expressing other emotions. I did everything I could not to feel pain."

The "outlandish" garb achieved the desired results: "It was mostly appearances. We would make fun of anyone who stared. If we knew that they were going to walk around to take a better look at our mohawks, we'd give them the finger or something. It was just an attitude. And it made us in some way feel better than everybody else." The violence often associated with the punk movement was never the point of the exercise. "I never took it to the extreme that I was a huge vandal or beat up on people. But the inside of that went as deep as it could go."

When she was 13 Anderson lost her virginity to "a punk guy. It was awkward, stupid, unadulterated crap. I think you'll find that most people's first times are less than mind-blowing." And when she was 14 she hooked up with a 24-year-old penniless punk musician. She lied to her parents about his age. "I used to give him cans of food from our house and buy him Big Gulps and cigarettes." They used to sleep rough "in warehouses with no heating and on friends' apartment floors. I guess I felt comfortable in that relationship because I felt dirty and grungy and angry. I used to not like myself. I spent time overweight, underweight, wearing black, hiding." She says now she identified with Jane Horrocks' character in *Life is Sweet* (a film about a family with twin daughters, one of whom is deeply self-critical), and she mentions "hurting myself in different ways," adding, "I was angry and it was my way of keeping people at a distance."

Of course the punk scene in Grand Rapids was miniscule compared to a city like London, and Gillian and her boyfriend became known as the "couple" in the town's alternative scene. The punk movement spread to nearby Kalamazoo and Gillian would go there to hear the underground bands play, bands with such deliberately provocative names as Butthole Surfers and Circle Jerks. Other favorites included the Dead Kennedys, Lords of the New Church, PiL, and the Velvet Underground.

Gillian was 16 when her brother Aaron, aged 3, was diagnosed with a medical condition called neurofibromatosis (NF). "It's been a big part of my parents' and my life for 12 years. It's been a major part of my growing up and Aaron's growing up because of the potential devastation of the disease." NF is a neurological disease that can cause tumors to grow on the body, inside and out.

Rosemary eventually helped to found an NF clinic in Michigan which offered support for patients and their families. In her adult years Gillian directs much of her energy and celebrity towards fund-raising for medical research on NF. In May 1996, Gillian flew to Washington, D.C. with her mother to make a speech requesting research funding from Congress on behalf of Neurofibromatosis Inc. She says now that "Aaron has been very, very lucky so far. Usually during puberty the disease grows rapidly, but he hasn't had that problem yet. Aaron has regular check-ups, and so far it's been relatively uneventful for him. Aaron is incredibly intelligent and athletic and beautiful. His illness has certainly affected us in a strong way and brought us much closer together as a family."

Rosemary sums up Gillian's teen years by saying, "her anger over the move and frustration with all the changes were partly responsible for her turbulent years. She definitely had a chip on her shoulder when we brought her back to America. It was the last thing she wanted to do. But a lot of it was just a part of growing up." But Gillian herself says, "moving into such a small town after growing up in London gave me a feeling of powerlessness, and it was a rebellious time that I went through and needed to go through. I think back now and feel it was a statement to myself. It was a feeling of power, saying something instead of nothing, that was necessary for me to go through . . . in my life."

This rebellious feeling and this need for self-expression is not something Anderson is willing to characterize as a "stage." According to Anderson, "It was a part of me already and it *continues* to be a part of me. When I was at college, and when I moved to New York, I still had unbrushed straggly hair down to my bum, wore combat boots and black thrift clothes. I always had that feeling of not fitting in and not caring what anyone else thought of me. It's funny because the anger or angst that propels it is real and comes from a place deep down inside. To really feel OK you have to reach down there and see it for what it really is. There's not much of that in the world of punk . . . in terms of understanding the self or bettering yourself."

The media have made much of this colorful period in Anderson's life. Nearly every interviewer gets around to the topic of her "punk days." "Some people were surprised by the things I've said recently. Many of the things have been blown way out of proportion. I honestly have *nothing* left to reveal. I try to be open and talkative about things in interviews. Everything, like my punk phase, seems to me to be old news now." Now, when asked about being a punker she replies, "Boring," and when asked about her childhood, she responds, "It was just growing up."

TWO

CITY HIGH SCHOOL, GRAND RAPIDS, MICHIGAN: CLASS OF '86

Anderson continued on in high school despite her rebellions, despite her choice of boyfriend and despite her punk lifestyle. "I was voted class clown, and most likely to be arrested."

When she was 16 she started auditioning for community plays, having begun to enjoy her small parts in the high school productions. There was a revolution about to begin in her life. "In 11th grade I decided to audition for a community theater play and I got the part, and then I felt extremely happy, like I had found my place." Her grades went up and she was voted most improved student.

Writers have asked Anderson if the acting bug "saved" her from her punk lifestyle. Gillian responds, "Well I guess, in a way, it did save me from it — not that I needed to be saved. But it changed my focus, I think, for some reason. Well, for whatever reason, when I started acting, I suddenly had found something that I was intrinsically excited about and enthusiastic about, so it made me want to learn and want to study and made me just feel happier in general. So my grades went up when I was in school and I'd found my place in a sense."

Gillian's mother noticed signs of her daughter's interest in theater even earlier. "From the start," she says, "Gillian had a real flair for the dramatic. That has simply always been her personality." But the first time she became conscious of her daughter's potential talent occurred when Gillian was only 14. A teacher assigned her the role of Juliet in the balcony scene from *Romeo and Juliet*. In spite of her having no background in Shakespeare, nor any family history of acting experience, Gillian mastered the scene almost effortlessly. "When she performed it for me my jaw just dropped. I was incredibly impressed and knew then that she was going to be an actress. After that, nothing Gillian did surprised me."

Anderson herself cannot point to one event that led her to the decision to go on to study acting and make it her life's work. "I'm not exactly sure when the decision was made. It was something that I guess I always felt like I knew; it was just there." But the process became an important element in her growth as a person. "Gillian learnt to portray a whole range of emotions by going through her problems and it helped her grow," says her mother. "To be honest, though, I don't remember her being quite as wild as she says she was."

Her grades may have gone up and her focus may have shifted but Gillian was still able to fulfill her high school yearbook's prediction with one final prank. She and some friends had decided it would be fun to glue all the locks shut in the school. On graduation night she went to the school with her boyfriend and some others and attempted to get inside. While her boyfriend finally gave up and went home, Gillian persisted, only to be there when the police arrived. Trying to get away, she stepped on a nail; needless to say that slowed her up. The cops arrested her and she spent several hours in custody before her boyfriend came to get her out. When the cops asked her to name her accomplices, she refused. "I did refuse to say who else was there and they threatened not to let us graduate, so I had to do public service for a week. It was really humiliating, I had to wash windows and mop floors . . . my purple hair and all."

The year before graduation, in the fall of 1985, Anderson also tried her hand at film acting. A young musician named Mike Kuhn was looking for actors for a film school project. The band in which he played sometimes played with Anderson's boyfriend's band. The film was called *Three At Once*; it ran about eight minutes in length and was shot in black and white over a three-day period. The action mainly consisted of three actors talking about their hopes and fears. The film was shown at a local film festival in Grand Rapids in 1986, and at a Seattle festival in 1996.

CHICAGO

By the end of high school Anderson was fully immersed in high-school theater, involving herself in all aspects of production. The rest of her time was spent hanging around the local community theater. She knew this was the thing for her and decided to apply to the Goodman Theatre School at DePaul University in Chicago. A major theater conservatory, the school had a stellar list of alumni, including Karl Malden, Harvey Korman, Geraldine Page, Joe Mantegna, Elizabeth Perkins, and Kevin Anderson. Applicants had to go through an intense audition process, but the signs of Anderson's early talent were visible to the faculty and she was accepted into the four-year drama program. During her time there she would also attend a summer program held in 1986 by the internationally famous National Theatre of Great Britain at Cornell University in Ithaca, New York.

Each year the school produced more than 35 full-length plays. Each spring they put on a festival of new plays and new works in progress. Their two mainstage seasons, the Showcase and the Playworks, were presented at the Merle Reskin Theatre in downtown Chicago.

One of Anderson's favorites while at university was a brilliantly giddy comedy by the French playwright Georges Feydeau called *A Flea in Her Ear*. Ric Murphy, a teacher from the school, recalls, "being with Gillian was like going to a surprise party. Gillian had an eight-line part in a French farce but turned it into a star role just by the attitude she brought to it. She has an incandescence." Anderson developed a love for comedy but she also appeared in productions of "In a Northern Landscape," "Last Summer at Bluefish Cove," "Serious Money" and "Romeo and Juliet."

Gillian also appeared in another student film, *A Matter of Choice*, by director William Davis. The film was shot in 1988 and is another black-and-white short piece. The five-minute film is a silent study of a young woman who waits outside an abortion clinic and whose emotions pass across her face as she paces in the alleyway. The film took only two hours to shoot, largely due to Anderson's talent and understanding of the director's goals for the piece.

For all of Anderson's growing talents and recognition of her promise by her teachers, she still struggled with demons and insecurities. "When I was younger and I lived in Chicago and New York, I was struggling financially and emotionally, and although I had a relatively strong belief in myself, there were times when I questioned my abilities and my sanity about going into this field."

And she struggled with all the issues that most young people do: sex, alcohol, relationships, family. What is unusual, however, is Anderson's candor about this phase of her life, particularly her sexual attitudes. "I think I felt that if somebody liked me, then I was supposed to. I didn't realize I had a choice in the matter. If they liked me, even if they were a complete asshole, I thought that I had to sleep with them! It was another way of getting attention. I think that people really didn't find me attractive — or I never really felt attractive — or I never really felt attractive for years and it was only when I started to shave my head and dressed differently that I realized I had a voice as to who I was and what I stood for, and that made me feel attractive and made people attracted to me. I always dressed in black and in combat boots and had hair that stood up six feet, but still guys were attracted to me and so it was like, 'Oh, okay, sure, why not?' "

"I didn't really enjoy it . . . I don't think I enjoyed it back then at all. When did I start enjoying sex? . . . For a long time I felt it was something I had to do, and it wasn't really a place where I could be free and experiment and enjoy. It was something that one did, you know. So I think it wasn't until I was about 22 that I started to realize that, 'Hey, I can enjoy this. Yeah . . .' "

She made another discovery about herself in university: "I loved alcohol. I actually like alcohol a bit too much. I gave it up because it was becoming . . . it was just getting too much. I just realized that all I wanted to do was drink. I was very introverted. It would've been fine after the first three drinks if everybody just left. But also it was a sexual stimulant for me. It made me feel much stronger and more confident and sexier, and I relied on that for a while." But she wasn't happy with the way it masked her feelings. "It's not necessarily the amount, it's what's underneath, what's driving you to do it. Those things distracted me from being present in my life. They numbed me. And it became important that I become awake and make conscious choices."

"The threat was that I was not going to do the things I dreamed about doing, because there was stuff getting in the way. I was covering up my feelings — the pain, the angst, the frustration and everything — and I needed to face them in order to move forward. So I did. And I know that if I hadn't taken that step, I wouldn't be here today." The honesty of her work and a growing ambition to succeed changed her whole way of thinking about herself. She'd found her path and her life's work and had no doubt she was in it for the long run. "One fear of many actors is that if they give up the crutch of an addiction, they'll lose the edge. But it's not true. There's more honesty in an actor who's had that experience and has come out of it. It takes more guts to remain in this business as an awake and conscious person."

So just before her 21st birthday Anderson gave up alcohol.

FOUR

NEW YORK

Success at university does not always transfer to the real world. And young actors who become known on campus are still a big step away from a life in commercial theater. That is why, every year, actors' showcases are held in which student performers get a few moments to strut their stuff before scouts for the big talent agencies. A very few talented and lucky young actors will find themselves with a contract offer from an agent.

For her own spot at a showcase, Anderson prepared two pieces — one about her father, and the second about a park bench. She showed up in an outrageous vintage dress far too big for her. "It was seven sizes too big, light blue and see-through, made out of this really stiff material, so I looked like a fairy. My hair was really long and straggly and I had these sandals on. Looking back, I don't know why they considered me."

In the audience that day were scouts from the William Morris Agency, among the largest and most powerful agencies in the United States, with a roster of famous stars on its client list. Impressed by what they saw and heard, they offered to have William Morris represent her. But she would have to go where the work is for most theater actors: New York.

She packed everything she had into her Volkswagen Rabbit and set off for the Big Apple. "I had it in my mind that I should leave on a certain day but it took longer to pack than I expected. The car was packed so high that I couldn't see out the rear-view mirror." It was 11 o'clock when she finally hit the road. "And when I stopped to sleep, I had to crouch up in a fetal position."

As she traveled eastward she made a vow that she would audition for film or stage work only. If she were going to be taken seriously as an actor she would have to work hard and hone her craft and keep away from television work. Television might put food on the table but it wouldn't help her mature the skills that had caught the notice of her new representatives from the William Morris Agency.

And so, like every other aspiring actor, she made her way to New York and started auditioning for theater work. And like every other aspiring actor she paid the rent by waiting on tables. She worked for a time at Dojo's, a student hangout on St. Marks Place, in the East Village.

Meanwhile, in Chelsea, rehearsals had begun for a new production at the Manhattan Theater Club on West 16th Street. One of the few subscription theaters in New York, the Manhattan Theater Club, produced first-ratc off-Broadway plays, with decent budgets and well-known actors. Artistic director Lynne Meadow had found great success with the comedy *Woman in Mind*, by British playwright Alan Ayckbourn, a few seasons previous. Stockard Channing had delighted audiences in the lead role of a woman slipping into schizophrenia. Now although American audiences do not always warm to the unusual hilarity characteristic of Alan Ayckbourn's plays, Meadow knew her long experience with British drama would allow her to translate the foreign sensibilities to her actors and the audience.

Absent Friends, one of Ayckbourn's early plays, had its debut in London in 1975. The playwright was now an established hit-maker and producers felt the comedy would do well off-Broadway. Mary Louise Parker had been cast in the role of Evelyn. The cast was getting to know one another, costumes were being prepared and blocking was falling into place. Like many actors, though, Parker had been auditioning for film work too and a big break presented itself when she was offered a chance to work with Steve Martin in *Grand Canyon*. How could she turn it down?

Producers released her from the play and scrambled to fill her part. Gillian was one of several hopefuls who won an audition, but her slim résumé must have made Meadow pause. Unlike Mary Louise Parker, who had already done a good deal of theater and film work, Gillian had no professional experience. But Meadow was won over by her anyway. "I didn't realize we would find someone quite this green," she says. "But it is one of those great stories, where someone is cast purely on ability. Gillian's background is largely

Gillian on stage in *The Philanthropist*, at
the Long Wharf Theatre, New Haven.

Gillian Anderson as Celia in Christopher
Hampton's *The Philanthropist*.

improvisational, and she worked those instincts into a highly technical style that fit in perfectly with the specific way the play was written." Her early years living in England, her facility with accents and her summer training with the National Theatre of Great Britain at Cornell University came together with her comedic skills and made her the perfect choice for the gum-chewing Evelyn. Finally, a big part, off-Broadway, working alongside a mix of American and British actors: Peter Frechette, Brenda Blethyn, Ellen Parker, David Purdham, and John Curless.

The play revolves around a tea-party thrown by friends for Colin (Frechette) whose fiancée has recently drowned. The friends, Diana (Blethyn) and Paul (Purdham), who give the party, and John (Curless) and Evelyn who attend with Marge (Parker), all believe they are there to console Colin. Colin, in spite of his loss, seems oddly resigned, and ironically sentimental about his friends whose marriages are all fiascoes. Evelyn is bored and is having an affair of sorts with Paul; John keeps silent about it to maintain a business relationship with Paul; Diana tries to keep up appearances; Marge is at the mercy of and at the call of Gordon, her absent hypochondriac husband. The piece is about misunderstandings and essential miscommunications and offers a deft satire of contemporary suburban life.

The production ran for 64 performances between January 29 and March 15, 1991 as part of the theater's eight-play schedule. The play did well and caught the critical attention of writer Richard Hornby who reviewed the production for *The Hudson Review*, the prestigious periodical for literature and the arts.

Hornby was pleased to see another Ayckbourn play presented in New York and felt "Gillian Anderson . . . was hilarious as the surly Evelyn." Her performance also won Gillian the 1991 Theatre World Award for Outstanding New Talent and on May 16 she was honored at the Equitable Auditorium along with fellow award recipients Marcus Chong, Jane Adams, and Adam Arkin (who currently plays a doctor on the CBS television show *Chicago Hope*).

And, as a side note, Peter Frechette currently plays a computer hacker working for the FBI in the, some would say Chris Carter-inspired, NBC television program *Profiler*.

But no award is a guarantee of work and it was back to waiting on tables to make ends meet. At times Gillian had two jobs just to get by. But true to a pattern of "feast or famine" that would frequently repeat itself in her career, Gillian's constant auditioning paid off with three job offers: another off-Broadway play, a role in Christopher Hampton's *The Philanthropist* at the prestigious Long Wharf theater in Connecticut, and a part in a low-budget feature film called *Home Fires Burning*. The scheduling allowed her to work in two of the projects: the film and the Hampton play.

The film, currently known as *The Turning*, was directed by L.A. Puopolo and Gillian was cast as April Cavanaugh opposite Karen Allen, Tess Harper, and Raymond J. Barry. Anderson won praise from her director for her professionalism during a difficult location shoot and under the challenges of nightly re-writes. The film has been variously referred to as "Home Fires Burning" and "Pocahontas, Virginia" and was released on video in the U.K. as *The Turning* in

October 1996 and more recently hit cinemas in Los Angeles in May of 1997, no doubt because of the new drawing power of Gillian Anderson's name. A romantically enticing picture of Anderson adorns the cover of the video box and various pictures from a short love scene in the film have made their way on to the Internet, but the picture had never been seen by American audiences until recently. The careers of Raymond J. Barry and Gillian did cross paths again years later in *The X-Files*. Barry played Senator Matheson, Mulder's government connection and protector in the first three seasons.

After the film wrapped in early December 1991, Anderson headed to Connecticut to prepare for the New Year's Eve opening. She joined the 27th season of the Long Wharf Theatre in New Haven, to play Celia in *The Philanthropist* opposite actors Tim Choate, Margaret Gibson, Ronald Guttman, Lily Knight, Don Reilly, and Sam Tsoutsouvas. Gordon Edelstein directed Anderson in this early Hampton play, first performed in 1971, about a group of unfeeling university friends who barely notice the suicide of a fellow faculty member who shoots himself right before their eyes. Celia is the fiancée of Philip, a self-absorbed philologist, obsessed with anagrams, but hopeless with the complexities of human relationships. Celia is betrayed by Philip and seeks to avenge herself in the arms of a lecherous colleague, Braham. The two have a showdown, Celia decides to leave Philip, who barely misses a beat before moving on to figuring out his next new anagram. The production ran to February 9, 1992 and Anderson received excellent reviews again.

Gillian's personal life was enriched as well when

she became romantically involved with one of the actors in the cast. In interviews she still will not name the gentleman but she took the relationship seriously enough to follow him to Los Angeles and begin a new chapter in her life and career.

FIVE

A FEW WEEKS WORK

Finding herself in L.A., Gillian decided to make the best of her time there. Work was scarce, especially for someone new to the city who was still basically an unknown. She took waitressing jobs and waited to find work as an actor.

Luckily, Gillian was being represented by the William Morris Agency, a firm with real power in Hollywood. However, while the agency was putting her name out there, it wasn't yet making a major effort for her. She now had a slim but solid portfolio which showed her range, from theater to film work. She was determined and ambitious, willing to work hard for the career she had chosen to pursue. Many actors have said that their profession is often hard on the ego. Sometimes, fine actors must suffer years of "dry spells." Success in acting, and especially in the movies, was a matter of grit and good luck, but Gillian was equal to the task.

Gillian and her mother

It was a time of waiting and working. For months, she lived with a friend, waitressed for money and went to any casting calls her agent could get for her. When the invitations came, she turned up and did the audition. Even so, she was out of work for almost a year before she started going to TV auditions. She was loath to even look at television scripts, she says. "My agent had been warned to be picky in that respect." Some of the shows were awful enough that she says: "I would pray that I wouldn't get [it] because I didn't want to be involved in it." She wanted film work, not television, and she admits to having "a very snobby view" of the small screen. And yet Gillian faithfully went to the casting calls even for TV work. She needed the money.

She once estimated that she went to three or four auditions a day at one point, but later said she had been exaggerating. But Gillian admits, "I was going to a lot of auditions." Though her efforts had not yet brought any job offers, the frequency of auditions was fairly encouraging. Even though some casting directors will audition dozens, even hundreds of actors for one part, the odds are still not in your favor of even getting invited to come. Your looks, experience, portfolio, and agent have a lot to do with it, and there are innumerable young actors out there just dying to get a part. If Gillian got even *one* audition a day, that's saying something.

But the whole thing worried her a little, or at least wasn't what she'd originally wanted to do.

"First of all, I swore I'd never move to Los Angeles," she says, "and once I did I swore I'd never do television."

Gillian got a guest spot on a TV show called *Class of '96*, a short-lived series shot on the grounds of the

University of Toronto. The series was canceled after about half a season, but in its short lifespan it attracted some critical plaudits.

She also nearly got a job playing a very young girl. "I went for this mini-series or something, where I had to play this 14-year-old girl. I got down to a shortlist of two and we had a lot of work sessions with the director and he called my agents to say a lot of positive things about me. They kind of pricked up their ears."

It seems likely that the result of this feedback was that Anderson's agency began to take more notice of her. She feels the event somehow "shifted things up a gear." Shortly afterwards, she received the script for a TV pilot called *The X-Files*.

It was a creepy, well-written script with a part Anderson could really feel good about playing. And the character was interesting, trying to make reason of the macabre events she witnesses. "I was reading something that, for the first time in a long time, involved a strong, independent, intelligent woman as a lead character." And it was truly scary. In fact, one of the Fox executives said of his first reading of the ten-page treatment: "I was scared shitless!" As Gillian says: "I remember exactly where I was sitting when I read it, how I was dressed and — it had a very strong effect on me. I was sitting in bed, my then-boyfriend was lying next to me. It was in the evening. I remember what bedcover was on the bed! It's just that I was very strongly affected by it."

It was the story of two FBI agents, Fox Mulder and Dana Scully, whose job is to investigate cases of a paranormal or unexplained nature. Apart from the basic facts of the script, Anderson knew very little else. She had little idea of how a TV show was made. This show was the pilot, so, even if she had wanted to do so, there was no one Anderson could ask for tips on how to approach her role, or the casting people she would face. She had to simply be herself.

She turned up at the casting call dressed very casually, with her hair down. There were 15 or 20 other women waiting to audition. At that time, her hair was its original color of blonde and hung halfway down her back with some natural wave in it. She has described herself as looking "scruffy" at that audition, and perhaps it was a mistake, but Scully is a medical doctor and some doctors are distinctly scruffy. Anderson didn't know that the 'type' network people were looking for in Scully was very much like Jodie Foster's character in *Silence of the Lambs*. Cool, intense, and brave, with a professional veneer over the feminine interior. This was not the look Anderson had dressed for. But Chris Carter, the show's creator, saw in her a quality that he had envisioned for the character.

"When she came into the room, I just knew she was Scully, I just felt it. . . . She had an intensity about her; intensity always translates across the screen."

Carter may have been convinced that Anderson was his woman, but the network casting people weren't. Unbeknownst to Anderson, a small war erupted over whether or not she should be cast as Dana Scully, with Carter championing her to the point of heroism. Carter has said: "I had to put my career on the line to put Gillian on the show."

The problem was that network executives wanted a more traditional television babe. Gillian seemed too normal, too girl-next-door. It has never been revealed who the other actress was that Fox executives wanted for the role of Scully, but the pneumatic form of Pamela Lee Anderson has often been invoked as a clear example of what Gillian Anderson *didn't* look like.

"I had no idea what the character was supposed to be like, nor did I know what the producers were looking for," Anderson says. "At the time of the casting, I knew nothing of Dana. It wasn't until later that the producers told me that the Fox network execs had wanted a sexy blonde with long legs and [who] looked like a super-model. . . . I really didn't have the kind of body they were looking for."

As Duchovny has said: "You look at Gillian and she's a beautiful woman," and, he adds (perhaps thinking of Mulder's famous pool scene) "how often do you see Scully in a bathing suit?"

Adding to this was Anderson's lack of experience. And her youth — the role called for a 29-year-old. Anderson's agent had said her age was 27, when in fact she was a mere 24 years old. But as Carter has said, Gillian "plays older than her years" and she passed as 27.

Chris Carter has always been very definite about his lead characters, as well as other elements of the show. In a way, there are parts of Carter in each of the two leads, elements of his own life and philosophy. Fox Mulder's name is a mix of a childhood friend's first name and his mother's maiden name. Like Mulder, he loves sunflower seeds, hopes to find something 'out there,' and has a youthful energetic drive. Dana Scully's name is a mix of a soft, feminine first name and a reference to the L.A. Dodgers' baseball announcer, Vin Scully, who Carter (interestingly) describes as "the voice of God." Scully is perhaps Carter's inner skeptic, his need for balance.

Carter had, even at such an early stage, a clear image of what he wanted in Scully, and, unlike many other such creators of shows, he seemed tenacious enough to keep that image clear and free of others' meddling.

Anderson's looks weren't a problem for him. He has described her features as "classic." What he saw in Gillian was "a seriousness, a believability as a scientist." Also that strange gravity she can summon so easily was a big factor for him.

"I believed in her in the role, I believed her when she spoke scientific terms, I believed her as a doctor. I think she looks the part."

As well, Anderson herself has said that she and Carter have always had similar notions of what the character of Scully is all about. It is possible that, at that particular audition, her own interpretation of the character, as off-the-cuff as it necessarily was, also said something to Carter about Gillian's suitability as Scully.

Carter has, by now, proven himself to be unusually talented at identifying what will work, in a TV series, in a character, in a story line. Whatever he thinks will work usually does. Carter's background was in writing comedy but his real interests lay in darker material, like *The Twilight Zone* and *Kolchak: The Night Stalker*, which had scared him as a kid. He'd wanted a show that was just as scary, and he had specific ideas about how to achieve that goal. But Carter didn't have the success of *The X-Files* to back him up at this point. He asked the network to trust him, but network executives are not generally a trusting — or adventurous — bunch. Still not sold on Anderson as the Scully they had envisioned, they asked to see more actors.

Gillian received a call-back where she auditioned with yet another group of young, hopeful actors. "We looked at a lot of actresses," one network executive recalls, and another admits there was a "tremendous negativity" toward the idea of casting Anderson.

As she herself recalls: "I didn't have any money, I didn't have any clothes, other than 'vintage stuff' and I borrowed a suit from a friend of mine. I don't know if she was bigger than me but she looked very good in oversized suits and clothes, so I walked into the first audition for *The X-Files* in a very oversized suit and looked somewhat 'frumpy' in that way. So that's how the Fox executives first saw me and it was hinted to me that I come in with a *little bit* of a shorter skirt and something a little bit more form-fitting."

David Duchovny had already been flagged as the likely winner of the role of Fox Mulder. His contender, whose reading of the character had been cooler and a little more "tortured," would be eliminated soon. The network has said that they favored Duchovny early on, but Carter says he had to guide them a little in Duchovny's direction. Duchovny himself hadn't thought much was going to come out of this job. So many TV shows don't get past the pilot, and many of those that do are canceled after six episodes or so. Looking at a show about paranormal phenomena, David Duchovny didn't see a six-year blockbuster hit before him.

In fact, Duchovny wasn't initially sure he wanted to accept the job at all. That is, until Chris Carter flew to see him and talk to him about it in person. The gesture impressed Duchovny and he agreed to come on the project, however long it would last. But he didn't think it would last long. "I thought I could go to Vancouver for a month and get paid, and then go on and do my next movie," he said.

After the first day of network auditions, the first call-back for Anderson, Duchovny was chosen for the role of Mulder. Anderson has said:

"I was there and read with him. But I think the network was still pretty freaked out at the possibility of casting somebody with as little background as I had, so they flew in some more girls from New York, and I had to sit in the hallway with more girls from New York [laughter], and go in again and read with him. It was pretty hair raising."

But the two actors clearly had a chemistry right off the bat. When asked about this later in an interview, Anderson recalled: "He came over to me in the hall-way at the network audition and asked if we could read through the scene together. We did, and it was amazing. Better than anything that we've done since."

At Carter's insistence, Fox executives thought it over, watching the only film footage they had of Gillian, her appearance in the episode of *Class of '96*. Time was running out and there was a lot of money being gambled on this venture. The tension was rather high.

Finally, Carter put his foot down and said she was his first and only choice for Scully, and the network, still unconvinced but impressed by his force of character, relented.

"Gillian had done relatively little work," Carter has said, "and it was harder to convince the people whose money I was spending that she was Dana Scully, but ultimately they believed that I knew what I was doing."

SIX

A NICE
TRIP TO
THE FOREST

Gillian got the news that she had been given the role
the same day as her last unemployment check arrived.
Two days later, she was on a plane to Vancouver to
begin shooting. It was a period of sudden excitement
and upheaval for her. Leaving L.A. where she had
friends and had made a place for herself was reminiscent of the many other times she has had to leave
"home." As well, she discovered that Vancouver is a
green, rainy place, quite unlike sunny, dry Los Angeles.
That very dampness adds a sense of atmosphere, perhaps not a cheery one, to the show itself. "There just
seems to be a constant cloud or a constant feeling in
this city that gets to you after a while," she says,
hurrying to add that "Otherwise, it's great."

At first, Anderson knew nobody in Vancouver, had
only just met the people she had signed on to work
with, and didn't know her way around the city. As

exciting as it all was, this was a big change and she admits, "It was difficult, at first."

The work schedule was heavy, 12 to 16 hours a day, six days a week. Anderson has often said that the schedule is hard for her even now. "Your body gets used to it," she says, but, in those early days, she didn't know what to expect. Gillian turned up for work very early each morning, sat while her makeup was applied, donned what some people have called Scully's "dowdy" wardrobe and was ready for work. At night and during any breaks they were given, she would study her script either alone or with Duchovny.

It was at this time, too, that she was "made over" to look more like the Scully Carter imagined. Her hair, which hung to the middle for her back, was cut, dyed and styled into a bob. Over the years, this bob has grown more sleek and soft, and the bangs have disappeared. "That was weird," she says. "They cut it and I looked like my mother, for Christ's sake! It was a big transformation. I'd never styled my hair. I never went through the curling-iron-every-morning kind of thing." For Anderson, who confessed on an on-line chat that "I didn't brush my hair for about four years," this felt very odd. "For the longest time, I couldn't stand to feel soft hair on my head. I couldn't stand what it was like when I first washed it, so I put as much gunk in it as possible. Even now, it drives me nuts when it flows nicely as I'm walking down the street on a weekend. I just want to, you know, gunk it."

She didn't know very much about the network reactions to her, but she knew that this was a personal test. "Let me tell you about tension and stress: I was a mess," she has said recalling those weeks. "It's taken me a while, and I'm still learning every single day I work." Sometimes, she says, she had to fight the 'impostor syndrome,' a sense that many successful people get in which they feel they are not worthy and soon will be exposed as fakes.

"For a long time," she says, "there was this feeling that they were going to find out they'd made a really big mistake."

Twenty other pilots were being shot in Vancouver at that time. The available crew support was severely diminished and there was lots of competition for good technical people. Carter hadn't been given much time to complete his project and everything was riding on the pilot. Anderson knew very little about how a TV show worked. "I naively assumed we would be picked up," she said. Still, she didn't expect it to go very far. She anticipated committing a short while to the pilot, perhaps a year at most to the show, maybe doing 13 or so episodes. What she hoped was that this work would put her in a different and higher category in the casting world and that it would lead to other jobs. With this in mind, and true to her character, she worked very hard.

It was interesting and challenging work. The outdoor shots were particularly hard for both leads and, in one scene, the two agents had to stand in the pouring rain next to an open grave, shouting through the downpour to one another.

"It was absolutely *freezing*," Anderson recalls, "and they were drenching us with rain machines — at times I couldn't even open my eyes, the water was coming down so hard. It was a horrific night."

Duchovny, who had quite a bit of movie experience,

mostly remembers it as a moment of insight into Anderson's grit:

"She stood there, wanting it to be colder and wetter. She was actually turning her face to the rain machine, saying, 'Hit me with more water.' "

As the rushes from the first few shoots came in, the network continued to gripe about Anderson. Was she going to be a character people could identify with? Was she not sexy enough? Was she too cool and professional? In fact, there is a scene in the pilot that seems to contradict this theory. Scully rushes into Mulder's room to show him two strange marks on her back, identical to the ones found on the victims of the story. She is in her bra and panties and she pulls her robe off to show him.

"At that point, it was the pilot and it was my first job, and that's how the scene was written. I have my own opinions about that. There really wasn't a reason for it . . . the bites could have been on my shoulder or something."

True to Carter's direction, however, Mulder's reaction is at first clinical, then amused. The marks turn out to be mosquito bites, and the whole thing turns into a chance for Mulder to expose himself in return to Scully, which, in Mulder's terms, means trusting her and telling her about his life's mission and his belief in extraterrestrials. Carter, himself, says "I love that scene." In a sense, the scene deals with the problem of sexuality right away and quickly diffuses it. "As soon as you have them looking googly-eyed at each other," he has said, "the relationship will supplant or subvert what's going on to make the show great," which is the unusual subject matter of *The X-Files*. So clear was he on this subject, that a near-to-end scene was removed from the pilot because it showed Scully in bed with her boyfriend (named Ethan Minette). As Gillian put it: "It didn't fit into the structure of the show . . . we were too different."

So sex was off-limits. In fact Scully and Mulder almost never use each other's given names; when Scully tries it once, Mulder laughs and says, "Even my parents call me 'Mulder.' " And yet, they have been voted "most romantic couple" by Internet fans, perhaps because of the very chasteness that seems to infuse their relationship.

If Anderson or the viewers of *The X-Files* wondered whether Scully was just an adjunct to Mulder's ego, that possibility was quickly dispelled in the second episode, "Deep Throat," in which Scully literally saves Mulder from a fate worse than death. Although some Internet fans have been counting who saves whom more often, Mulder having the leading edge, the early identification of Scully as a protective force is entirely deliberate. This kind of scene would be repeated several times, in several ways, in the seasons to come, and, in one stunning moment, Scully even shoots Mulder — for his own good! Hardly an adjunct.

Once the pilot was completed, Carter had to sell it, not only to network executives at Fox, but to Fox's owner and president, Rupert Murdoch. As usual, a screening was set up and a group of high-powered people gathered together to watch Carter's creation. He had a few great admirers at Fox, but Murdoch had the final veto. As the pilot ran, there were a few nervous titters, which was unnerving. But when it was over, these jaded executives who had already been asked to watch pilot after pilot that season, broke into spontaneous applause — a very rare event. Chris Carter got the go-ahead. *The X-Files* and *The Adventures of Brisco County Jr.* (a now-defunct Western) were the only one-hour dramas picked up by Fox in 1993.

The seemingly arbitrary circumstances that led Gillian Anderson to this place were unusual in retrospect, but not too far removed from Anderson's own philosophy of life. She knows her life could have gone in a different direction at any given moment along that path. Her decision to come to L.A. Her decision to accept TV offers. Carter's attention to her and the network resistance to her. It was hardly a sure thing. "I'm not sure," she says, "if I hadn't made those choices that I would be doing *The X-Files* right now." And she'd be right.

"Once in a while" she says, "I'll be driving down the street in Canada and think, 'I'm in Canada. How did I get here?' "

SEVEN

OLDER THAN HER YEARS

When shooting began for the first season, Gillian Anderson poured herself into the work.

"When I shot the pilot, it was only the third time that I'd been in front of a camera. There was *so* much that I didn't know. I didn't know about marks, about angles, I didn't know about hitting the light — I mean, the basic things."

She was dealing with the vast differences between television and theater and it was, to say the least, a challenge.

"I had a terrible time with learning lines. It's one thing to work on a theater production and move on a daily basis through the scenes; your body remembers what's going on. But when you have to stare at a page and practically soak it in, it takes training." Rehearsal time was minimal and sometimes the episode was still being written as it was being shot. This is the nature of television, but in theater that would be the definition of a disaster.

"In theater," she said, "you have time; in a film you have more time than this, at least. It was a very different thing, and it took a while for my brain to latch onto making quick choices and being okay with it."

Anderson was very new to the whole process, and she knew she had to find a way to adapt. So she applied herself full-thrust to the work at hand, took direction, and spoke to Carter about her character. "Chris has a very, very strong idea about who Mulder and Scully are, and he was very particular about how he wanted us to act in terms of their degree of intelligence, seriousness, and what drove them. He was very adamant about that. . . . But I think we both have a similar idea who the character of Scully is, anyway."

During this time, David Duchovny proved himself to be a generous, supportive friend. "David took me under his wing," she has said in several interviews, and she insists that his support and advice "meant a lot to me, and still does, because it was a scary time."

In fact, she was learning many things about David, and about herself. Despite the fact that Fox clearly ranked *The X-Files* as second-fiddle to *Brisco County Jr.*, Anderson and Duchovny were thrown into publicity chores to promote the show. The usually reserved, wryly funny Duchovny turned out to be a hoot in front of journalists.

As Anderson puts it: "We were sitting in this room on couches in front of these affiliate people — they were shooting questions from the floor. He turned into this comical person; he was absolutely hysterical. I had never seen that side of him before."

Anderson and Duchovny had an immediate "chemistry" together as actors. Despite their difference in height, looks, and delivery, they seem to go together; not exactly like a couple, but not just like partners, either.

Anderson says that chemistry is not something that can be created, and it's not something that happens often.

"I think that Fox was very lucky to find two people who just had that, no matter what is going on on the outside, no matter what moods we're in. It's just something that, when the cameras go on, we just have."

Besides the professional challenges facing Gillian, there were the personal ones. It's common for an interview with Anderson, or Duchovny, to include a mention of the incredible workload involved in shooting a weekly TV show. Quite recently, Anderson described the schedule as "pretty grueling," but she has been more definite: "It's insane! It's 12 to 16 hours a day, five days a week, ten months of the year. And then I spend my holidays working."

During this first year, she had not yet been asked to participate in promotional tours (no one knew if the show would even last a year), neither was she dealing with a baby — all that was yet to come. But just getting used to waking up so early and coming home so late, was very difficult.

"I'm not out much," she told interviewers, "I work and I go home. I work on the scripts. I wake up and come to work. And in between I try to get my bills paid."

Because this kind of job was so new to her, she had to quickly form coping mechanisms, ways to deal with the pressures, and she had to do it in a kind of social vacuum. She knew people in L.A., in Chicago, but not a soul in Vancouver. Although it is on the temperate west coast, Vancouver is often cool and rainy. As green and mild as the winters can be, the summers often lack the sunshine Anderson had been used to in L.A. The Canadian city was unknown to her and she had almost no time to explore. This was hardly an easy, comforting environment. "I have a support system in L.A., which I don't have here," she says.

But, Gillian is a strong, outgoing person, and she quickly found a way to ease into the hectic pace and the new setting. "I think she's very independent emotionally," Carter has said, "very adult and mature." She made the best of her situation, found her energy, and, true to form, was soon known as a light-hearted, generous presence on-set. Her mother has said that Gillian seems to prefer to keep her troubles to herself, rather than talk about them, and she cares about other people. One interviewer noticed Gillian's natural kindness. When director Rob Bowman seemed tired and upset about a shot, dropping his headphones in disgust, Anderson hurried over to him. "Rob, sweetie," she said, "are you all right?"

Playing Agent Dana Scully was a different and fascinating acting challenge for Gillian, and, thanks to Carter's clear vision, she was able to see a way into the role.

For this show, Carter wanted a controlled performance from both leads. Both Anderson and Duchovny have adopted an understated acting style, so much so that during that first year the agents often looked like aliens themselves, walking among hot-blooded humans. Some critics liked this, others didn't. But

Duchovny sums it up: "To me, underplaying is reality . . . I've never met anybody who acts like the people on *Melrose Place* . . . when we talk about creating realistic characters, we try — I think both of us — to react realistically and not dramatically." Anderson joked that she and her co-star were just too fatigued to put any more into it.

This style of acting isn't Anderson's usual style; she is known as a very good comedic actor and her energy is high, her presence very strong. So this was new to her, and it was something she and Duchovny continued to develop as the show progressed. But Gillian had very little trouble with that element of the role. Carter has said: "She has, first of all, a tremendous acting ability. Secondly, she has an intensity both as a person and an actress which really serves that character well."

Although, in the pilot, Scully laughs at Mulder's outrageous theories while the two agents are standing in the freezing rain, that laughter was not repeated in the next episode, or the next. In fact, that is one of the identifying features of Anderson's character. (Even so, Anderson herself estimated once that Scully had smiled a total of three times. But that all depends on what you call a smile. Scully's amusement or disbelief or panic seems to peek out from beneath her self-control.)

This understatement has its effect on an audience's nerves, too. When Scully inspects a corpse and puts a delicate hand to her nose, we don't need to see the putrescent thing itself — we get the picture. And when she slams her hand on the table in "Beyond the Sea" and shouts at manipulative death-row inmate

Luther Lee Boggs, ". . . no one will stop me from being the one to throw the switch and gas you out of this life for good, you son of a bitch!" the scene is a real shocker, simply because this kind of explosion so rarely happens. The whole show seems to make a virtue of understatement. Even the credits are smooth and creepy and oddly dreamlike. There are no out-takes from the show depicting car crashes, men punching each other, or people kissing. What *The X-Files* imparts to viewers overall is a strange sense of dislocation and eeriness, and it is this atmosphere in which Scully and Mulder must operate in their low-key way.

It was this carefully constructed production that met viewers when *The X-Files* premiered in September, 1993. By the time the pilot aired, the *The X-Files* team had shot eight episodes and were in the middle of making the almost universally reviled episode "Space." Using footage he had bought from NASA, Carter pasted the episode together, while his career, and the jobs of his cast and crew, hung in the balance.

Fox was still not set on the whole package, either. They felt that the endings of the shows were a bit too loose and enigmatic. Carter had a virtual shouting match with one Fox executive who believed that the endings "didn't make sense." "There's no sense to make!" Carter retorted, "you make the sense yourself!" However, the writers did add what is now a staple to the show, Anderson's voice-over as Scully writes her final report into her beloved laptop, summing up the extraordinary events she has witnessed and assessing the degree to which they can be explained by science. This kind of scene reasserts Scully's basic role in the show, which is as witness to events, a kind of stand-in for the audience. It also adds a tinge of the "overseer" to Scully's presence, as if she is still true to her original assignment, writing what Mulder, in a paranoid funk, called her "little notes" (which had a horrible resonance in the final episode of season four where Scully appears to be making her final report on Mulder). But mostly it added a certain degree of closure to the hour's bewildering events.

Ratings for the series were a respectable 7.9 on the Nielson rating system, which meant that over 7 million homes were tuning in. If Gillian Anderson knew this, or was tempted to let this information influence her, she showed no sign. And she had no time to reflect. The schedule was as heavy as ever. By May, the ratings had risen again to 8.8, despite the Friday night slot, which is not a choice one. In fact, the show had slowly become what network people call "an appointment series," one that viewers organize their schedules around. As Carter said, "I always said that we would have to create an audience on Friday nights, not steal one, and I think that's what we have done." The Fox network, which had been focusing on *Brisco County*, suddenly realized that *The X-Files* was taking hold and began to promote the show more aggressively. Fox's Friday slot hadn't exactly been stellar but *The X-Files* seemed to offer a remedy for that.

Anderson, meanwhile, was beginning to sense a stasis to her character, a repetition of a standard scene, where Mulder presents her with his bizarre theory for the night (virtually always correct) and she insists in vain that it is impossible.

"It's hard to keep being the skeptic. I've had this conversation a couple of times with Chris Carter, where I've just said, 'I have a feeling that the audience is laughing at me because I'm saying essentially the same stuff over and over again.' And the answer, via Chris, is that she is a scientist; she is a forensic pathologist; she is a medical doctor. And he's right: I mean, that's the formula that works."

But it was a formula that was a challenge to breathe life into. "There are times," Anderson says, "when it's frustrating being the negative energy in a situation." So what she did, and does to this day, is to return to the defining features of her character: faith in science, reason, and justice and an unholy appetite for hard work. When asked how the writers will be able to deal with the problem of Scully's continuing skepticism, despite all she has seen, Anderson points again to logic. "It comes down to the fact that, in order to write these field reports, Scully has to basically shut her mind to what she has learned, and keep it to herself. There are episodes where she starts to see his side of things and begins to open up a little more to those realms of possibilities. But she deals with reality and what is tangible. If you look at every episode, there is a *logical* reason for the things that happen."

Another thing that Anderson found a struggle was the scientific and medical dialogue she had to get her tongue around. While Duchovny seemed to have no trouble with his lines (he apparently has a fairly powerful memory), Anderson kept struggling with hers, which caused a little frustration on-set and gave her considerable anxiety. She was used to being able to work with scripts until she felt fairly comfortable. But in TV, as she says, "There's not time to get hung up on getting the lines right." Nonetheless, she felt she had to keep up with Duchovny, keep pace with the shooting schedule, and find a way to deal with the dialogue. The best way seemed to be to relax and trust in herself as an actor.

"It is hard to connect . . . there's only so much of it that you can comprehend and understand from day to day as you're working on these lines, and then you just have to let go and trust that, as an actor, you can make it seem real and make it seem like you know what you're talking about."

It was little things like this which were new to her. Things like the fact that she'd never handled a gun before and had to be taught how to do it. "My hand was practically covering the whole gun," she says, laughing, "but people reminded me not to do that."

In the second episode, they were asked to imagine that strange lights were flying overhead, probably UFOs, and Anderson and Duchovny had to match their sight-lines so as to appear to be looking at the same objects. Take after take, they had to appear to be amazed. She said it was difficult, "reacting to special effects that aren't there or exaggerating something that you know is fake and reacting to it as if it's the most horrible thing you've ever seen in your life."

The X-Files rarely has continuity problems and even the hard-core nitpickers on the Net are often (but not always) reduced to analyzing tiny details: briefly glimpsed signatures, computer monitor passwords, or the changing birthdays of secondary characters.

She was also performing some of her own stunts, which she enjoyed immensely and calls "doing my own tumbles." But she recalls a scene in the episode "Young at Heart" where her character was wearing a bullet-

proof vest when she is shot by multiple murderer John
Barnett. Scully is thrown violently backward and lands
limply on the floor, unconscious. Anderson had to
throw herself backward and land in a dead faint, over
and over again. It was exhausting work. "I didn't
realize till later," she says, "that I was pregnant at the
time." But the scene worked well.

Gillian knew she was working on a good show, with
an intelligent producer and strong writers. "I had a
very good feeling that this show would be successful,"
she said, but she never had a chance to really find out
how the show was doing. In fact, she rarely got a
chance to watch herself on TV because the shooting
schedule meant that she was still at work when the show
aired in western Canada. She could tape the show and
watch it late at night, or watch several on her day off,
but her experience of the show wasn't the same as that
of *X-Files* fans.

Even from episode to episode, the pacing was a little
skewed, various crews working on various scenes and
several episodes being shot or in production at the
same time. The leads were called upon to act for
the main scenes in which they appeared, to be available for re-shooting if the script changed, be available
for voice-overs (eventually even Duchovny got his
own voice-overs for the ending of the show). And on
top of all this they had to work on the next script.

As Anderson puts it, "when we get scripts we are
still working on a previous episode, so that's where
the focus is. But it is exciting. Sometimes we get
scripts that we hear a lot of buzz about from people
who have read them or crew members who have
already started work on the scripts, and we get excited

about the possibilities of the next ones coming up or what kind of work it will entail for David and me on different levels. It's neat. It's a neat process to be involved in."

EIGHT

CLYDE

Sometime just after the pilot was shot, in September of 1993, Gillian met an artistic director for *The X-Files* named Clyde Klotz. One day on-set, she invited him into her little trailer for some sushi. By all accounts, Anderson loves sushi, and that day she had a tray of it on hand. It seems that they got along well, because when Clyde left, he admitted to Gillian that he hadn't really wanted any sushi, he just wanted to talk to her.

"It was Clyde's smile that first attracted me," she said, "he was very quiet, rugged and cool, but I soon realized he had a lot to say and that he was a very intelligent man."

Clyde must also have been fairly good at his job, because, despite its newness, *The X-Files* was a show with a lot of money and talent behind it. Also, after working on *The X-Files*, which is known for its gorgeous look, he moved over to YTV's *Reboot* which was the first computer-animated show of its kind. Several similar shows exist now, but at the time *Reboot* was the only one to use computers to create all the art involved in a show.

For his part, Clyde seems to have felt something unusual was at work in their attraction to one another: "We felt like we'd known each other a long time, and we'd just finally met in person," he said. "Gillian is very spiritual, in search of whatever explanations might be out there."

But, as Gillian is quick to point out, this was a very normal, nice thing, not a cataclysm: "It wasn't love at first sight. I was very attracted to him and assumed he was to me as well. We went out on a couple of dates and he asked me to marry him. No, that's not true," she says laughing, "it was pretty close to that though — we had a few dates to feel it out — it wasn't *bang* or anything . . . I didn't faint."

Gillian and Clyde dated for a fairly short time, less than four months, before Clyde proposed to her. It was a scene which seemed to have an element of spontaneity to it: "We were in my kitchen when Clyde asked me to marry him. For some reason, the TV was on, showing a couple in bed and the guy was proposing to the girl. That's when Clyde popped the question, and I knew it was right."

Gillian has been quoted as saying that she married Clyde after a romance that lasted "more than a week, less than a month," but in fact it was the engagement she was referring to. The romance itself was closer to four months old when they got married. In fact, it was not the first proposal she had ever received.

"I had gotten engaged before, with a ring over a

fancy dinner, and it was a very uncomfortable thing." The event she is referring to dates back to when she was living in L.A. Her boyfriend at the time took her out to dinner. Obviously a romantic fellow, he had decided to do things in a traditional way — but it wasn't a good idea.

"He presented me with a ring," she says, "while the waiters and other diners looked on. I should have said no. I didn't want to marry him. But how could I, when everyone was watching me and willing me to accept? So I said yes, but it was stupid because, looking back, I was simply accepting the marriage proposal just to please the waiters. It was only when I went to Vancouver to film *The X-Files* that I realized it was all a mistake. It was the first time I'd been away from him and could think clearly. I realized I wasn't meant to be this man's wife and I put a stop to any wedding."

Gillian and Clyde flew to Hawaii on one of their rare breaks. It was warm and sunny and very beautiful. Once there, they found a Buddhist priest who agreed to perform the ceremony for them. Gillian is obviously open to alternate forms of spirituality and different ways of expressing faith, so this seemed like a natural choice for her. It was a very casual and enjoyable event. "It was so fabulously simple," she said of the whole thing, "it was just one of those channel-changing moments interrupted by wedding vows." The Buddhist priest drove his two guests around in his Ford Explorer, looking for just the right place to perform the ceremony. The humor and charm of this image, a holy man in a four-by-four, was not lost on Gillian, and she has laughed out loud recounting the tale to an interviewer. Finally, since Gillian and Clyde were unable to find the perfect site, their host suggested the 17th hole of his private Kauai golf course, by a cliff over looking the ocean. At that spot there grew a particularly beautiful tree and it was under this tree that Clyde and Gillian were married. The event was videotaped, the camera being set way back in order to take in the beautiful setting. The light was such that the bride and groom appeared at times to be just silhouettes. When the priest said "You may now kiss the bride," Clyde and Gillian kissed, and then embraced for a very long time. The scene was beautiful and loving, but the video didn't record the exact nature of the event. Instead, as Gillian said laughing, "It looked like we were making out in front of this priest. But we weren't! We were just hugging."

The next task was to break the news to people. Besides all the folks back in Vancouver, there were Gillian's parents, Rosemary and Edward.

"We sent a letter to my mum and dad, with a strict instruction not to open it until New Year's Day. My Mum had already met Clyde and my Dad was in a good mood that day, so they were happy."

When the couple flew back to Vancouver, Gillian too was happy. She was a co-star on a successful television show. The ratings just seemed to climb as a larger and larger "cult" fan-base began to take hold. The Internet was the home to many sites that celebrated *The X-Files*, some of which were devoted to Gillian Anderson alone. She was in love and recently married.

But, she was also pregnant. She didn't know it yet. But when she did find out, her own life would change forever. So, in time, would *The X-Files*.

NINE

PIPER

When Gillian discovered that she was pregnant, she and Clyde were stunned and thrilled, but they also knew exactly what the implications were. They did the math and realized Gillian would be due in September, right at a critical time in *The X-Files'* shooting schedule. No matter which way they looked at it, there was no way for this to be a decision the two of them could make unmolested by outside opinion. They were forced to deal with two clashing realities: a baby requires a great deal of a mother's time; Gillian barely had time to sleep as it was.

Suddenly, everything was up in the air, especially Gillian's future place on *The X-Files*. It was a very worrying moment in time. They were halfway through the first season. She knew she was so new to the show, so new to TV, that there was a good chance she might be replaced. There was no way to guess what would happen once the news came out. Laid out before her were a series of awkward moments: the one where she tells Chris Carter, the man who had cast her against network opposition; the one where the crew finds out; the moment when she hears what, ultimately will be her professional fate and the fate of the show as a whole.

Clearly, the couple, and Gillian in particular, had to consider the future and come to terms with it in some way. She had to make her own decisions before she asked other people to.

"I knew I needed to make my decision about the pregnancy first, before broaching the subject with the producers. I couldn't be wavering."

Rosemary, Gillian's mother, has said of her daughter that she tends not to complain out loud, especially in a time of personal difficulty. Like many people, Gillian turns inward and searches for a way to deal with the problem. Her husband knew this about her, too, and it seems like he needed some time to think, as well.

"We'd sit in silence and think, Oh my God, what could the repercussions be? I imagine all the worse-case scenarios were flashing through her head, but Gillian is not the type of person to verbalize them. She wouldn't want to tempt fate in that way."

And fated it seemed to be. It wasn't until later, when Anderson was further along in the pregnancy, that she remembered that someone had predicted this — not the marriage, but the baby, including its sex.

"I was at a party that Fox gave at a Burbank Airport hangar, and there were fortune-tellers. So I sat down, and the fortune-teller said to me: 'You are going to have a little girl soon.' And I said, 'I am not!' A month or so later, I started feeling nauseous."

As happy as she was, it was hard to know what to
do, but Gillian chose to go to David Duchovny first
and confide in him. Apparently, her conversation with
Duchovny wasn't what one might be justified in expecting; no shouting or accusations. "I went into his
trailer," she recalls, "and I said, 'David, I'm pregnant.'
It looked like his knees buckled. I think he said, 'Oh,
my God.' And he asked me if it was a good thing. I said,
'Yeah, it is.'"

Next, Gillian had to break the news to Carter,
which was going to be far from easy.

"Having this baby was the right decision for my
husband and me. But it was like, 'Oh, my God; they
did all this for me and now look what I'm doing to
them.' So many things go through your mind. So yes,
I was worried."

Reports vary as to what happened once Anderson
told Carter that she was pregnant. "Well, he was
shocked," Anderson says. "Understandably. I mean,
everybody was. . . . I don't think Chris was too happy
about it." Nonetheless, it seems clear that, once again,
Carter stood behind Anderson and behind his vision
for Scully. He agreed that, somehow, they would work
around the problem. How, exactly, he wasn't sure,
but as he says, people like him are in the business of
solving problems: "As a director, you have to solve
them practically. As a writer, you have to solve them
creatively."

So, it was agreed that they would keep Anderson
on, keep *The X-Files* as it was, as a balanced, two-
character show, and find some way to work with this
new situation. For the first while, however, the network and crew would know nothing about it until

Carter had developed a strategy. "It was a huge risk," Anderson said, "for all of us to just go ahead with it." But they did. And, though none of them could have predicted it, the changes forced *The X-Files* into territory that ultimately enriched the story, the depth of the characters and, by implication, the show itself.

What followed was a very interesting period for *The X-Files* team. Once the crew and, more importantly, the Fox network, had been informed, smoothed out, and brought on-side, everyone got to work in an effort to keep the show from suffering. One of its two integral characters was going to *have* to miss an episode or two, and certainly, they would have to conceal her changing physique from the audience. If any optimists in the group thought that this would prove to be a positive challenge, an opportunity to learn, it seems likely that few people thought it would turn out to actually make the show better.

In dealing with the lost time necessary for Anderson's maternity leave, the writers created a two-part strategy. First came the closing of the X-Files by shadowy forces high above Mulder and Scully, suggesting that they had got too close to "the truth." Mulder was given a series of pointless surveillance assignments and Scully was sent to Quantico Training Center to teach. This separated the two agents, and necessitated their meeting in secret. All of which added suspense, heightened the already sky-high paranoia, and reaffirmed the relationship between the two lead characters. But it also got fans used to seeing Mulder alone — seeing more of Mulder than Scully. As Anderson seemed to drift away, turning up for a meeting here or there, the camera seemed to close in on her face in a kind of nostalgic focus.

Of course, what the camera was really doing was avoiding showing the changes in Gillian Anderson's body. At first, she just wore the regulation FBI trench coats, which, by the end of her pregnancy, barely concealed her girth. There is one scene in "The Host" where the two meet in secret at night on a park bench. Anderson is clearly huge, fatigued, and very glad to sit on the bench.

"There were so many things I couldn't do and the camera couldn't do because there were only certain ways they could shoot me. But on the other hand, I think they did a fabulous job with what they had."

Scully sat behind desks, held file folders before her, was shot from the shoulders up, and gradually changed her wardrobe from a fairly conservative and tailored business suit style, to (depending on the setting) parkas and baggy raincoats. In fact, to draw attention away from Anderson's shapeless wardrobe, both agents began wearing what is now practically a signature: dull, expansive FBI trench coats.

"It's funny," she says, "because David and I wear raincoats about the same amount of time in the series, but it's me that gets the comments about it. Actually, they're very necessary in the cold and wet of Vancouver, and I'm glad of them."

Another challenge was dealing with the fact that Scully is supposed to be just as active as Mulder, chasing bad guys around in alleys and warehouses. As time went on, Anderson just couldn't perform to the physical standard she was used to. Stunt doubles had to take her place for simple things, like running past a door or down some stairs. Luckily, *The X-Files* is not a show that relies on action as much as narrative and atmosphere, and the writers could minimize the rough-and-tumble Scully got into.

And there were the usual, strange things that happen during pregnancy. "When I was pregnant," she says, "something happened to my hair. I *hated* my hair then. If I could have shaved it all off, I would have been happy." She also found that she felt differently about some of the storylines they were pursuing, specifically the appearance of the alien fetus in "The Erlenmeyer Flask. "To have a life inside you and pretend that you don't — as well as all the hormonal things that were happening at the time — was very difficult during that episode. I think, on a psychological level, the storylines have worn on me a bit, but on the whole my work is very separate from my private life . . . I approach it in a very technical way, and I don't pay so much attention to the meat that's underneath that could maybe scare the hell out of me."

But Anderson has a powerful imagination anyway, which sometimes gets the better of her: "Once, in college, I overheard a bartender saying that his girlfriend had run off with his best friend. He described in, like, two seconds what he wanted to do to her, and I had to go to the bathroom and throw up. The image had such an incredible effect on my physiology that I couldn't handle it. It's like something inside me needed to get it out."

During all of this, Gillian felt an encouraging amount of support from the cast and crew of *The X-Files*. Many of them had families of their own (which, due to the nature of the business, they didn't see very often) and so they understood what she was going through. Duchovny himself had to pick up much of the workload as she eased off. As the pregnancy progressed, everyone found ways to make her work hours easier to bear.

"I had a lot of support from the crew and they kind of acted as my extended family," Gillian said, "they helped me a lot and brought me boxes to sit on, made a bed for me to sleep on between the shots. They were very supportive and that made it a lot easier."

Near the end of her term, Anderson's physique also allowed for a kind of free special effect. At the end of "Ascension" Mulder imagines that Scully is the unwilling subject of medical experiments. A tube is attached to her belly, inflating it. The image simultaneously suggests torture and — conveniently for the trajectory of the Scully story-line — impregnation. "I'm not sure whose idea that was," Gillian says, but she adds, "I liked the idea."

Finally, writers had to find a way to give Gillian at least *some* time off to actually give birth, and what they settled on was that her character would actually be abducted. In the episode "Ascension," Scully the skeptic would disappear, leaving a stunned and panicking Mulder behind. She would be missing for the episode "3," in which Mulder has a fling with a vampire, and she would reappear, in a coma and apparently dying, in "One Breath." This event would echo the abduction of Mulder's sister, Samantha, as well as bring fruitful secondary characters, like the duplicitous Alex Krycek, into the mix. In retrospect, Howard Gordon says, the move opened up "a whole new avenue of possibilities for the show."

Anderson herself feels that she brought something to *The X-Files* that no one could have guessed at, but which was positive and a big part of the creative development of the show. "There are certain people on the show who are aware of that," she says, "and there are certain people on the show who don't want to admit that." Even Duchovny says *The X-Files* wouldn't be the thing it is without the added wrinkle of Gillian's pregnancy. "The monster-of-the-week episodes are fun," he says, "but what makes the show really great are the extended stories, and I'm not sure that we would have discovered those otherwise. I think Gillian would agree."

But writer Howard Gordon, who was in on creating some of what is now called the "myth arc" story-line, makes no bones about it: "We were able to block out not only the episodes that would exclude her, but ultimately it sort of was a blessing in disguise because it forced us to contrive something that has been grist for the mill and will continue to be, in terms of her abduction or disappearance, whichever it was."

In fact, the whole thing threw the idea of Scully's skepticism into question: how does she reconcile her experiences with her ordered world-view? And, apparently, there was some disagreement among writers about all that.

In the fourth season, writer Glen Morgan discussed Mulder's similar disappearance in "Anasazi" and said he thought there was the chance that Scully could step into Mulder's shoes. "It's almost as though she's in the position where she would have that cynicism," he said, "that darkness, yet she would now have the hopeful, believing edge. . . . To me, Scully's in a position to become Mulder. I just don't believe she's a skeptic anymore. I thought there was a possibility after 'One Breath' for her to come out of it and be thrown back to her skeptical state, her really hardcore position, because she was in such denial over what had happened to her. But it didn't come out that way."

But Carter stuck to his guns. "My feeling is that she feels there is definitely someone trying to keep certain things from us. But her bias is a scientific one. She believes that there is surely a conspiracy afoot, but is she able to take Mulder's place? I would say no. She's not willing to take his place as a believer. She's still a skeptic."

TEN

THE TOOTH
IS OUT
THERE

When Anderson did have the child, a healthy girl named Piper Maru Anderson, she was late in delivering and eventually had to have a caesarean section. Strangely, the fans on-line somehow knew about the caesarean right away. "They knew within three hours. Maybe it was leaked by someone in the hospital," she says. "They heard about it before my *mom* knew."

Although it would have been a relatively routine operation under normal circumstances, these were not normal circumstances. Anderson had been given just enough time to recover from a normal delivery, but a c-section is surgery and requires a hospital stay. It is harder on the mother and can take several weeks to recover from. Anderson had distinguished herself as a tough person, but it was a harrowing time. "I worked until about a week before the delivery," she said, "and had to be back at work by the time Piper was ten days old."

Her first episode back was "One Breath" in which Scully appears without explanation in a hospital, in a coma, hanging between life and death. As Mulder rages (an emotional explosion the likes of which is rarely seen from this character), Scully slowly seems to die. Of course, she comes out of it in the end, but this all gave Anderson a chance to rest for the first day or two. Literally hooked up to the bed with tubes and monitoring devices, she was unable to do anything but lie there, exhausted, and she found herself sleeping through a lot of the filming. She also found herself wishing she could be with her daughter, and the fact that she couldn't do so was painful.

The next section of filming entailed Anderson sitting for hours on end in a rowboat, bobbing around on a misty lake. The boat was tethered by a long painter to a dock; a metaphor for her soul's desire to float away (the rope is cut at one point and she does, indeed, disappear). For Anderson, this scene was cold and tiring. The crew did their best to help. They put a pillow at her back and concealed a blanket at her feet to ease her situation, but it was not a pleasant time for her. Still, Anderson was glad of the time she was given to simply sit, or lie down and rest.

But, she says, "The next episode ('Firewalker') entailed a lot of running and jumping. It was physically difficult, and emotionally — well, I shed a lot of silent tears. It was horrible. There were plenty of times that all I wanted to do was quit and be with my baby. But then I would have had a lawsuit on my hands, for breach of contract."

"I did have post-natal depression, except there was no time for it, which made it worse. And I was breast feeding," she says.

As tough as this period was, it would pass soon enough. And it was worth the effort. She had gained people's respect for her efforts and dedication and she had made a point to the network that had been so undecided about her at the beginning. Not least of all, she had justified Carter's belief in her.

"I thought it was really a testament," Carter said, "to both David and Gillian's dedication to us. First of all, David had to carry a tremendous amount of work because Gillian's workload was limited. But Gillian was such a trooper in that she wanted more work and worked right up until she couldn't anymore. Then she came back 10 days after giving birth. Although her work in that episode, 'One Breath,' was minimal by design, she was such a trooper to come back so quickly."

Once back, and once she had recovered fully from the birth, Gillian would bring Piper with her to the set every day, or, if that was not possible due to scheduling, a nanny would bring the baby along later. Given the choice of leaving Piper at home, or bringing her onto the set, Anderson didn't want to lose any time with her new daughter. "That's the time you just want to be with her all the time," she says.

Anderson's trailer got one size larger, in proportion to her growing family, and when she had a break, Gillian would spend time with her daughter. One journalist painted a sweet picture of Gillian collapsed on a couch on the set of "Aubrey," only a few episodes after the fact, with Piper on her lap and a large coat thrown over both of them. "I have a fabulous nanny," Gillian is quick to point out, "and although I have to work ridiculous hours, one of the blessings of the show is having Piper on the set."

On top of her usually grueling schedule, Gillian (and Clyde) had to deal with the demands of a new baby. In all of this Clyde was doing his best to get used to being a new father.

"He's doing OK," she said. "It's a much greater shock for any husband. It's easier for the mother because you have all that time to prepare: your body prepares, your mind, your hormones. Men don't really have the preparation for sleep deprivation that women do. But he's handling it very well. He loves her to death."

Some time around this period, Clyde moved from his job at *The X-Files* to his new position at YTV's *Reboot*. The people who work on shows like *The X-Files* often live a fairly nomadic life, taking jobs as they come up, working with companies or directors who are up and coming. As Carter has said about his own industry, "this is a business of failure," and the best way to survive is to stay mobile, interested, and keep learning. Despite the attempts of tabloids to find a meaning in this move, it is more likely that there was nothing in it but an exciting job opportunity. However, if Anderson and her husband had a chance to pop in on each other while working on the same show, that option disappeared with Clyde's leaving *The X-Files*.

Although it had felt like a long time, in just a few months Gillian's life had altered considerably, and these changes altered her perception and portrayal of Scully. "There was a huge chunk that kind of shook things up when I was pregnant. And everything that happens to a woman's body when she becomes pregnant — the hormonal changes, your mood changes, your personality changes. I mean, I was a very different person. And I think Scully became a different person in a way during that time, too."

In fact, Gillian has said that the change came at a strange time for her, one where both she and the writers were beginning to see new avenues for Scully, and in a way, those avenues had been cut off by the sudden necessities of shooting around her pregnancy. The episode "Beyond the Sea" was a kind of showpiece for Scully. As Glen Morgan said: "It was time to grow Scully's character, because she was doing the same kind of thing too often." And James Wong was even more specific about what he'd hoped. "Gillian needed to show off her talents," he said.

"I think I was just starting to find out who she was. I think in the beginning it's perfectly natural that I was still trying to figure out who she was." But then, she says, she got pregnant and "there was this big change."

Although she is thrilled with Piper, and with her own career so far, and although she has said that, hypothetically, she would want more children, Gillian is quick to say that she will not go that route again soon. "I wouldn't want to do it the same way again. It was one of the hardest things I've ever done."

The crew lavish attention on Piper when she is on the set. She has been given an alien doll with a missing tooth, and a matching t-shirt with "The tooth is out there" written across the front. She has been seen toodling around in her own little FBI jacket. She seems unconcerned by the gore and scary special effects surrounding her, and has allegedly been seen carrying a latex severed hand about with her wherever she goes.

"She's been on the set since the day she was born," says Duchovny to an interviewer, "so she's used to seeing squirming alien worms. . . . But when she saw Santa Claus this year, she went apoplectic — screaming and crying." (This scene will sound familiar to any parent who's had to take a hysterical child off Santa's knee at the mall.)

To ward off loneliness himself, Duchovny got a puppy from the owner of the dog that starred in "Ice." The dog is a mutt, called Blue. As Duchovny says, "Piper's cuter, but Blue has nicer hair. Blue used to be smarter, but Piper has eclipsed her in that area." And he adds, perhaps sadly, "I don't see Blue gaining."

For her part, Gillian is finding life — and herself — quite changed. "I am a much happier person since she came along," Gillian says. "Nothing is quite so important any more." And she adds, "Piper keeps me in check. My husband has grounded me as well."

Although her relationship with Clyde would eventually end, she is always generous with her praise for his love and care of Piper. Little is known of the reasons for their separation. And honestly, little is known of their life together previous to the break-up. On the subject of their time together, Gillian has said: "The stuff that the public knows is pretty surface stuff, it's pretty run-of-the-mill, basic information. They don't know the other stuff. The whole courtship and marriage and pregnancy was such a communal thing with the crew and everybody. It was something that was happening to all of us, so I was used to it not being just a personal family thing." In fact, she enjoyed the idea that the few fans in the know were sharing in this communality, as well. "What I've gotten from the fans who know the information has been nothing but support, so it's been like they've been sharing in the magical nature of it, which is wonderful."

Despite a basic lack of information, Anderson's life often ended up in the tabloids, which didn't bother her at first — in fact, it often amused her. "I love rumors that have no basis in reality that are funny; [they're] not hurting anybody." But she soon began to think of it as Duchovny does. "I think gossip is hurtful," he says, and then he affects nonchalance. "You know, it doesn't matter to me." But after two years of having her life played with in a strange kind of public forum, Anderson began to put the brakes on — mostly to protect her daughter. The official news of her separation from Clyde Klotz hit the media the day she won her first Golden Globe. Since then, there have been many more awards, movie offers, interviews, and fan appreciation for Gillian. But she has not changed *that* much as a person.

"At least once a week," she says "I lie back in the bathtub and laugh at the ridiculousness of it all."

X-FILES CONVENTION

In January of 1996 Anderson made her first appearance at an *X-Files* Fan Convention. It was held in Burbank, California, and thousands of fans lined up to get the chance to see Dana Scully live and in person, or, at least, the actress who portrayed her every Friday night. Chris Carter had already attended several conventions, as had several of the show's regular guest stars, to sign autographs and satisfy fans' curiosity at the regular question-and-answer sessions. *The X-Files* prop and special effects teams created displays of items used during the filming of the fans' favorite episodes. Lucky attendees have even had the opportunity to view the official *X-Files* blooper reel: "The Gags Are Out There."

Anderson, apparently, holds her own on a set filled with pranksters. She startled viewers and crew members alike when she ate a live cricket during a scene in second season's "Humbug." It went unquestioned that she had actually swallowed the bug for some months, given Gillian's proclivity for gags, but she has more recently confessed that she spat out the bug off-camera. On-set there is a running gag, a contest really, to clip as many clothespins to a victim's clothing without him/her catching on. "Last year Rob Bowman and I would try to pin clothespins on each other regularly. I won with 37 at once on this big red coat of his."

During the filming of "The List," maggots were used in a particularly gruesome scene that required a stuntman to be covered in the little creatures. Cast and crew were horrified by the larvae but when one of the insects headed for the stuntman's eye Anderson nonchalantly picked it off his face. Duchovny could not let an opportunity slip by; he sneaked away and returned with a handful of white rice from the caterer's supplies. He tossed the larva-like grains at Anderson. She shrieked and Duchovny burst out laughing.

"I can goof around with other people right up to when we shoot," she says. "If it's a scene that needs more from me emotionally, I'll focus more. But we've been doing this long enough that we can fall into it at the drop of a hat." Mitch Pileggi describes the quality that best distinguishes her from Agent Scully: "Her sense of humor. Once she gets the giggles, it's like, forget it." And Gillian, herself says, "I'm more spontaneous. I laugh. I'm crass. I'm raunchy."

Before going on stage, Anderson felt nervous. There were at least 3,000 fans listening and laughing as Dean Haglund, a stand-up comic in real life, got the crowd roaring. "I don't have anything funny to say," she groaned backstage. Later she recalled, "I went in thinking it was going to be weird and I was going to hate it. But everybody was so loving and so normal, I was overwhelmed, touched. I didn't prepare a speech. I wanted to just react to the moment. It wasn't exactly the right choice, because I had nothing to say. I went right to the questions and answers."

She continues, "I was very nervous going in, I wasn't sure what to expect and I came out feeling much less nervous about it. The audience was wonderful. They were terrific. They were all very sane — most of them were — very sane and just very sweet and wonderful. And they were just there because they love the show and it ended up being a wonderful experience."

It was a real coming out, of sorts, for Anderson. A real opportunity to separate herself from her TV persona and to separate herself from her costar in the public mind and the media. When a boy from the crowd stepped up to the mike and asked her why David Duchovny has more magazine covers, she replied, "Maybe it's my time now."

[See page 119 for a transcript of Anderson's January 1996 X-Files Convention appearance.]

TWELVE

LOTS AND LOTS OF PHILES

Just how famous was *The X-Files* — and Anderson herself — becoming? In the summer of 1996, she found out.

Among the crowd waiting for disembarking travelers at Sydney airport, where Gillian Anderson was scheduled to emerge from the gates, was a car rental agent holding a sign with "SCULLY" written on it and a small "X" scrawled in the corner. Unrelated to Anderson's trip, this man was waiting patiently for a family of the name of Scully.

On her way to do a promotional tour in three Australian cities, Gillian had just flown in from holidaying in Bali. In another odd coincidence, she was spared a ride on Garuda Flight 865, thanks to a last-minute reschedule. That flight made it to Japan but crashed soon after taking off from Fukoka, losing the tail, both wings, wheels and the engines, and leaving a trail of debris on the ground behind it. The miracle is that, although the fuselage burst into flames, all of the nearly 300 passengers survived the disaster. It was pure luck that Gillian was not on that plane.

Stepping out of the gates and into the arrivals area of Sydney airport, Gillian Anderson was greeted by a crowd of photographers and journalists. Wearing a long black sleeveless dress, sandals, and glasses, she paused briefly for photographs, but answered only a few questions. When asked about her recent holiday in Bali, she answered simply, "It was good." She was friendly, but busy. Sensing that it was strange to see this celebrity and devoted mother in an airport without publicists, "minders," or her child, one journalist asked Anderson why Piper wasn't with her.

"She is," Anderson replied, smiling, "we're just protecting her from you guys." With that, she made her way to where a white limousine was waiting, slipped inside, and shut the door. Shortly after that, Piper and Anderson's "minders" hurried through the crowd, into the limo, and away.

It was clear Gillian was beginning to have a following. Fans on the Internet debated everything from her true hair-colour to her latest date at a public function. She was deluged with fan mail, requests for interviews, magazine photo shoots, profiles, and public appearances. She was asked to give her endorsement to foundations and products. She offered her energies to many things. She was virtually always cheerful, open, and giving of herself, fun in an interview, laughing a lot of the time. She was not stuck up and often described herself as "goofy." When asked by a Sydney journalist what fame means to her, her answer was oddly rueful: "suffocation," she said, and yet, even this answer was given with a laugh. It all seemed to be a kind of pleasant shock to her, a mixed blessing.

"I tend to be very private, so I don't get off on the paparazzi following you around, or the intrusion aspect of it. Or being in places where there are lots of people. I don't like big crowds."

Well, crowds were certainly what the hard-working actor got in Australia. And it was perhaps the first time she got a really clear idea of her own celebrity.

A large, calm man stood outside a hotel room door. His name was Andrew Tatrai and he was a security guard whose job was to keep the curious away from Gillian Anderson. His other clients included Elle Macpherson, Joan Collins, and Claudia Schiffer. Andrew was used to dealing with sneaky paparazzi and hysterical fans, but at the moment, everything was calm. It was close to sunrise and he could hear nothing more exciting than Piper chattering to her mother. Gillian, her close friend Bonny Hay, with whom she was traveling, Piper, and Piper's nanny were sharing a quiet breakfast before the busy day began. (Bonny is on the *X-Files* production crew and often acts as Gillian's stand-in.) Later, Gillian would meet with Kristen McGrath and Jane Nagel, publicists from Twentieth Century Fox Home Entertainment and Foxtel, who were acting as Anderson's hosts during her visit to Australia. She would tour three large cities, Sydney, Brisbane, and Melbourne, to promote *The X-Files* TV show, as well as the release of the new *X-Files* videos which hit the stores June 12, 1996. This set of videos came in the form of a Special Collector's Cube and included a new video, a 45-minute special episode called "Secrets of *The X-Files*," and eight large-format collector cards. Gillian had three mall appearances set up, where she was to sign copies of the new merchandise. As well, she would do print, radio, and television interviews.

Gillian and *The X-Files* show already had a large fan base in Australia. In fact, many Australian interviewers had traveled to Vancouver to interview Anderson, Duchovny, and other *X-Files* personalities. When one such journalist asked her whether she gets fan mail from Australians, she said yes. Lots. But it was distinctly different from the fan mail she gets from Americans.

"They're all very polite and usually the fans have a lot to say, as opposed to the States. Sometimes you'll get letters [that say] 'Hi, I like your show, can I have your autograph?' But from Australia they talk about shows they enjoy or why they like the show."

The fans in Australia were loyal, interested in every detail of the show, and, apparently, rather numerous.

In the early days of the trip, Gillian and Piper visited the Sydney Zoo, one of the best zoos in the world. The animals are kept in conditions as near to their natural habitat as possible, so that they can find privacy if they want it, and are surrounded by familiar land forms and plant life. Later, Gillian and Bonny went scuba diving at Manly's Ocean World. Gillian had tried scuba diving for the first time while vacationing in Bali, and had loved it.

"As soon as I put my head under the water for the first time, there was so much to see it was like . . . overload," she said. This time, though, Anderson was in an indoor tank, swimming with sharks — literally. The tank was full of gray Nurse Sharks which are a benign, though massive species of shark (they can grow up to 14 feet long and weigh as much as 500 pounds).

Anderson also made herself available for interviews in this first day or two, and there were a lot of interviewers waiting. In the enormous conference room of one of Australia's grandest hotels, she curled up on a couch and sipped from her bottle of water as journalists lined up to interview her. She spoke to as many as she could, patient with the repetitious questions ("Will Mulder and Scully ever get together?"), charming and affable with everybody, until it was time to go. She had to pack and get ready for the trip to Brisbane.

After arriving in Brisbane and settling in to the hotel, Gillian left Piper with her nanny and went off to an interview on the Martin/Molloy show, a popular FM radio show on the Austereo network. Among other stations, Austereo carries Fox FM. Crowds outside the station were not huge and Gillian carried on a fairly silly, up-beat interview with the two hosts, Tony Martin and Mick Molloy. One thing the hosts do is to ask celebrities something about themselves that they have not told other interviewers. Gillian, who has learned not to give it up easily, slyly said: "I have size seven feet," and left it at that.

Next stop, the Midday Show on channel 9, where, as if to illustrate that all Australian media hosts are silliness embodied, the host Kerri-Anne was holding a Christmas show, the set festooned with snow. Skiing was on the roster for later in the show and Gillian was expected to join in. When the host asked her, "You have skied, haven't you?" she looked down at her size-seven feet and said: "I've never skied in heels, though." Some of the audience members were sitting on the floor because there were not enough seats, and, earlier in the day, the more eager fans had been literally climbing over fences outside the studio to get in. In fact, the crowds seemed to be gathering, almost as if news of Anderson's presence had been spreading by word of mouth. By the time she left the TV studio, people were lining the streets, and later, at an in-store appearance in Brisbane, an estimated 10,000 fans turned up for a chance at an autograph or a glimpse of Agent Scully.

Anderson has said of being in the spotlight that it is clearly flattering, a wonderfully positive trade-off for the hours of hard work, but that it is a little bewildering. Her every expression and gesture begin to take on such heavy significance that it is hard to be casual about anything. Some American sport figures have complained about being set up as role models for kids, only to have the less-than-heroic facts of their lives trotted out as crimes against their own image. A few have even returned the gift unopened, saying it is their job to be athletes and that's all; it is the job of parents to be role models. Anderson will not go that far; she seems to appreciate her own position as a female role model and she understands the incredibly positive effect a thing like that can have on the world young girls live in. However, the pressure can get pretty high.

"If you're in a vulnerable state of mind in any way," she says, "it can be incredibly intrusive and disorientating to place yourself in a situation where there are hundreds of people who want your attention and want you to live up to their standards. It gets emotionally exhausting."

But most of the time, she says, it's flattering.

Once finished in Brisbane, Anderson moved on to Melbourne on June 28. In the morning, Piper visited a place called Kids' Sport which was filled with lots of jungle gyms, trampolines, and other fun items. At 1:30, Gillian was to make an appearance at the Southland Shopping Centre. The event would be covered live on Fox FM and she would be interviewed by two hosts, Grubby and Dee-dee. Neither Fox personnel nor the Southland organizers could have predicted the response to the advertising. By the early afternoon, when Gillian walked onto the stage, most fans had been lining up for many hours, some die-hards even camping out on-site since 4 a.m. When she came into view, the crowd began to roar and continued to roar throughout Anderson's radio interview. At one point, one of the hosts simply gave up, remarking with awe, "This is just berserk!"

When the interview was over and the time came for Anderson to sign autographs, the crowd surged forward, some people waving videos or photographs, desperate to get closer to the stage. In a crowd of nearly 10,000 (one of the hosts estimated closer to 15,000) most people knew she would only sign a fraction of the items, and so they pressed forward to get closer to the front of the line. As this happened, the people at the edge of the stage began to get crushed. In the excitement, people, most of them young, began losing belongings, became close to hysterical, and some people were in grave danger of being hurt.

Although one source said there had only been three security officers on duty before the event, police were quickly called in to manage the crowd. From her vantage point on stage, Anderson could see what was happening. Clearly alarmed, she watched young fans fainting and being lifted from the crowd, and she tried in vain to calm people down. Invoking the cool, unflappable character of Scully, she shouted appeals for calm into the PA system.

"People are getting squashed," she shouted, "we do not want to do any autopsies."

As it was, two people were injured and 24 suffered from hyperventilation and had to be treated by ambulance medics. One medic blamed it on the fact that people had been lining up since the early morning without sufficient food or water. "Their breathing rate changed when the lady from *The X-Files* came on stage," he said.

Since the pushing and hysteria showed no sign of stopping, organizers decided the event had to be cut short to prevent any further injuries. Thirty minutes before she was scheduled to leave, Anderson was ushered off the stage.

Sitting in her hotel room later that afternoon, Anderson described the event to yet another group of journalists. Clearly shaken and perplexed, she described the whole thing as "unbelievable."

"The welcome here has been overwhelming," she said, "absolutely incredible."

It seems that Anderson did not have a clear idea of her own level of celebrity, the degree to which she was known and, for many different reasons, adored. "I've not experienced anything like it," she said, adding, "I've never made a mall appearance before, so I really have no point of reference."

She had been to *The X-Files* convention. "When I did the convention in the States we had about 3,000 people. But that was all the place could hold."

When told by a journalist that she, more than the show she was on, was the reason for the hysteria, she reacted very strongly.

"I'd go insane if I thought that. If I honestly allowed myself to believe that 12,000 people would show up to see me, then I'd be somebody I'm not. . . . It would be too much to handle if I started believing it. I try to be humble in the midst of everything and appreciate everything that's come my way."

This is admirable modesty, but it likely also proceeds as a side-effect of the kind of work schedule Anderson, Duchovny, and the rest of *The X-Files* team have. There is a blurred sense of how all this work is going over in the public arena. You work, you go home to sleep, you work again the next day. There is very little time to cruise the Net (let alone learn how to do that), little time to read magazines or newspapers, to sit back and channel-surf and get a really good idea of just how often *The X-Files* in general, and Gillian Anderson in particular, comes up. *The X-Files* team must, in some ways, take it on faith that the work they do is appreciated. Even cruising the Net isn't enough since, despite all the hype, not everybody has access to the world wide web. The gradual shift from cult success, to mainstream success, to genuine hit, is just that, gradual. The momentum of the show was growing and there was very little Gillian could do to gauge its growth.

It's one thing to sell something to lots of people. It's another thing entirely to see all those people in one place, all wanting more. So it must have been a bolt of reality for Gillian to walk onto that stage and literally see the scope of her own public appeal. As pleasant as the knowledge might have been, it came in an astonishing package — and it wasn't over. If Gillian had any doubts that the event at the Southland Shopping Centre was just an anomaly, those doubts evaporated when she walked on stage at the Westfield Miranda mall in Sydney.

Anderson was expected at Westfield Miranda on the 29th of June. She spent the day before at a party at Planet Hollywood. The party had a Rocky Horror theme, was noisy and fun. For the first while, a photographer followed Anderson around, chronicling her participation in the event. She allowed him to shoot several rolls of film before she turned and, with a raised hand and stern Scully-like glance, drew the line. She knew it was her job to make herself available for publicity purposes, but Anderson was learning by experience when to assert her right to be left in peace.

The next day, she was to do an interview via satellite link with a New Zealand interviewer. But the interviewer seemed preoccupied with a fictitious romance between Anderson and Duchovny and wouldn't get off the subject. On top of this, the interview was very nearly terminated due to technical difficulty. The whole process briefly baffled and unsettled Anderson, who often has to answer these kinds of questions.

"I guess the most obtuse question I was asked in that regard," she says, "was: 'David's such a sex symbol . . . what's it like working with a god?' How could somebody answer that question?"

When rumors of an off-screen romance between Anderson and Duchovny didn't pan out, rumors of a feud took their place. Her separation from her husband was big news and her life was scoured for men who might be the "cause" of the breakup. Anderson sees the artifacts of her own fame as being separate from her own private life. What bothers her now is that that very private life is coming increasingly under scrutiny. Unfortunately, loss of privacy is the by-product of fame, and very hard to control.

At 1:45, fifteen minutes after she was scheduled to arrive, Gillian Anderson walked onto the stage at Westfield Miranda. A roar of adulation rose up as she stepped forward, waving. "Hello!" she said into the mike, "You guys look great," and the crowd became deafening.

By some accounts, there were 10,000 people staring back at her. The sea of people began at the stage and went back into the shopping centre, heads waving and bobbing in a congregation that seemed never to end. Fans tossed flowers and stuffed toys onto the stage at her feet. One young woman close to Anderson had "Scully" written on her forehead and an "X" on each cheek. Some waved videos, t-shirts, collector's cubes, and other merchandise, and everyone hoped to get close to Gillian Anderson. Judging by the excitement and noise, there was certainly the possibility of more trouble. Wide-eyed and no doubt apprehensive after her experience in Melbourne, Anderson carried on, smiling and cheerful. She told stories about working on the show, enthused about the incredible loyalty of Australian fans ("You guys are amazing!"), made jokes and waited to see what would happen.

But the organizers of this event were ready for the huge number of people, warned perhaps by the news that had recently come from Melbourne. There were ambulances standing by outside the shopping centre. Security officers and more than 100 Sydney police officers were positioned strategically throughout the crowd. Organizers had issued a warning that any undue pushing or jostling would result in termination of the event. As well, to control the vying for position, official autograph tickets were given out to the first 350 people. If you didn't have a ticket, you would not be able to get Ms. Anderson's signature. Still, people lined up, ignoring customer service officers who told them there was no point. One representative of the Miranda shopping centre said, "This is the biggest crowd I've seen here."

Despite its being a well-organized and successful event, some 80 people fainted from the heat and excitement and had to be pulled to safety and treated by ambulance workers. Again, people had lined up since the early morning and others had even camped out overnight to assure being close to the front. In many ways, it was a repeat of the Southland event.

In all, Anderson attracted over 30,000 fans in Australia and the implications, for her and for Chris Carter and the rest of *The X-Files* team, must have been very heartening. As clear and encouraging as TV ratings systems might be, and as suggestive as it might be that Anderson and Duchovny had turned up in dozens of magazines, there is nothing like a near-riot to really bring the news home: this show is a success and Gillian Anderson is a star. One can only wonder whether any of them, working away in Vancouver, Canada, actually *knew* this. But if they didn't know it before Anderson went to Australia, they sure did after.

Anderson's modest self-appraisal of her reception in Australia was an attempt to hold on to a healthy sense of balance:

"There's a huge temptation in this business for people to allow stuff like that to go to their heads, so it's really important to keep it in perspective."

She knew that *The X-Files* show, and the solid and attractive character of Scully, had a lot to do with the adulation. She was always quick to give credit to Carter and *The X-Files* team:

"Because of where Australia is, they don't get that many celebrities visiting, so when they do come, the people get so excited about it. I showed up as the representative of *The X-Files* and that's what the people were responding to. Maybe they thought I was the only one from the show who would make it there."

Maybe. Then again, maybe it really was all about her.

THIRTEEN

A MATTER
OF
PRINCIPLE

Now that she was feeling more confident of her position as a leading actor on television, Anderson decided to use the opportunity of contract renegotiations to address some of the inequities prevalent in Hollywood film and television business dealings. Male actors have always been paid more than female actors. And although there is a trend in the film industry to hand out some big pay cheques to a few "privileged" high profile women, as Anderson says, "They'll never earn what their male counterparts are earning. Women in Hollywood are constantly shown that there's a difference between them and men, and that that's okay. But it's not okay."

The common wisdom is that it is the men who create a box office success. Television executives follow their film counterparts and the big money-makers in television are predominantly the men. "There are huge differences in the way male and female actors are perceived," Anderson explains. "Women have to be a certain size, in order to get good roles. The only successful, larger-than-average female actor I can think of is Kathy Bates. And once women reach a certain age, they can only expect one or two good roles per year, whereas male actors can continue working regularly well into their forties. Then there are the types of roles available to women. We're constantly depicted as sidekicks, ingenues, and hangers-on, rarely as independent and capable individuals. And the enormous, huge discrepancies in pay. . . . The amounts that some male actors make are astronomically obscene."

So as part of the natural course of renegotiating the terms of her contract with one of the most successful shows on television and a huge money-making vehicle for Fox, Anderson asked for a raise. "I knew — going into this [fourth] season — that was the way it was going to be. It was something that I was attempting to handle privately and just make some kind of statement about the lack of equality not being OK. And somehow it got public. I haven't actually talked about it that much at all."

The topic of TV stars' salaries has always been a hot one for the media (mostly because the figures are less routinely reported than are those of film actors) and *Entertainment Weekly*'s cover story in August 1996 stirred up the public's interest in time for the new fall season. Duchovny's estimated $100,000 per episode was plastered across the cover while inside the magazine the article reported Anderson's salary to be five figures, not her costar's six. She told an Australian reporter that she makes "a little more than half of what David makes."

Of course, as an unknown actress, hoping for regular employment, Anderson saw the difference in her pay and Duchovny's as reasonable. "Actually, I originally got even less than half as much as David. It was OK at the time. He was coming off 10 features, and I was coming off of nothing. But things have shifted, in that we're now in the fourth season of a two-person show. And we're continuing to do the same amount of work. A lot of people have actually come up to me, just kind of quietly, and said, 'I'm glad that you're taking a stand.' On the other hand, it's obviously not doing any good."

FAME

Filming in Vancouver meant that, for the most part, the cast and crew were removed from the atmosphere of hype and pressure associated with Los Angeles. And, for the first season, everyone could concentrate on the job at hand — producing a television show unlike any other. For Anderson, it also meant that feedback from the audience came in the form of fan letters.

There was, and still is, a mix of adoring male and appreciative female writers. "I've gotten quite a few letters from young girls saying I'm a role model, and this is probably one of the best compliments I could get as an actor. It's terrific because of what the character represents: honesty, justice, hard work and dedication and passion — and if that's what they're tapping into, that's fantastic." A lot of the online, male attention came from, she proudly declares, "computer geeks." "There's an intelligence to the attraction. I actually enjoy that I *don't* get letters from guys saying, 'Oh, you're so beautiful, I want to marry you, I can't wait till you take your clothes off.' I think I might throw up if I got something like that."

And, in keeping with her widely reported sense of the absurd, Anderson also receives her share of eccentric tokens of appreciation. She was sent a tape of a song written and performed by a fan: "Oh, Scully, When Will You Kiss Mulder?" — "It was this twangy hillbilly song. It was fabulous."

But as the show has grown in popularity the quantity of mail has grown exponentially. "There used to be a manageable amount and now it's not manageable at all, and we haven't quite figured out how to remedy that. I can't see myself hiring somebody to fake signatures. I'd rather grab at a few when I get the chance and write a note myself." Which is what she did recently when an online fanclub pooled their resources and efforts and sent her one long letter with submissions and signatures from its two hundred or so members. Her reply was hand written and gracious and was posted online in keeping with the spirit of the Internet community.

Although she owns a computer, she admits that her time is so limited that she does not log onto the Internet. From time to time downloaded material from the fan sites makes its way onto the set and although Anderson, along with Carter and Duchovny, has participated in moderated IRC (chat) sessions, she says, "I haven't actually logged on myself, but I'm aware of their presence. It's pretty amazing how involved it gets. I think it's wonderful. I mean, it has been helping the show and it's wonderful that we have a constant following. I see myself, if I really got involved, spending hours reading stuff. But my energy needs to be in other areas right now."

She has also made time between takes to sign autographs and chat with fans on many of the occasions that the show has been filming on location in and around Vancouver. But the demands on her time with a young daughter and the long hours of shooting don't always leave her with much personal privacy. "In a way that's par for the course . . . I'm more than happy to make kids happy, or make someone happy by signing an autograph; that's great. There are certain times when I feel it's more an invasion of privacy than others. But that's just something that I have to deal with," she says. "I'm not sure exactly what it means to me. I try not to think about it too much."

Fame, as a goal or as an entity unto itself is something she does not feel comfortable with. "I tend to be a very private person and want to let people in when I want to let them in, not when they want to be let in," she says. "There is something vulnerable about being in the public eye, to a certain degree. Having that feeling, hearing 'Scully' whispered as you pass people. It reminds you constantly that you're not in your private little world."

But she has learned to deal with the attention and she credits her daughter with lending her the perspective. "It hasn't really freaked me out. It's a separate entity from who I am. So having it in that reality, in that perspective, I am who I am. When I go home at night, I am with my daughter. There's this whole other being who's perceived of in a certain way, and to keep myself separate from that entity is, I think, essential in survival in this particular type of situation."

Anderson has also had to deal with some of the darker sides of notoriety. As Scully stepped out of her partner's shadow, and as Anderson gained confidence in her work and in herself, the actress began to consciously reveal herself to the public eye in a new light. She did several photo shoots early on that revealed what was distinctly non-Scully about Gillian Anderson. Most of the early pictures were romantic, like those in *Starlog* magazine, April 1995. In February, 1996 she made the cover of *Entertainment Weekly*, looking very glamorous, as did she in the American TV *Guide* a few months later. But it was her photo shoot for FHM, a British men's magazine, that put her on the map as an "object of desire." The April '96 issue sold out in record time from the newstands, which is not surprising considering the cover depicting an alluring bedroom shot of Anderson in black lingerie. Inside the issue, the pictures took on a more aggressively sexual look with shots of the actress in an outfit of black lace and a jumpsuit made of blue rubber. At the photo shoot someone suggested that it would be funny to shoot Gillian hancuffed to the bed. To the surprise of everyone in the studio, she grabbed the cuffs and said, "Great, where do we start?" "This is very un-Scully," it was observed, to which she shot back: "Good. That's the point."

The photos from this session are, easily, the pictures most often posted and downloaded on the Internet. And this means they are the ones most frequently altered to make it appear that Anderson's session was a nude photo shoot. But, as usual, she greets this part of her life with humor. "I've seen one picture from that shoot on the Internet that somebody has doctored where I am meant to have pulled my bra down to expose my breasts! They've put in these two implant-filled breasts in place of my not-so-huge non-implant ones. And it's meant to be real. My manager rang me and said, 'Gillian, you didn't really do this, did you?' "

Not all of the pictures online are as easily dismissed. "There's another one where I look like I'm on-set and I'm sitting there with my legs open and you can see my knickers are showing. So naturally the first thing you think is, 'Oh my God, how did somebody get this picture,' and then I thought, 'Hang on, I never sit like that.' And I wear nylons anyway, so you wouldn't be able to see what I had or didn't have on underneath. But I kept thinking, 'When did I sit there with my legs open?' "

Not surprisingly, the pictures attracted the attention of another men's magazine: *Playboy*. "I felt like I'd arrived when, after I'd done FHM, I got offered a *Playboy* cover! They called my manager when she was in the car with me. We had it on speakerphone." She won't say exactly what the six-figure offer was but it was "a lot. I turned them down. But it was very flattering, I must say." FHM readers also voted her the Sexiest Woman in the World in 1996, much to her surprise. And she won *People Online's* Most Beautiful People poll.

She and Duchovny also fulfilled the fantasies of fans who would love to see Mulder and Scully's relationship become more intimate, when they posed in bed together for the cover of the Australian edition of *Rolling Stone* magazine. "It was just something that was

thought up and agreed to by us because it sounded like
it would make a great cover and the photographs
ended up being very risqué and beautiful, and we
loved them. Scully is so strait-laced that it was refreshing to do something different." She adds, "For me,
it was a conscious choice as an actress to get away
from the stereotype of Scully. I wanted to show that I
had other sides to me."

Her most prized response to her "exposure,"
though, came from a source closer to home, revealing,
perhaps, from where she inherited her sense of humor.
"This is a letter from my grandmother," she told Jay
Leno and his NBC talk show audience. "Dear Gilly,
I was very, very sorry to hear that you ran out of
clothing. Maybe I should send you some money so you
can buy a new dress or two. I am going to plant several
fig trees so that in the future we will have plenty of fig
leaves to cover you if you ever run out of clothing
again. Loving you very much, but wondering why you
stripped, or flipped, or whatever."

With the photographic exposure has come tabloid
exposure and some real intrusions on her family's
privacy as well as her own. Her mother, Rosemary,
described some of the changes for a *Washington Post*
reporter in May '96. "Last week, for the first time, a
reporter showed up at my door, from England —*from
England* ! — yes, in the pouring rain, came charging
up. My girlfriend was in the driveway and she practically pushed her out of the way, and said, 'I'm from
London and I'd like to interview you about Gillian
and her childhood and have some pictures and use
some of your time.' " The reporter remained in Grand
Rapids, and "she has called everybody we've ever

known. She has been over to the high school, going through the yearbooks."

The knowledge that one's every public move is going to be scrutinized or photographed is hard enough to get used to. But even worse is the invasion of privacy. "When it bothers me is when I know that I can't go on vacation without being followed by cameras. Twice now I felt certain nobody was around taking pictures and I was wrong, pictures showed [up]. And that's disturbing, really disturbing." So it's also not surprising that Anderson's feelings about her notoriety have changed a little over the years. "I'm not as tolerant as I used to be. I like my space. I don't like crowds on set. I'm less tolerant of signing autographs in the break I have between takes, and I'm less tolerant of people trying to snap pictures of me in the street. But basically I've stayed the same. I'm just here to do the work."

"The obligations of fame are interesting. I remember a period of time when I was pregnant. That's when it really hit me that the show was getting successful. I felt for the first time that I had a certain responsibility to the audience to maintain at a time when I couldn't maintain it anymore because I was pregnant, tired and I was going through the whole hormonal thing. So, that was the first time any obligation really hit me. I have an obligation to do the show, to play this character and, beyond my contract, to Chris Carter. I try to do good work and to remain a good person. No fan of *The X-Files* or any TV show, I think, wants to hear that star of a show bitch about their life or bitch about the fans. So, I try very hard to maintain a positive frame of mind about everything."

"This is my life's work, this is what I know how to do and what I care about as much as anything in my life," she concludes. "I'm not going to give it up because I can't handle the attention. It's about following one's heart and one's dream. It's not about fame."

X-TRA CURRICULAR ACTIVITIES

AUDIOBOOKS

1993   Records "Exit to Eden," by Anne Rice. Audio-book for Random House.

1995   Records "Ground Zero," (*X-Files* novel) by Kevin J. Anderson. Audiobook for Harper Audio.

RADIO

Although she has done a number of radio interviews around the world, Anderson's first interview for CBC Radio in Vancouver set into motion some new experiences for her and the station.

1994   *November 19th*: "The First Time" in Studio 4 CBC Vancouver

1995   *September 16th*: "Hello Gillian?" — Gillian made broadcasting history the with the first ever *global* celebrity call-in show on RealTime.

| 1996 | *March 16th*: "DJ for a Day" — Gillian played DJ and spent hours setting the play list with producer Loc Dao. |
| 1996 | *September 21*: "DJ Gillian returns" — Anderson produced another two hours where she played music, took calls and answered e-mail. |

TALK SHOWS

Anderson began her talk show "career" on American television with a popular morning program. Her appearance was notable, for although she was not talkative she was very open about herself and her youth. She has since gone on to make appearances on shows all over the world displaying with ease her quick sense of humor and readiness to share herself. Here are some notable U.S. appearances:

1995	*April 18*: Her first TV talk show interview on *Regis and Kathie Lee*
	April 18: *The Jon Stewart Show*
	April 26: *Conan O'Brien Show*
1996	*February 19*: *David Letterman*
	September 30: *The Late Show with David Letterman* (her second appearance)
	October 9: *Rosie O'Donnell Show*
	December 16: *Jay Leno*

OTHER TELEVISION WORK

Since May of 1996 rumors have circulated that Anderson, like her costar, Duchovny, will be contributing a story-line for an upcoming *X-Files* episode. Until then we'll just have to look out for her other work:

1993   *Class of '96*, episode #8, "The Accused"

1995   *December 30*: Always ready to make light of her success, Anderson agreed to do the voice-over for CGI Agent Data Nully in episode 22 of *Reboot*, a computer generated animation show for young adults. In the episode, titled "Trust No One," (an *X-Files* parody) the Bi-nomes and Sprites of Mainframe are being terrorized by an energy-siphoning "mouse." Two CGI agents, Fax Modem and Data Nully, who specialize in cases known as the ASCII Files, are called in to solve the puzzle.

1996   Hosts TV special *Why Planes Go Down*

1996   Hosts TV special *Spies Above Us*

1996   *June 13*: Hosts *Future Fantastic* a nine-episode U.K. documentary; soundtrack by Hal

1997   Anderson and Duchovny did the voice-overs for a *Simpsons X-Files* parody called "The Springfield Files"

PUBLIC APPEARANCES

Nothing prepared Anderson for her three appearances in Australia in the summer of 1996, but she has kept busy back home too:

1996   *January*: Anderson made her first appearance at an *X-Files* Fan Convention in Burbank, California. Her appearance drew a crowd of 3,000.

May 3: Washington, D.C., Anderson makes speech requesting research funding from Congress on behalf on Neurofibromatosis Inc. *November 2*: Webstock96 Celebrities and Activists gathered at the House of Blues in Los Angeles to encourage voting and political awareness in young people.

1997 *March 15*: Attends the GameWorks Seattle Grand Opening

COMPUTER PRODUCTS

1996 Performs the role of EVE (Enhanced Virtual Entity) in Microsoft's futuristic game Hell-Bender.

1997 Anderson, along with co-star David Duchovny have filmed new *X-Files* footage to be incorporated into an interactive CD-ROM, slated for release in 1997. Developed in conjunction with the show's creator, Chris Carter, this interactive odyssey features a new *X-Files* storyline geared to engage both X-philes and interactive gamers.

MUSIC

1997 *April* — Anderson has recorded a song, "Extremis," with a British techno band called Hal, which features a spoken word performance by Anderson. "Extremis" was recorded in Mushroom Studios in Vancouver, Canada before Christmas 1996. Three mixes of the song were completed — a contemporary version, a dance treatment, and an industrial mix.

1997 *May 5* — "Extremis," which will be the first single off of a Virgin Records U.K. compilation of techno artists: "Future: Journey Through The Electronic Underground" which is out on May 19, 1997. The selections for which were made by Anderson herself.

MOVIES

The long-awaited *X-Files Movie* began shooting in the summer 1997. A summer, 1998 release is anticipated. The film may tie in with the fifth season cliffhanger; Chris Carter says the story will stand on its own. Meantime Anderson has moved into a film career on her own.

Hellcab is based on Will Kern's play, chronicles a day in the life of a cabdriver during the Christmas holiday. Filming took place in Chicago. Produced by Suzanne De Walt & Paul Dillon & Jamie Gordon. Directed by Mary Cybulski & John Tintori. Written by Will Kern.

Cast at time of publishing (in alphabetical order):

Gillian Anderson
John Cusack
Paul Dillon
Moira Harris
Laurie Metcalf
Julianne Moore
Kevin J. O'Connor

The Mighty is the film adaptation of Rodman Philbrick's novel *Freak the Mighty*, about the journey of a boy whose physical growth stops at the age of six. Peter Chelsom will direct this film for Miramax Films. Gillian will be playing the role "Loretta Lee," who is described as a "scrawning haired" "biker chick." The release date is set so far for December 1997.

Filming Locations: Toronto, Ontario, Canada; Cincinnati, Ohio, U.S.A.; Covington, Kentucky, U.S.A. Produced by Simon Fields & Jane Startz. Executive Producer Sharon Stone. Directed by Peter Chelsom. Written by Charles Leavitt & Rodman Philbrick (from his novel *Freak the Mighty*).

Cast at time of publishing (in credits order)

> Gena Rowlands
> Gillian Anderson
> Harry Dean Stanton

and (alphabetically)

> Kieran Culkin
> James Gandolfini
> Sharon Stone

Cinematography by John de Borman. Music by Peter Gabriel.

SOURCES

BOOKS

Bassom, David. *Anderson & Duchovny: An Extraordinary Story*. (Hamlyn, 1996).

Brooks & Marsh. *The Complete Directory to Prime Time Network and Cable TV Shows*. (Ballantine Books, 1995).

Edwards, Ted. *X-Files Confidential*. (Little, Brown, 1996).

Genge, N.E. *The Unofficial X-Files Companion*. (Crown Trade, 1995).

Genge, N.E. *The Unofficial X-Files Companion II*. (Avon Books, 1996).

Guernsey, Jr., Otis and Jeffrey Sweet, eds. *Best Plays 1990–1992*. (Applause, 1993).

Lovece, Frank. *The X-Files Declassified*. (Carol Pub. Group, 1996).

Lowry, Brain. *The Truth Is Out There*. (HarperCollins, 1995).

Lowry, Brian. *Trust No One*. (HarperCollins, 1996).

Mitchell, Paul. *The Duchovny Files*. (ECW Press, 1996).

Rooney, Terrie M. *Contemporary Theatre, Film and Television*, vol. 14. (Gale).

Shapiro, Marc. *The Anderson Files*. (Boulevard Books, 1997).

Willis, John (Ed.). *Theatre World, Vol 47*. (Applause, 1992).

Willis, John (Ed.). *Theatre World, Vol 48*. (Applause, 1994).

MAGAZINES

America. Torrens, James S. "Absent and Lost," (May 4, 1991), 496.

American Cinematographer. Probst, Chris. "Darkness descends on *The X-Files*. (June 1995), 28–32.

Axcess. Whitworth, Dan. "Into the unknown," 120–125.

BC Woman. Melcombe, Lynne. "Supernatural SuXXess." (October 1995).

British GQ. Gale, David. "X-Drive." (November 1996), cover, 156–159, 26.

Broadcast Week. Doyle, John. "Extreme Close-up." (March 9, 1996).

Broadcast Week. Knott, Shirley. "Millenium madness." (October 28, 1995), cover, 8.

Cinefantastique. Vitaris, Paula, et al. Miscellaneous. (October 1996), cover, 16–41, 62.

Cinefantastique. Vitaris, Paula, et al. "X-Files." (October 1995), cover, 17–89.

Cinescape. "On a right wing and a Prayer." (February 1995), 14.

Cinescape. "X-Files & conspiracy TV," *XF* issue. Entire issue.

Cinescape. Letters, 8–9

Cinescape. Letters, November 1995

Cinescape. "X marks convention spot."

Cinescape. "X-Files." (Fall 1995), cover, 8–22.

Cinescape. Gross, Edward. "X-Files: The truth is here." (November 1994), 6, 34–45.

Cinescape. Gross, Edward. "X-Files: After a season in the sun . . ." (August 1995), cover, 8, 24–34.

Cinescape. Gross, Edward. "Fright Stalkers." (May 1995), 54–59.

Cinescape. Gross, Edward. "Zero Tolerance." (January 1996), cover, 74–75.

Cinescape. Gross, Edward. "Alien Invasion." (August 1996), cover, 10, 20–32.

Cinescape. Perry, Douglas. "Big time." 40–41.

Cinescape: X-files. Miscellaneous. (November 1996), entire issue.

Cosmopolitan. Grant, James. "Red hot right now: DD." (October), 144.

Cult Times. Eramo, Steven. "Need to know." (November 1996), 5, 8, 50–53.

Cult Times. Richards, Justin. "Super Nature Christmas." (1996), cover, 49–50.

Details. Cohen, Scott. "The X Man." (October 1995), cover, 120–124, 188–189.

Details. Saban, Stephen. "Creep show." (February 1995), 69–72.

Details. Udovitch, Mim. "Lord of the Files." (June 1997), cover, 118–123, 166.

Dream Watch. Davies, Hugh, et al. "X-Press #4." (April 1997), cover, 31–46.

DreamWatch. Hughs, Dave, et al. "X-Press #3." (January 1997), cover, 25–38.

Dream Watch. Toth, Kathleen. "Good Wins Over Evil." (April 1997), 26–30.

DreamWatch. "Emmy coverage." (November 1996), cover, 2, 3, 5, poster.

DreamWatch. "Xpress #2." (September 1996), cover, 4, 23–35.

DreamWatch. "X-Files at the Emmys." (November 1996), cover, 2–3, 27, 54, poster.

DreamWatch. Kendall, David. "DK talks with Jane Goldman." (December 1995), 42.

DreamWatch. Robb, Brian J. "The Howard Gordon files." (December 1995), cover, 22–26.

EntertainmentWeekly. "10 reasons TV is better . . ." (October 20, 1995), 26.

Entertainment Weekly. "Veneration X." (November 29, 1996), cover, 24–58.

EntertainmentWeekly. Miscellaneous. (November 29, 1996), cover, 24–58.

EntertainmentWeekly. "Millenium," "X-files." (November 8, 1996), 55, 57.

EntertainmentWeekly. "Rankings and files." (October 13, 1995), 34–35.

EntertainmentWeekly. "TV: The week." (October 13, 1995), 66.

EntertainmentWeekly. (December 1, 1995), 26.

EntertainmentWeekly. "'Twas the season." (June 2, 1995), 21, 25.

EntertainmentWeekly. "This week: TV." (April 28, 1995), 52.

EntertainmentWeekly. "This week: TV." (September 1995), 100.

EntertainmentWeekly. "Thursday: getting a little wired." (5th), 40–41.

Entertainment Weekly. Bonner, Tom. "Fox's Den." (September 1996), 40–43.

EntertainmentWeekly. Browne, David. " 'X'ecutioner's songs," 61–63.

EntertainmentWeekly. Fretts, Bruce. "Emmys . . . Stay healthy." (September 1995), 15, 28.

Entertainment Weekly. Fretts, Bruce. "Generating 'X.' " (April 5, 1996), 89–90.

Entertainment Weekly. Fretts, Bruce. "The truth is really out there for Duchovny." (December 2, 1994), 32.

Entertainment Weekly. Fretts, Bruce. "G-strings to X-files." (December 1996), 64.

EntertainmentWeekly. Gordinier, Jeff. "Flashes: G-Wizards," 12.

Entertainment Weekly. Kennedy, Dana. "The X-Files Exposed." (March 10, 1995), cover, 18–24.

EntertainmentWeekly. Letofsky, Irv. "Additional 'File' Copies."

Entertainment Weekly. Malone, Bruce. "X-tra credits." (February 9, 1996), 22–25.

Entertainment Weekly. Malone, Bruce. "Gillian to one." (February 9, 1996), cover, 18–21.

EntertainmentWeekly. Natale, Richard. " 'Fences' X'd out. (December 9, 1994), 12.

Entertainment Weekly. Newman, Bruce. "Leaving Normal." (September 8, 1995), 2–3, 8–9.

Entertainment Weekly. Svetkey, Benjamin. "No wonder he's called Fox." (September 1995), cover, 20–26.

Entertainment Weekly. Svetky, Benjamin. "Cult Favourites: Twin Peaks." (Summer 1994), 74.

Entertainment Weekly. Tucker, Ken. "The X-tra Files." (September 1996), 59, 62.

Entertainment Weekly. Tucker, Ken. " 'X' marks what's hot." (January 21, 1994), 40–41.

Entertainment Weekly. Tucker, Ken. "The proof is out there." (December 1, 1995), 56–57.

Entertainment Weekly. Watson, Bret. "Pay Daze." (August 16, 1996), 32.

Entertainment Weekly. Watson, Bret. "Friday – The X-Files Factor." (September 1995), 74–76.

Esquire (UK). Williams, Greg. "Woman of the year: GA." (Dec/Jan 96/97), cover, 5, 60–63.

Face, The. Garratt, Sheryl. "The Lone Stranger." (June 1997), 156–164.

FHM. Noguera, Anthony. "Second Coming." (January, 1997), cover, 136–142.

FHM. Noguera, Anthony. "Close Encounters." (April 1996).

GQ. Glock, Allison. "David Duchovny's X-cellent Adventure." (January 1997), cover, 94–99.

GQ. Rafferty, Terrence. "Into the Heart of Darkness." (April 1997), 107–113.

GQ (UK). Gale, David. "X-Drive." (November 1996), cover, 156–159, 267.

Here. Ewbank, Tim. "The Night I said Yes to Mr. Wrong." (August 19, 1996).

Hudson Review. Hornby, Richard. "Theatre." (Summer 1991), 285–286.

Mad Magazine. Letters. (August 1995), 2.

Mad Magazine. "Ecch-Files." (May 1995), cover, 44–48.

MAX. Translation: "Gillian Anderson: X Symbol." (1996).

Melody Maker. Wills, Dominic. "Agent Provocative." (May 1997), cover, 36–38.

Movieline. Campbell, Virginia. "Agent of Fortune." (June 1995), 64–65.

Movieline. Frankel, Martha. "Hiding in Plain Sight." (May 1997), cover, 46–51, 88–89.

New Weekly. Jarvis & Webster. "Gillian: The Disease that Threatens My Kid Brother." (September 1996).

New York. Leonard, John. "Teens and Sympathy." (January 25, 1993), 56.

Newsweek. Kantrowitz, Barbara. "The truth is X-ed out there." (December 5, 1994), 66.

Omni. Bischoff, David. "Opening the X-files: behind the scenes . . . ," 42–47, 88.

Omni. Parsec. "Parsec brainteasers – XF." (April/May 1996), 42.

Omni. Benedict, W. Ritchie. "The truth can be found, inside book." (April/May 1996), 15.

Omni. Daniels, Calvin. "Freakish luck lands, Regina, man on *XF*." (April/May 1996), 13–14.

Omni. Hetheringto, Janet. "Xtreme paranoia." (April/May 1996), cover, 8–12.

People. "David Duchovny," 102.

People. "Pre-Fab Stars." (April 28, 1997), 49.

People. "50 Most Beautiful People, 1997." (May 12, 1997), 141.

People. "Star tracks." (November 18, 1996), 14.

People. Baker, Calvin. "Senior G-Man." (May 6, 1996), 213–214.

People. Gliatto, Tom, et al. "X-ellence." (October 9, 1995), cover, 72–78.

People. Lipton, Michael, et al. "Going to X-tremes." (April 25, 1994), 59–60.

Playboy. Hitt, Jack. "X-Factor actor." (November 1995), 92–94, 158–59.

Playgirl. Higgons, Jenny. "Making contact with DD." (April 1995), 42–43.

Realms of Fantasy. Persons, Dan. "Chris Carter scares the bejabbers out of his . . ." (February 1995), 21–24.

Rolling Stone. Lipsky, David. "All Gillian Anderson Wants . . ." (February 20, 1997), cover, 32–33.

Rolling Stone. Wild, David. "X-files undercover." (May 16, 1996), cover, 21–22, 38–34.

Saturday Night. Headlam, Bruce. "Closing the X-files." (December 1995), 101–103.

Scarlet Street. Lilley, Jessie. "The truth is – Chris Carter," 69–70, 72.

Scarlet Street. Lilley, Jessie. "Reasonable Doubts: Gillian Anderson," 73–76.

Scarlet Street. Lilley, Jessie. "Squeeze play: Doug Hutchison," 77–79.

Scarlet Street. Lilley, Jessie. "Deep inside the *XF*," 79.

Scarlet Street. Sullivan, Drew. "Stalking the X-files," 67–68.

Scarlet Street. Sullivan, Drew. "True believer: David Duchovny," 71.

Sci-Fi Entertainment. MacCarillo, Lisa. "The truth is out there." (October 1995), cover, 54–58.

Sci-Fi Entertainment. Reed, Craig. "The XF Are Out There." (April 1997), cover, 52–64, 102.

Sci-Fi Universe. "Universal report: X-franchise." (June 1995), 16.

Sci-Fi Universe. Stevens, Kevin. "Uncovering the X-Files." (August 1995), cover, 20–36.

Sci-Fi Universe. Stevens, Kevin. "X-men," 34–36, 30–33.

Sci-Fi Universe. Stevens, Kevin. "Investigating the X-files." (October 1995), 20–21.

Seventeen. "17 questions: David Duchovny." (December 1995), 10, 66–68.

SFX. Golder, Dave. "X-Appeal." (July 1995).

Shift. Leiren-Youn, Mark. "X-treme possibilities." (Nov/Dec 1995), cover, 18–22.

Shivers. "Making of Duane Barry/Ascension." (August 1996), 32–36, 37–38.

Shivers. Fillis, Michael. "*XF*: 20th century mutant." (January 1995), 37–39.

Shivers. Nazzaro, Joe. "Darin Morgan: life, laughs, Clyde Bruckman." (June 1996), 3, 8–11, 38–39.

Sight & Sound. Pirie, David. "In the cold." (April 1996), 22–23.

Sight & Sound. Ross, Jonathan. "Talking with aliens," 61.

Sky International. Hughes, David. "Discreet Agent." (October 1995), cover, 30–38, 43–50.

Spectrum. "The Rapture." (July 1996), 25–27.

Spectrum. Miscellaneous. (June 1995), whole issue.

Spectrum. "A discussion with Chris Carter." (June 1996), cover, 16–21.

Spectrum. "A discussion with Chris Carter." (May 1996), 12–17.

Spectrum. Miscellaneous. (July 1995), cover, 1–35.

Starburst. "X-Files Report #3." (May 1996), cover, 25–57.

Starburst. "X-Files Special." (October 1996), cover, 1–32.

Starburst. Eramo, Steven. "X-Files '96: an extraordinary year." (December 1996), 17–21.

Starburst. Hill, Annette, et al. "Home Is Where the Heart Is." (April 1997), 29–40.

Starburst. Hill, Annette. "The King of Pain." (December 1996), 22–23.

Starburst. Killick, Jane. "The X-files report #2." (April 1996), cover, 25–40.

Starburst. Mount, Paul. "UK TV '94 Yearbook." (1994/95), 4–5.

Starburst. Nazzaro, Joe. "Sleepless nights." (September 1996), 7, 21–24.

Starburst. Nazzaro, Joe. "Creating the X-files: CC." (May 1995), 16–19, 46.

Starburst. Nazzaro, Joe. "The X-men." (January 1996), cover, 27–30.

Starburst. Nazzaro, Joe. "Creating the X-files: Chris Carter." (Special #24), 16–19.

Starlog. Counts, Kyle. "True disbeliever." (Platinum), 30–33.

Starlog. Counts, Kyle. "Scientific American." (April 1994), 76–79.

Starlog. Florence, Bill. "Keeper of secrets." (February 1995), 28–30, 74.

Starlog. Florence, Bill. "The X comics." (March 1995), 58–60.

Starlog. Garcia, Frank. "Prince of Darkness." (November 1995), 76–79.

Starlog. Lee, Julianne. "X-Symbol." (June 1995), cover, 27–30, 71.

Starlog. Lee, Julianne. "The X novels." (Platinum #5 1995), 15–17.

Starlog. Lee, Julianne. "Mutants, Psychics & Freaks." (May 1996), 52–54.

Starlog. Lee, Julianna. "X heroine." (April 1995), 32–35.

Starlog. Miscellaneous. "Inside The X-Files: Yearbook." (August 1997), 1–41.

Starlog. Spelling, Ian. "X-Factors." (December 1996), 42–46.

Starlog. Spelling, Ian. "X-Factors." (December 1995), 42–46.

Starlog. Vitaris, Paula. "X writers." (January 1995), 61–64.

Starlog Sci-Fi Explorer. Swallow, James. "American Skeptic." (February 1996), cover, 6, 12–15.

Starlog: X-Files #1. Miscellaneous. (December 1995), complete.

Sunday Times Magazine. Miller, Russell. "The Odd Couple." (May 5, 1995), cover, 36–39.

The X-files Magazine. Miscellaneous. (Summer 1996), whole issue.

TV Guide. Nollinger, Mark. "20 things you need to know . . ." (May 4, 1996), cover, 15–18.

TV Guide. Saddy, Guy. "Entertainer of the year." (December 1995), cover, 11–17.

TV Guide. Saddy, Guy. "Out there." (March 11–17, 1995), cover, 15–21.

TV Guide. Slotek, Jim. "Sci-Fi Boom." (May 27, 1995), cover, 15–25.

TV Guide (US). Mansfield, Stephanie. "Gillian looks like a million." (July 6, 1996), cover, 2, 6–14.

TV Hits. "X-Files-Travaganza." (March 1996).

TVWeek. Cooney, Jenny. "Gillian's Alien Past." (October 7, 1995).

TVWeek. Cooney, Jenny. "Gillian in Alien Territory." (May 25, 1996).

TVWeek. Lipworth, Elaine. "Gillian's X-Generation Baby." (May 13, 1995).

TVWeek. Sexton, Jim. "No Rest for the Eerie." (June 3, 1995).

TV Zone. Calcutt, Ian. "Taking it Personally." (March, 1997), 4–10.

TV Zone. Miscellaneous. "X-files Dossier." (May 1996), cover, 4–13, 24–41.

TV Zone. Nazzaro, Joe. "David Nutter directing more X-Files." (December 1995), 45–47.

TV Zone. Shapiro, Marc. "Television special effects are hell." (June 1995), cover, 39–42.

Us. Lee, Ricky. "Faces & Places: Quiz show." (December 1995), 22.

Us. Mundy, Chris. "David Duchovny & Gillian Anderson." (May 1997), cover, 7, 44–52.

Us. Pond, Steve. "Strange Brew." (September 1994), 58–59.

Us. Pond, Steve. "Secret agent man," 80–83, 92.

Variety. Edmunds, Marlene. "Dutch to hit L.A." (May 27, 1996), 46, 48.

Who Magazine. "Occult Leader." (March 1995).

Wrapped in Plastic. "X-Files Extra!," 40–44.

Wrapped in Plastic. "X-Files Extra!" (December 1996), 25–32.

Wrapped in Plastic. "X-Files Extra!," 29–31.

Wrapped in Plastic. Miller, Craig. "Don Davis delivers the message." (December 1996), cover, 2–7.

Xpose. "2Shy, NL, season 2." (September 1996), 16–22, 34–37, 54–57.

Xpose. Miscellaneous. (November 1996), 2–3, 4, 8, 16–21, 34–37, 54–57.

Xpose. "Conduit, season 1." (August 1996), cover, 16–21, 44–51.

Xpose. Brooks, James E. "Field of Dreams." (May 1997), 36–41.

Xpose. May, Caroline. "The X-Man." (February 1997), 12–21.
Xpose. May, Caroline. "I Believe." (January 1997), cover, 12–19.
Xpose. Zonkel, Phillip. "Willam Tells." (March 1997), 44–50.

NEWSPAPERS

Australian Newspaper, The. Williams, Sue. "Cyber Pin-Up With X-Appeal."
(June 28, 1996).

Daily Telegraph, The. "Spooky Arrival as X Marks the Spot." (June 24,
1996).

Guardian, The. Jeffries, Stuart. "The Return of the X." (August 28, 1995).

Herald-Sun TV Guide. "Fanning the Flame." (July 23, 1996).

L.A. Times. Matsumoto, Jon. "In Search of the X-Factor." (1996).

Melbourne Herald Sun. Fidgeon & Lewis. "Chaos as Fans Go to X-
Tremes." (June 29, 1996).

Observer, The. Billen, Andrew. "X-Ceptional." (July 9, 1995).

Seattle Times. Tu, Janet I-Chen. "Inside the X-Files." (May 13, 1996).

Sun, The. Collins, Lisa. "The Sex Files." (January 6, 1996).

Sun-Herald. "X-posed and Loving It." (June 23, 1996).

Sunday Telegraph TV Extra. Idato, Michael. Interview. (1996).

Sunday Telegraph, The. "X-Files Star on Alien Soil." (June 23, 1996).

Sunday Telegraph, The. Idato, Michael. "Star Prefers Some Space." (June
30, 1996).

Toronto Star. Mietkiewicz, Henry. "X-Files still out there." (October 4,
1996).

Toronto Star. Zerbisias, Antonia. "The end is near, on TV at least."
(September 1995).

Toronto Star Starweek Magazine. "Starweek reader survey." (April 29,
1995).

Toronto Star. Bawden, Jim. "Bawden's picks and pans of '94." (December
31, 1994).

Toronto Star. Knutzen, Eirik. "TV talkback." (May 27, 1995).

Toronto Sun. "Aussie fans frighten X-Files star." (June 29, 1996).

Toronto Star. "Being on a hit show 'weird.' " (September 1995).

Toronto Star. "Sleepless in Vancouver." (March 14, 1996).

Toronto Star. "Vancouver facing ban on violent film shoots." (December
6, 1996).

Toronto Star. "The X-File." (November 21, 1994).

Toronto Star. Bickley, Claire. "Weirdness rules – finale." (May 19, 1995).

Toronto Star. Bickley, Claire. "X-Files plagued by flat, black disk."
(February 20, 1996).

B
I
O
G
R
A
P
H
Y

Toronto Star. Bickley, Claire. "X-Files' Anderson goes future-tech."

Toronto Star. Bickley, Claire. "Global scaring up weekend schedule." (1996).

Toronto Star. Bickley, Claire. "Opening the X-File on Krycek." (October 17, 1995).

Toronto Star. Bickley, Claire. "The gouge file." (September 7, 1995).

Toronto Star. Bickley, Claire. "X-Files extravaganza coming to Metro next month." (September 4, 1996).

Toronto Star. Bickley, Claire. "Production file: X-Files." (January 16, 1995).

Toronto Star. Bickley, Claire. "Dis-X-tion on the Internet."

Toronto Star. Bickley, Claire. "Anderson files." (July 13, 1996).

Toronto Star. Last, Eugenia. "Happy Birthday." (August 6, 1996).

Toronto Star. Last, Eugenia. "Happy Birthday." (August 9, 1996).

Toronto Star. Slotek, Jim. "TV viewing tips."

Toronto Star. Stevenson, Jane. "X marks the musical spot." (March 30, 1996).

Toronto Star. Stevenson, Jane. "Music of alien nation." (October 18, 1996).

USA Today. Roush, Matt. "X-Files new mom Anderson Has No Time for X-haustion." (1995).

USA Weekend. Sexton, Jim. "No Rest for the Eerie." (May 12, 1995).

Washington Times, The. McCain, Buzz. "Skepticism All an Act for X-Files Agent." (January 6, 1994).

ONLINE

IRC, Delphi Internet's FOXtalk (January 1995).

IRC, *XF* channel Undernet (September 16, 1995).

News service, Mr. Showbiz.

News service, CNN Showbiz (May 1996).

News service, CNN Showbiz (October 13, 1995).

Press release, FutureMedia.org (March 1996).

Press release, The Seattle Times Company (March 1997).

Radio transcript, Austereo Martin-Molloy Show (June 1996).

Radio transcript, Midday Show, Australia (June 25, 1996).

Radio transcript, Fox FM at Southland (June 28, 1996).

RealAudioPop Talk (December 1996).

Transcripts, L.A. Times articles (1995).

TV interview, Sci-Fi Buzz, Sci-Fi Channel (February 19, 1995).

Web Site, DePaul University.

GILLIAN ANDERSON CONVENTION APPEARANCE: BURBANK, JANUARY 1996

by Autumn Tysko

In January 1996, Gillian Anderson made her one and only appearance at an *X-Files* convention in Burbank, California. Autumn Tysko was there, and reported her experience to friends and *X-Files* fans on the Internet. Her report captures the excitement such an event holds for the fans and, apparently, for Gillian herself; with Autumn's permission, we offer you this inside look at a very special *X-Files* Convention.

Right before Gillian Anderson came out, to torment us a bit with more wait they played a video compilation of scenes highlighting her talents from: the pilot (initial meeting), "Ice" (the joint examination), "Beyond the Sea" (hotel room), "Irresistible" (you know what scene), "The Blessing Way" (metal detector scene), "War of the Coprophages" (7–11 scene), "2Shy" (fight sequence).

GILLIAN ANDERSON then emerged to an astounding number of paparazzi — you would not believe the press there; the flashes were blinding. She was genuinely overcome with emotion at the tremendous crowd reaction to her appearance and stood smiling and laughing, looking stunned and slightly teary eyed. She was wearing black slacks, black shoes with those very high heels, a navy long-sleeved blouse that buttoned up the front with large gold buttons, and glasses (more oval than Scully's). I know I won't get the inflection right in typed word, but suffice to say there was much fun and laughter during her whole appearance. She has good comic timing and was quite funny.

Her first words were, "Holy cow! I have no idea what to say right now! It's unbelievable. I'm completely *verklempt*." After more screams she said, "You know, I wanted to prepare about 10, 15 minutes of something extemely witty and charming, and honestly, if I had, I wouldn't remember it right now." So she decided to just take questions "if anyone had any" (LOL!) and then laughed as a huge crowd rushed to stand in line (including yours truly).

The first question was, "What was it like to eat that bug?" She told the story of The Enigma eating all the bugs and how she thought after seeing him do that she felt she should at least try to put one in her mouth. Then she came clean and said, "I didn't actually eat it — sorry!" Despite all the other stories, we finally got the truth — she put them in her mouth then spit them out. (Actually you see David doing it too in the blooper reel.)

In answer to what was the most difficult part of her job, she said the long hours and the dialogue — the long words and complex lines she has to deliver constantly (you know that can't be easy).

Much to the crowd's delight the next girl told her that she had the "greatest hair" (so there, TV *Guide*!). She also asked if she'd made any films ("A few very small ones that never even made it to video"). She wants to do something over the next hiatus. The next girl asked, "What was it like to do that *Rolling Stone* picture with David?" To which Gillian replied, "She means what was it like to have my naked breast against his chest," then proceeded to tease the cheering crowd with, "It was fun! David's got very soft skin. He's very fit. And we had a very hard time that day. It . . . it was work."

The next person said, "Oh, my God, I'm so nervous," and got a "Me too" reply. She asked if GA knew about her online "brigade." GA said yes, and that she thought it was great, especially when she was pregnant and got so much support from the fan clubs and that she likes the support that she gets from her brigade — both men and women.

She was asked her middle name. "Leigh."

The next guy that got up mentioned her glasses, that she wasn't wearing Scully's glasses and that we didn't see Scully in her glasses enough. To which she replied, "No, these aren't hers, these are mine. But if Scully were here she wouldn't be wearing them, because she only wears them at her computer . . . and sometimes she doesn't wear them at her computer and sometimes she wears them when she's reading . . . and sometimes she doesn't wear them when she's reading. . . . But you know, probably she wouldn't be wearing them up here."

The next question was the Bambi question (Bambi was *not* a popular character this weekend and was the butt of many jokes). The girl asked, "Uh, last week — could you tell us about Bambi?"

GA: What exactly would you like to know? [The girl asked if she was actually trying to convey that Scully was jealous or were we all trying to read too much into it.]

GA: I think that because of how intimately and intensely Scully and Mulder work together, that anytime there is anybody that comes up around the other character it causes a little bit of tension. Needless to say, uh, Bambi caused a little bit of tension. [This exchange was *real* funny.]

The next guy asked her what type of film she'd like to do during her hiatus — what genre, etc. "I don't have any particular thing planned. It would be nice to play a character that is very different than Scully, and hopefully I will get that chance to do that. The things that I'm interested in are — a wide range of things. I love period movies, I love *Pulp Fiction*, I love smaller films, I love foreign films, and I love independent films. But, you know, anything that is well written and really speaks to me."

At this point something *really* funny happened. DOUG "TOOMS" HUTCHISON had just shown up at the convention (as the "Fire" star Mark Sheppard had, and the "Eve" twins were also there Sunday), and he got to the mike to ask a question as a dweeby alter-ego.

DH: Hello, Ms. Anderson. [Many screams and laughter from all, GA included — she was cracking up with the audience.] My name is Norbert Weiner, and I'm a big fan of yours and of the program *The X-Files*. I would like to thank you for being here today, and my question is as follows. During the first season, you did a particular episode called "Squeeze." It happens to personally be my favorite episode and I was just wondering, Ms. Anderson, there was a very talented young actor in that particular episode by the name of Doug Hutchison. Quite good-looking young fellow, too. My question for you, Ms. Anderson, is in the final scene in the bathroom when Doug Hutchison as this character Tooms was on top of you — what was that like? I would only like to guess that it was the most thrilling experience of your life. [She is just losing it at this point and can't really answer.] I'm a little nervous, too.

GA: Let me tell you all a little about Doug Hutchison. I hope he's not here right now. Um, no.

DH: No, I don't think he's here either — I looked for him, but . . .

GA: I have no — I'd love to tell a little story about . . . . Um, it was my birthday. . . .

DH: Yes.

GA: You know, he was a great guy. [One senses the story might be a bit risque.]

DH: I thought as much.

GA: He was a sweetheart, you know, and it was really sad to have him die so [gesturing] — you know . . . blood . . .

DH: Rumor has it your blouse kept popping open. Your brassiere was exposed. I just heard that, I don't know.

GA: That's very possible. I'm trying to remember that particular night. . . . Yeah, you know, there's a lot of stunts that are involved and it is very technical when you're doing that kind of . . . [looking toward audience]

DH: Uh, I'm over here, Ms. Anderson; I didn't go nowhere.

GA: When you're doing that kind of stunt there are a lot of other people around, and you hit each other in a certain way, and it's not a very intimate experience.

DH: Oh, right. Well, I do appreciate you answering my question and welcome to lovely downtown Burbank, and anytime you are in the area again, Ms. Anderson, if you'd like, I would love to take you out for some liver.

GA: Thank you. What a day!

The next guy with a question says, "And I've got to follow that!" then asked how she got talked into doing the Kevin & Bean Christmas album and who wrote it.

She said that "they wrote it, and we were shooting in a train station somewhere up in Vancouver, and I remember them there in their shorts in very cold weather, and we sat in the back in these pews. Pews? Why would there be pews in a train station? Long seats, and we sat back there and did this interview that they had written, and the point was too be as 'actorly' as possible. I mean, hopefully it's an odd tape then."

Q: It was different hearing you say "It's reindeer crap."

GA: It was basically a little sketch. Personally, I wish we had taken it a little bit more seriously and not joked around as much as we had with it, but that's beside the point.

The next question was, "How are you handling all this [gestures to audience] — people adoring you, everyone yelling 'I love you'? Is it, like, different for you?"

GA: [Looks back at audience] I guess so.

He continues, "I mean, when you are filming are there just drones of people all around you?"

GA: No, no, there's not. Well, sometimes there are; it depends on where we are. If we shoot in the studio it's pretty secure and no one is really allowed in, but in neighborhoods, which we often do, there's usually a crowd of people around standing in the middle of the street.

Q: Do you get used to it?

GA: Uh . . . this is a little hard to get used to. I'm shaking in my boots a little bit. But, it is, you know, I mean — cool!

The next question dealt with the fact that Mulder and Scully are supposed to be equal partners, but it often seems like it is Mulder who gets to do most of the fighting, etc. [references scene in "Die Hand Die Verletzt" where Mulder fights someone, but she gets taken out by a bookcase], and he wondered if she found that equal treatment.

GA: That's interesting, coming from a man. I think that the character of Scully has made so many strides forward in the nature of women on television [applause] that it is hard to bring up any of those issues, but certainly there are situations where, you know, Mulder kills the bad guy more often or Scully can't . . . . [refering to "2Shy"] That was one of the first scenes where we actually see Scully beat the sh . . . [covers mouth] . . . beat somebody up. So, that stuff comes up every once in a while, but the writers are trying so hard to develop a great script, something that flows, and that builds and builds and builds, and sometimes it is necessary for those things to take place, for both of us to be knocked down at the same time in order to carry the through line of the script out. I mean there are some. In the beginning it was a bit different — there were more times when Scully had to walk three paces behind Mulder and stuff like that. It doesn't really happen anymore as much, so I don't really find it a big issue.

Q: How do you feel about David having more publicity, such as being on Letterman and Leno and your being on a somewhat less . . . [drowned out by crowd booing].

GA: You better get out of here fast. [Much applause] I'm sorry, I didn't mean to — you can stay here. Well, hmm, how to answer that question. You know, David has been in this business for a lot longer than I have. He was around for almost 10 years before I was, or five years, or something longer than I was. And he's done quite a few features and he's a man. It's true. A spade's a spade — you know what I mean. So it's natural for one character at a time to get more attention than another. On ensemble shows that becomes more difficult when everyone is working just as hard and one actor is getting all the attention and the others aren't. But I was talking to a reporter this morning for an interview, you might like to know, and he was asking me, "Was that David's time and it is now your time?" and that might be so. I don't know; I mean David has had his fair share of coverage and stuff and maybe that will happen to me. [Much applause]

The next question was along the lines of, "How does it feel to be part of such a successful TV show, and all the fans?"

GA: I don't think I still get it — I don't think it is going to hit me actually until sometime next year. When I first started auditioning for the show, I didn't understand what the odds were for a show to get picked up. I thought that all shows were picked up. I didn't watch television very much — I didn't know what a season was, you know, I didn't know that some show aired new shows then they aired old shows for a while and then they started airing new shows again. I didn't understand any of that stuff; I was completely naive about that, and for somebody who did my business you'd think I'd know. If you don't know, it's OK, but I just didn't know. So coming in on it, I kinda expected it to be picked up and I expected it to run for a couple of years. The odds were that that wasn't going to happen, and the odds certainly were that this was not going to happen. I mean, it's been a shock for everybody, for Chris, for David, for everybody on the crew. The crew that works on the show is so happy to be a part of something that is so successful and so well respected and liked; they're all just tickled to death about it.

Q: We do have to say it is one of the most outstanding shows in the history of television. [Much cheering.]

I'd like to agree you could kill more on the show.

GA: I could kill more on the show? [Someone from the audience yells, "Yeah, get Bambi!" to laughter.]

Q: Well, you know, with Mulder killing five times and you killing once. [At this point, as I was near the questioner, I corrected the poor misguided thing with, "Twice." Gillian smiled at me and the crowd laughed.]

GA: I think that what is expressed, in all fairness here, isn't killing. Maybe if I, like, beat people up more often; but I don't exactly kill them. I mean, if they're really, really bad guys, maybe I could kill them; it would be nice to do a few more stunts more often and kill people more often. [Laughs] Thank you.

Q: How did it feel to have been a punk?

GA: Uhhhhhh. You know that was something that I needed to go through at the time. [Someone in the crowd yells, "How long?"] How long was I that way? I guess it started when I was 15 and went on until I was 21. Well, it is still a part of me — I mean, what it was at the time was an expression of — an attempt at expressing feelings, it was a very angry phase that I went through and it served me at the time. It was something that I needed to go through, and it gave me a sense of self — of who I was, and I started to make opinions about how I wanted to dress and what I believed in and what kind of music I wanted to listen to, and I think on the whole it made me more independent and a stronger person. Even though it was a crutch, so to speak, at times. I'm talking about mohawks, combat boots, swearing at people on the street. [Some cheers from audience.] Why is that so appealing to you? Now I can't do that anymore — anyway, it is always something that is inside me, and

once in a while I'll put on a Circle Jerks album or something. [Someone yells, "What is your favorite band?"] Right now? ["Then."] Then? Lords of the New Church. What about now? Gosh, I don't know. I like all different kinds of music. I love blues, I love jazz, I love Alanis Morrisette. I love all kinds of stuff.

Q: Hi. I was just wondering what it was like for you the morning you woke up and realized your face is on everything — pictures, posters, even billboards around here.

GA: I don't know. Honestly, I've been asked that question a lot — not specifically that way, but I don't think that I really have thought about it because I think I'm afraid that if I really think about it I'll die or have a nervous breakdown or something, so I don't really think about it. You don't want to know what I'm thinking about then. [Said jokingly to much laughter] So, I don't know. It has been a nice slow transition being up in Vancouver and, you know, I think being down here it would have hit a lot harder and been a lot harder to deal with. It's great, you know. I honestly don't even know what to say about it — I'm kind of numb to it all.

Q: Thank you. I think you're a really great actress and I'm sure you'll be around for a long time. [Much cheering]

GA: Thank you.

Q: What do you think Scully's dog should be named?

GA: There were two names that I came up with for it. One was Clyde — but that's my husband's name, so . . . The other was Yappi. [Cheering] Which do you like?

Q: I prefer Yappi.

GA: You like Yappi? That's the most obvious one, I would have thought.

Q: I think I speak for all the women here when I say that your character Scully is a real role model for all women [much applause] and I wanted to ask you if you get to take Piper with you, like today, and what it's like to have her on the set with you?

GA: Sure, thank you. I do get to bring Piper with me every day; that's something I'm incredibly blessed to be able to do. What I usually do, if I have to leave really early in the morning is I'll — she'll be at home with the nanny, and then I'll have somebody come and pick them up like around maybe two hours before lunch and then she'll spend the rest of the day with me. And then, or usually later on in the week, if I have to go to work much later she'll come with me at the beginning and then I send her home early so she can go to bed. And she's there entertaining everybody. She's the most amazing little girl and I really miss her right now. She's really strong and she loves to be on set. She loves everybody. What's funny is that on the Friday nights that I have to work really late and she's at home with the nanny and the show's on, she'll like walk up to the TV and point to me and start to cry. She's changed my life and, I honestly don't know how women — I mean, I went back to work 10 days after I gave birth, but most women have to go back financially within three months of a baby. I don't understand how somebody can go through that and not be near that child for eight to 10 hours a day at that period of the child's development, and I feel for everybody who has ever had to do that and wish it weren't so.

Q: [This one is mine] You've talked a little bit about

stunts. Do you do your own stunts besides running in the heels? [Laughter]

GA: Um, it's funny, I did a lot more before I had Piper. When you get pregnant, your body changes and your knees get all out of joint and stuff. I came back and I wasn't walking straight, I wasn't doing anything right, and this was after I had Piper. It took a long time for my body to heal. And so it didn't feel safe to do any kind of jumping. It was one episode where a bullet just grazes my head. [She points to that poor abused temple]

ME: [Joking] That's almost all of them. [Laughter]

GA: What? It's one where I'm in my apartment and a bullet just grazes my head and I fall to the floor. [I'm guessing she is referring to "Anasazi"] And it was just after I had Piper and I remember saying, "You know, could you put pillows down there?" And, "You know, I don't want to do that anymore — I've already done that three times." And before I'd be like, "Yeah, go!" There was one time which is an interesting bit of whatever — what episode? It was the one with that salamander hand — I'm sounding southern now, "the salamander hand" — what episode was that?

ME: "Young at Heart."

GA: No, that's not it. Though you're right; that was the one with the salamander hand. The one where I get shot in the hotel.

ME: That's it.

GA: [Slightly confused, as crowd is responding]: Alright. [Laughing] It's a long life, honey. Yes, "Young at Heart." So, I was shot in the hallway and I had a protective vest on. I had hip pads on, and butt pads, and chest pads, and back pads, and I was supposed to be shot and they wanted to see my face — they wanted to see that it was me that was flying backwards. So what I had to do, which was part of the stunt, is out of nowhere just throw myself back off my feet onto my back onto the floor — we had to get into the rhythm of it and the shooting of it. I guess it was what I needed to do. So I did that, you know, quite a few times, and I had a couple bruises, and they were also shooting from a balcony up top so they really needed to see my face. So we did take after take after take and that was fine, but what I didn't know at the time, which I learned a couple of months later, is that I was pregnant at the time. So when I actually put that together, which might have been months later, it was just kinda like "Whoaa, is that ever weird." I mean, I had no idea.

ME: We're all glad everything turned out okay.

GA: Me too — thank you.

Q: We've all heard about the long tapings that you have to do, and I was wondering which episode was the hardest or which took the longest?

GA: I don't know which episode. You know, we shoot an episode in eight days and once in a while — I think it's only happened maybe two or three times where they've actually from the get-go said, "This episode is going to take longer; we have to have a nine-day shoot." Our film unit is called first unit, and it is the main unit and that's what shoots the show in the eight-day episode, but we also have a full second unit that shoots all of the shots of people's feet walking and — you know, I have a hand double so that if there is a close-up of me picking up a piece of paper that we don't want to waste the time on in a regular shooting they shoot it in second unit. That's a whole other unit — it's got the same amount of cameras, the same amount of people — you know, it's a big deal — and usually I think what happens is that it takes them about a week and a half to two weeks to prep a show — going through finding the location, where they want to shoot, what actors they are thinking about, how they want to do a particular stunt, how they want to do a particular special effect, how they're going to build this and that — it is very complicated. This is them prepping and preparing the show. And then after the eight days of main unit shooting that David and I are involved in, there's sometimes up to five, sometimes six, days of second unit shooting 12- to 16-hour days just to get all those other shots. So we say it takes us eight days to shoot an episode, but it takes a lot more than that. It doesn't happen that often, but David and I will be shooting something for the show for the eight-day episode that we are working on right now, then in the morning or the afternoon we'll go off to second unit to shoot something for the episode that we just shot that we didn't get, and then maybe later on in the afternoon after shooting the show we are doing right now we'll go back to a corner of the stage and shoot an extra scene that's been written because a show wasn't long enough to air on television so Chris has written a little extra scene to shove in here and there. And so we shoot something that was from three episodes ago and that can get very confusing so — God, I talk a lot — it takes a lot of time.

Q: Before I ask my question — someone else said that your character, Scully, was a great role model, but you as a person are also a great role model. [Applause] She just asked what the hardest episode was to deal with, so I'm going to ask what was the funnest stuff to do.

GA: Wow, um, I guess one way or another "Ice" was one of the funnest. It was one of the first fun shows that we did. It was hard work, and that whole thing about paranoia in there; it was just an excellent show to work on. And then came "Humbug." [Much applause — Darin Morgan shows were easily the crowd favorites that weekend.] Darin Morgan scripts are — you know, he's new for us, or relatively new, but it's great after working on these heavy-duty serious episodes to, once in a while, have these whacked-out episodes come along. It's been consecutive Darin shows — "Humbug," then "Clyde Bruckman's Final Repose," then "War of the Coprophages," that's been a lot of fun. There's a lot of humor on the set amongst the crew and amongst David and I. We goof around a lot, so there's a light-heartedness that takes place; it's not all dark and dreary. But when the scripts are humorous, it gives us an opportunity to really have fun — it's a treat.

Q: I've read in many magazines that you're the actual believer and David's the skeptic — could you explain that to us?

GA: Well, I'm not sure if David's necessarily a skeptic. I think that he has more reservations about believing than I do. It's not like I'm a believer-*believer*-believer, I just have always have had a fascination with paranormal subjects. I've always been fascinated by ESP and by psychokinesis and the whole subject of aliens and life on other planets. It is just something that I have been fascinated by. It's not something that I've sought out. I've haven't gone out and read books on it, I just find it fascinating and so, I guess because of that fascination, I've developed some sort of desire to believe in, or understanding of, that subject matter. I mean, I've had many experiences in my life — not paranormal experiences — as I'm sure many people have, where you think, you know, "God, that was a miracle that I just didn't get hit by that bus." Or when you say something at the same time as somebody else three times in a row — you know, that kind of stuff that, whatever that is, it's fascinating — it makes you think. Or when somebody in your family is near death and they come back to life — I mean all that stuff. It's life — it's fascinating stuff that happens all the time, and I think that if we pay attention to that stuff, and what I'm talking about is more on a spiritual than a paranormal level — I'm not talking about the evil stuff — that stuff doesn't attract me so much — I guess, just the things that we have to be grateful for in life, and how many times during a day we are reminded of that and pay attention to that. And I think that this whole craze of aliens and angels and stuff is people reaching out there and wanting to feel better, and for the pain to go away, and that's the stuff that is fascinating about it. I also think about it — in my mind, the odds that there is life on other planets is greater than there not being life on other planets. That's just in my head.

The next question was a real odd method-actor type question asking her if there was ever a time when she was doing a scene that "Gillian is gone and Dana is there and she is terrified." [Hey, we had to have one of these — it *is* L.A.]

GA: [looks a bit perplexed] Uh, I don't know when that has ever actually taken place. There's always the

copyright © CINDY STABILE 1996

safety of, like, 70 people around you, that you know that you are safe. . . . Oh, I'll tell you, that same episode that I was telling you where I was flying backwards and I was pregnant, I was really scared — and I guess that was just me, not necessarily as Dana. I was, because — to answer the question another way, there are not many times where Gillian is actually scared on the set. I mean, because we see everything that is going on and it is all technical. But there was that time when this guy had this gun on me and I didn't know — oh, you know what — this whole thing with Brandon Lee had just happened, and it was shortly after that and besides there was this gun on me and I had this jacket on underneath, but I was concerned that some kind of a mistake was being made. That was something that was honestly a fear for me, but that was like the first and only time, I think. There have certainly been times where I have read scripts when I have to put it down and go in the other room, or make sure that I am reading it long before I am going to bed.

Q: A little girl asks, "The episode where Tooms jumps out at you, were you really scared? When he jumps out and pulls you down?"

GA: [Smiling] Um, yes. [Laughter] You know what? I'll tell you a secret — I knew that was going to happen. Whenever you do that kinda stuff — what you want to do as an actor — because the character is not supposed to know that something is going to happen, so you're walking around pretending that you don't know that something is going to happen, and something does and it is always shocking. Whenever you know that a gun is going to go off, and you're waiting, you're waiting, you're waiting, and when it finally

goes off you jump out of your pants. You know it is
going to happen, but you are still affected by it. So,
fortunately, yes, it makes it easier for an actor to act
as if they are scared — but it is freaky when somebody
you know pulls your legs out from under you, no
matter what the situation is, whether you're acting or
not.

Q: Hi, I saw a picture of your daughter — she's so
cute.

GA: [Alarmed] You did? How?

Q: I don't know, somebody just told me that they
ripped it out of the TV *Guide* or something.

GA: TV *Guide*!? That wasn't my daughter. Oh no. I
never let anybody take a picture of her. I hope she was
cute, whoever's daughter she was. [Laughs] I'm sorry,
I don't mean to give you such a hard time.

Q: I was wondering if you were going to have any
more kids?

GA: Am I going to have any more kids? Um, I think
so eventually. It would have to be after the show is
over before I try to do that again. Yeah, probably a
good 'nother few years. Why, do you know somebody
or were you just wondering?

Q: I just want to say that male/female relationships
on TV are badly portrayed, in my opinion, because
they feel like they have to have a romantic relationship in order to make their job work. What do you
think makes Mulder and Scully's relationship with
each other unique in this situation?

GA: Well, it is different than that. They work incredibly intimately together on a daily basis, day in and
day out — they stay in the same motels together —
but they respect each other highly and they remain

friends. I think it's just — obviously, it's the writers — but I think that underneath it's who they are. I mean, they have very high morals, especially Scully . . . well, only Scully. [much laughter] Yeah, I mean, I think that they may take the platonic nature of their relationship out of respect and responsibility to their work and that's hard to do. It's a great example, but when you're working intensely with somebody, whether it's in school or in college or at work, and you have that kind of dynamic, it's hard not to take advantage of it when it's there, you know. I think it's kind of funny — so it's a good example of how to keep the boundaries very clear. When you know inside yourself that this is something that you are not going to take advantage of, that's a good feeling of power, of empowerment when you know that . . . it's all wishy-washy — let me shut up.

Q: First of all we all love you, Gillian — as if you didn't know that yet. Is there any special reason why you named your daughter Piper?

GA: Well, it's hard to find a name for a child, and I went through so many different names as I'm sure everybody does, and this little thing inside me — I started to really get an idea of her personality at about the seventh month, and she was jumping around, sticking at me. I mean, you could see her feet, you could practically see the imprint — she's got big feet — see the imprint of her feet on my belly. And I could tell from the feeling of the child growing inside me that she was very spunky, but she was also very strong. And after going through so many names and so many names, my husband was reading a list of names from an old yearbook of his and was just going down the list and he landed on the name and it was like [snaps fingers] bingo, you know — I automatically knew it was her.

Q: I bet it was really hard when you were pregnant on *The X-Files*, was it hard for you?

GA: Yeah, it started to get really hard when I gained a lot of weight. I'm short, and I gained a lot of weight. [Someone in crowd yells, "No, you didn't!"] What?! *I gained 52 pounds!* I'm 5′3. I gained 52 — I gained a lot of weight! Those big trenchcoats helped — they did — they hid me well, but I did, I gained a lot of weight. What was the question? Oh yeah, my feet got really swollen and it was hard to stay on my feet for so many hours at a time. I had to sit down a lot, and that's mostly when it became hard, and then after when she was born not being able to spend as much time with her those first few weeks as I would've liked to.

Q: You've done a couple of spreads in publications and what I've noticed is that they kind of exploit your feminine qualities a little too much — how do you feel about that? And if you were peanut butter would you rather be regular or crunchy and why? [This girl was odd.]

GA: Crunchy. [doesn't know why] . . . 'cause . . . it's . . . nutty? And what was the first question? The magazine question? I guess I haven't been aware of that? In what ways?

Q: Well, in magazines your cleavage has been kind of accentuated just a tad.

GA: I think that the object has been that this is Scully and that most of the time when we take photographs we concentrate mostly on Gillian and not that I . . .

Q: There have been some instances when part of your brassiere has been shown, and so how can we respect you. [She is soundly booed by the audience.]

GA: I think that there has been a heightened attempt to show that I am not as straight and as contained as the character is [much applause], not only so that more people can relate to me as human beings, but also that people can see that I might be able to play another character other than Scully — somebody who might be, uh [someone yells "You go, girl!" to much laughter] — That's been the attempt.

That was the last question, and GA said, "Thank you very much. [She gets a huge standing screaming ovation whereupon she seems to start to get a bit teary eyed again.] Thanks you, guys. I don't know what to say — I can't tell you how touched I am right now, and I . . . I don't know — thank you." [She starts to leave the stage and the crowd goes wild. She stops, smiles, and waves to us some more.]

I hope you all enjoyed this. I have always had a lot of respect for the lovely and talented Ms. Anderson, but let me tell you it grew tenfold at this event. It is something I will never forget. She is witty, endearing, genuine, and honest.

INTERNET SOURCES

Address: http:\\www.great-xfiles-info

BOOKMARKS

No list of Internet bookmarks could ever claim to be complete, so we are not even going to attempt such a Herculean feat. The passion and hard work involved in producing a good, let alone great Web site, cannot be overstated. These sites are produced by dedicated fans who selflessly offer the fruits of their labor to the rest of us.

So what we offer are a few places to start your online explorations. Remember that, like life, the Internet is ever-changing. The URLs offered here will change over time, so if you are having trouble with any of the addresses try one of the "Links Pages," or one of the many search engines or directories available on the Web.

Address: http:\\www.great-xfiles-info

Gillian Anderson Testosterone Brigade (GATB)
http://www.bchs.uh.edu/~ecantu/GATB/gatb.html
An organized, and secret, group of Anderson fans who rallied together, originally as a backlash to the David Duchovny Estrogen Brigade. The group maintains a web-site, ftp site, listmail, etc. Home of the "Gillian Anderson FAQ."

Gillian Anderson Estrogen Brigade
http://www.teatime.com/gaeb/
A site set up by women for women who admire the actress and her work.

Genuine Admirers of Gillian Anderson Association (GAGA)
http://users.cyberbeach.net/~jonmg/GA/GAGA.html
This group seeks to actively promote Ms. Anderson by writing to assorted print and non-print media and requesting coverage of her work, interviews, pictures, etc.

Welcome to #xf-GA
http://www.geocities.com/Area51/5922/
A home page designed to get you started in participating in one of the Anderson IRC (Internet Relay Chat) discussions. Everything you'll need is here: FAQ, software, list of users, help, etc.

The Gillian Anderson Web Site
http://www.ao.net/~gaws/
Possibly the best Gillian Anderson site on the web! This site is updated daily by site owner Cynthia Schmidt. She also maintains the NF Inc. site. In May 1997, the GAWS page held an online auction for NF and raised over $5,800 for the cause. This site reflects the hard work Cynthia puts into it. This is *the* site to start from — you may never leave!

The GAHP — The Gillian Anderson Home Page
http://www.blarg.net/~cynical/GAHP/
Extensive site offering a variety of information and download-able treats; some things here you will find hard to locate elsewhere. One of the first GA sites — Victor Chan and Mike Walter, site owners.

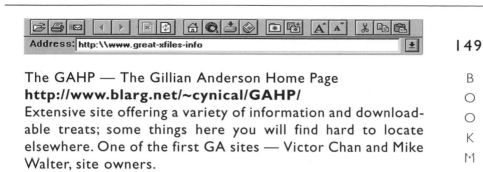
Order of the Blessed St. Scully the Enigmatic

Order of the Blessed Saint Scully the Enigmatic (OBSSE)
http://security-one.com/obsse/index.htm
Well you know you're in the right place when you visit Nancy Cotton's The Church of the Immaculate Gillian. One of the most fun sites on Scully you'll find. These guys take worship to new heights, so to speak. Filled with contributions of real fans who don't take themselves too seriously. Highly recom-mended.

LINKS

Mulder, it's me (MIM)
http://home.interstat.net/~tomveil/gillian.html
Huge list of Anderson/Scully-related links. Well organized, HUGE! Highly recommended. Created by Jack Witzig.

Yahoo — Anderson sites
**http://www.yahoo.com/Entertainment/Movies_and_
Films/Actors_and_Actresses/Anderson__Gillian/**
An enormous list of places to start.

B O O K M A R K S

Terminal X
http://www.neosoft.com/sbanks/xfiles/xmap1.html
A great site, and great-looking too. Great start to your X-Files
X-plorations on the Net.

The Ultimate, Biggest List of X-Files Links
http://www.geocities.com/Hollywood/Hills/2499/
fxfilesmain.html
An exhaustive X-Files directory, easy to navigate and HUGE.

GAWS Link-o-rama Page
http://www.ao.net/~gaws/lor/
Over 900 links as of June 1997, beautifully organized.

WEBRING — GILLIAN ANDERSON
http://www.webring.org

 RingWorld
http://www.webring.org/ringworld/ent/tv.html
The page from where you may begin your explorations of the
GA WebRing from an index, or let the server send you
randomly to one on the 44 sites (as of June 1997) participating.

GALLERIES

Gillian Anderson Images
http://www.snip.net/ganderson
A huge collection of regularly updated Anderson images. Links
to Duchovny pictures and pictures of the pair together.

Gillian Anderson British Association (GABA)
http://terabyte.virtual-pc.com/HawKSanD/gaba/
gaba.html or
http://www.hawksand.co.uk/gaba/gaba.html
A U.K. site of Anderson/Scully worship.

The Ultimate Gillian Anderson Image Gallery by Ron
http://www.worships.demon.co.uk/ga.html

The Thinking Man's Crumpet by Andy Robbins
http://www.webcom.com/andyr/ga.html
These sites share resources to offer sites containing hundreds
of GA images. Easy download of thumbnails.

The Gillian Anderson Classic Collection
http://www.iinet.net.au/~korn/ga/
This site is being reconstructed but be sure to check it out.
All the pictures of Gillian you could need.

OTHER ANDERSON SITES

Gillian Leigh Anderson Real Ecclesia
http://www.geocities.com/Hollywood/Hills/4965/
Great-looking site from Argentina, with lots of information,
easy to navigate. Includes a beautifully illustrated career bio,
humor section, and a picture gallery, collages designed by the
site owner, Leandro M. Rodriguez Sosa.

DIVORCX.HTML
SITE TITLE: **D.I.V.O.R.C.X.**
**http://www.geocities.com/Area51/Corridor/7171/
index.html**
Site opens with Scully wav: "I don't know how you think that
what they say is even remotely plausible." Site reports on
media coverage of GA's public "private life." Offers an "honest
and impartial summary of GA's relationship culled from the
world's press" — according to its own description. The site
is non-sensationalist and reports GA's presence in the media
while suggesting that you should not believe everything you
read. A good site to visit if you want to keep up your grocery-
store tabloid reading.

Welcome to My Gillian Anderson Home Page
http://www.pginet.com.au/~bmw/Ga/
The GA FAQ, some nice pictures. Scully wav files and a Scully
screensaver all make this site worth a visit.

Gillian FOREVER!
http://www.geocities.com/Hollywood/7299/index.html
Dave Chin's nicely put together site has lots to explore. Go
there!

The X-Files Experience
http://www.geocities.com/Area51/Vault/1411/
Although this is an XF site, there are some nice Scully elements. Also there is a page on Scully smiling and a page
devoted to "Irresistible," the site owner's favorite.

. . . Smart Is Sexy . . .
**http://www.geocities.com/Hollywood/3318/
gillian.html**
This is a fun page! One of the best things about this site: "101
Reasons to Love Gillian" — Gabrielle Wong has some original
and fun ideas.

NEUROFIBRO-MATOSIS

When Gillian Anderson's brother, Aaron, was three, he was diagnosed with the disease Neurofibromatosis. Life in the Anderson household changed from that day forward. Rosemary Anderson helped to found a Michigan clinic for NF patients and their families. Gillian, with her new-found celebrity, has worked to raise public awareness and funding for research.

On Friday, May 3, 1996, Gillian Anderson and her mother Rosemary flew to Washington, D.C., on a fund-raising and awareness-raising mission. What follows is the speech given by Gillian Anderson at a luncheon that gathered together scientists in the field of neuro-fibromatosis research. Her speech, these pages and the NF Inc. website (http://nfinc.org) are offered in the hopes that funding for research into this disorder can be raised. Every little bit helps. Please consider a contribution to this fund, especially if you are thinking of sending a gift of appreciation to Ms. Anderson for her work as an actress. Thank you.

Thank you. I am just listening to the very small list of my accomplishments. They seem so insignificant in the presence of such gurus as Dr. Collins and Senator Kassebaum. I'm very honored to be here. But I will say, this is much scarier than any X-File I've encountered. I'm going to read what I have written. I may be able to look you in the eye, but at this point it's written down and hopefully I can make some sense.

My first lesson with neurofibromatosis came when I was 16, after we learned that my three-and-a-half-year-old brother Aaron had it. My mother took me to the first meeting of what was to become the Neurofibromatosis Support Group of West Michigan. I remember the social worker there talking to the 40 or so people who had shown up. There were many who were too intimidated to speak, and there were many who were so excited about the prospect of communicating with people who for the first time understood what they had been going through, and also communicating the fears that they had experienced in their lives, that they couldn't stop talking. I remember in particular one young mother who had just lost her six-year-old daughter to an NF-related brain tumor, and I remember a 60-year-old woman who was trying somewhat heroically not to hide the many disfiguring tumors on her face. It was a very broad spectrum.

My mother tells me that some people never actually came back to that support group. I think for the many who remained over the past 11 and some years that the support group has been there, they have shared in the comfort of unbiased friends and fellow sufferers,

and in the slow but gradual understanding of NF and its unpredictable complications.

Zoe, Gillian, and Aaron Anderson

I have watched my brother grow into a sturdy 15-year-old boy. We are among the most fortunate of NF families. My brother is mildly affected by it; so far so good. But as we learned here today, if we didn't already know, with NF, it is never over. He has a couple of visible tumors, skin tumors, right now. He may have no more; he may have so many more that they are uncountable. We don't know at this point. And then there's always the threat of the more serious tumors which can come about at any time. And I guess my one hope, regardless of what happens in the future for him, is that the "Joke-meister," as we call him, maintains his wonderful sense of humor throughout.

But it is not just Aaron and the West Michigan NF community. NF is worldwide, and it can happen in any family. And I must say that if the horror of this disease isn't enough to promote its financial support, something that has — that is just as important, and something you might want to consider as an added bonus — is that the study of NF and neurofibromatosis research is already providing breakthroughs in understanding more about cancer. And we all know how to pronounce that.

I want to thank you for having me here, for joining me in an effort to raise awareness of a disease that is in dire need of acknowledgment, community education, and extensive research if we are going to find a cure.

Thank you very much.

Quoted material from the May 20, 1996, Congressional Record, pp. S5392-5394. Remarks of Gillian Anderson at Neurofibromatosis, Inc. Luncheon, Friday, May 3, 1996.

!PLEASE HELP! To send a donation is easy, make your cheque payable to

Neurofibromatosis Inc.
8855 Annapolis Rd., Suite 100
Landham, MD 20706-2924

or to

The National Neurofibromatosis Foundation
95 Pine Street, 16th Floor
New York, N.Y. 10005
1-800-323-7938

Our thanks to Mary Ann Wilson and Cynthia Schmidt for allowing us to reprint text from the NF Inc. website (http://nfinc.org).

INTERVIEWS WITH CHRIS CARTER AND GILLIAN ANDERSON

by Jon Casimir

Jon Casimir is a journalist living in Sydney, Australia, where he works for the *Sydney Morning Herald*. He met with Gillian Anderson and Chris Carter in November 1995.

CHRIS CARTER
INTERVIEW

JON CASIMIR: How did the episode I visited turn out?

CHRIS CARTER: "Revelations," it was called. It actually turned out really well. It was one of the favorite episodes this year.

JC: You were locked up writing last week when we were supposed to talk.

CC: I think every week it's safe to say I'm locked up writing.

JC: How much of the series are you doing?

CC: I have my name on seven of the first 15 for this year. And I do a fair amount of rewriting past that. So I do, I would say, more than the lion's share.

JC: Is writing the heart of the job for you?

CC: It is. Everything springs from that but there are numerous responsibilities that I have undertaken. I just got out of the playback room, where I reviewed the sound and music for episode 13. I did a final quality control on that.

JC: Is the writing where you get the most personal enjoyment?

CC: I think the biggest personal satisfaction for me is in seeing the final product. Everything else is done under such strict deadlines and time pressure that a lot of the enjoyment is just in finishing it.

JC: You've given yourself a job where you work 150 hours a week. Couldn't you pull back?

CC: I don't think I've got the personality to really pull back. If I felt that the show was going to suffer in any way or was not going to be the show I thought it could be, I couldn't pull back. And right now I feel that this isn't just obsessing or a neurotic compulsion, it's really about trying to make the show as good as it can be. I am really determined to never have the quality suffer. I would like to see the show keep getting better and better.

JC: Gillian said the third season had really found itself — that it has been through its adolescence and has now found its style.

CC: I think she's right. I think that this is the best year ever. The ratings reflect it. I think the quality of the shows this year has been excellent. And I think that has a lot to do with the directors that we have hired. We've hired a series of directors who have rotated. I think that helps a lot, takes a lot of the guesswork out. There's a communication that is built in in that situation.

JC: Does a TV show need to mature?

CC: I think the first year is a really important maturing process. I think it really finds itself. You find what works, the pacing, the rhythms. But I think that all too often TV shows age rather than mature. And that is not a good thing.

JC: How close to your original vision is what we get?

CC: I have to say that it's extremely close to what I imagined. Of course, when I was sitting and writing the pilot, I never imagined episode 73, which is where we'll be this year. Anyone who creates a show, I don't think, can look that far down the road. But I did, indeed, have an idea about how the Mulder and Scully relationship would progress. And how the stories would work. What is most surprising to me is the kind of stories we have told, the directions the show has gone in, in terms of the variety of stories we've told.

Other than that, the show is pretty much what I originally conceived of.

JC: So where has it taken you that you haven't expected?

CC: I don't know if you guys saw the "Humbug" episode, the freaks episode last year. That's just an ep that I never imagined. To tell you the truth, when it came in, I thought it was a pretty big departure from what we had done before, but I thought at that time, the 45th episode, that we had earned the right to stretch a little. If I can make a baseball analogy, we had been throwing fastballs and curveballs and this was a knuckleball, something new to our repertoire. In season three, you're going to get a few more of those kinds of episodes. They're very comedic episodes and I hadn't anticipated taking the show in that direction.

JC: Are you getting away with more than expected, taking it further?

CC: In some respects, yes. There were stories they told us we wouldn't be able to tell, about satanic cults for example. They thought that was viewer-unfriendly, territory they thought was not for television. We've gone into that and further. I think we have pushed the limits of standards. But other than that, I think we're not getting away with anything more than they would ever let us get away with in terms of detail, graphic elements. I think it's more that subject matter which may have been verboten before is now in play.

JC: Are the episodes gone over with a fine-tooth comb?

CC: Oh yeah. Every week there is a negotiation that is waged between the broadcast standards and practice wing, which is the censorship wing really, of the network, and me and the producers on the show, who fight for the things we think are very important to our storytelling.

JC: You've talked a lot about the influence of TV shows like *Night Stalker*. But are you now or were you as a kid a big comic reader?

CC: No, uh-uh, never. Never a big comic book reader. Never a science fiction fan. I just loved scary movies, good scary stories, good mysteries and thrillers. Even in my adolescence things like good political thrillers, *Parallax View*, *All the President's Men*, *Three Days of the Condor*, loved those kinds of movies.

JC: Scaring is not what it used to be in this age of gratuitous, over-the-top special effects. What are the rules of doing it now?

CC: Making it seem as if it really could happen. If it could happen to you. If it's a believable situation. We live in fear every day, we live in a lot of denial as well. If you can find the elements of everyday life that scare us and bring them into play, embellish or find new ways to look at the world, then you have naturally scary situations, which is what the best *X-Files* have.

JC: The really good shows, rather than a roller-coaster scare, have a profound sense of unease.

CC: Yes, that's what I'm always looking for.

JC: I love that story about there being three million people in America who believe they have been abducted by aliens. Anyone else would say, well, it's time to move away, but you thought, wow, a target audience.

CC: Not so much a target audience. If I had to go for three million people, I'd be off the air. Three million people is not enough to carry an American TV show. I didn't see them as the audience as much as I saw it as a quantitative analysis of a syndrome. For me it said that there is a legitimate way to present these people's cases to a larger public. So I never saw them as my audience as much as fuel for my stories.

JC: You've created a believer and a skeptic. Which are you?

CC: I'm a skeptic by nature. I describe myself as a non-religious person looking for a religious experience. So I'm like Mulder, who has that poster "I want to believe" on the wall. I really have a desire, as I believe we all do, to find a reason to believe, to have our skepticism tested, eroded, or our beliefs affirmed.

JC: Is it a search for meaning?

CC: I think it is, but it is indirectly. I didn't set out to deliver a message at all. And I still don't want that to be the purpose of any of the shows. I really want to entertain, scare and thrill.

JC: The motto of the show is the truth is out there. But you seem to be saying the truth isn't, that it's changeable, manipulable.

CC: I've always thought of it as a double entendre. The truth is out there to be found, and then it's so far out there that we'll never find it.

JC: How important is the sexual tension between the characters?

CC: I never wanted them to jump in the sack together because it was uninteresting to me. To me, the most sexual relationships are often the ones that are never realized, consummated or even spoken about. So I wanted this to be two smart people who work together, who happen to get along very well. Through their shared passion in their work, there is a natural chemical sexual tension that comes out of that, that doesn't ever have to be spoken about, but it works.

JC: Like in *The Avengers*?

CC: I loved *The Avengers* as a kid. That Steed/Mrs. Peel

thing was a sort of May/September thing. He definitely was more of a father figure to her.

JC: I like the fact that *The X-Files* is non-linear drama.

CC: Kind of. Sometimes it's very linear. Sometimes you really tell it in a very straight path.

JC: But it's drama which often works without resolution.

CC: Oh yes, in that way, there is rarely any kind of perfectly satisfying resolution. You may have an understanding of a situation or something may have been solved, but ultimately we never try to explain the unexplainable.

JC: That's a pretty radical step for television. There is an assumption that everyone wants a neat package tied up with bows.

CC: They only do if they think there is resolution to be had. But I think in this case people would actually call B.S. on us if we pretended to explain something or give them all the answers. We are dealing with subject matter beyond explanation a lot of the time. So I think it was the right choice. It's the natural choice for this kind of storytelling.

JC: It also gives credit to the audience for intelligence and imagination.

CC: Yeah, exactly.

JC: It's been a real zeitgeist show. Did you have any idea it would strike a chord?

CC: You never do. You just hope you get an order for your pilot script, an order for your pilot. You hope the pilot gets picked up for a series and you hope the series gets picked up for another. Along the way, you are, I call it taking the pig to the fair. You want to make it to the final judging, which is ultimately with the viewing public. You want them just to like it. You can never anticipate the kind of response we have had with *The X-Files*.

JC: Were you surprised at the level of paranoia and weirdness out there?

CC: No, I had anticipated that. But I wasn't prepared for the prevalence of a basic distrust of authority and the government.

JC: Around the time of the Oklahoma bombing, did you ever think, I am making a paranoid anti-government program, am I feeding into this?

CC: No, I think there's no connection. I am not saying overthrow authority. I am saying question it. We're not suggesting anything revolutionary. These people are obviously very militant.

JC: People talk of *The X-Files* as being like *Star Trek*, saying it will go on forever. Are you sitting on a 30-year job?

CC: No way. This show will never go for 30 years. There may be a movie now and again. I see it going for five years and anything past that is great. But if it lasted any longer than seven, I would be completely surprised. And it wouldn't be under my aegis.

JC: Has it made you as rich as Croesus and does this mean you are finally going to get to make that series of documentaries on the life of the boll weevil or whatever your personal fantasy has been?

CC: I think it will allow me to go surfing where I want to go surfing, when I get to go surfing again. So I'm looking forward to that. When you do this kind of show, certainly the paychecks fatten and start coming in. Am I rich as Croesus? Hardly.

Gillian Anderson and Chris Carter
on the set of *The X-Files*.

GILLIAN ANDERSON
INTERVIEW

JON CASIMIR: You were not going to do television,
were you? So how did you end up here?
GILLIAN ANDERSON: Yeah, I was somewhat pig-
headed about that. In a way. TV represented a kind of
a step down, or a sellout in some way to me then. I
think the whole framework and quality of television
has changed in the last four or five years. So yeah, that
was something I felt pretty strongly about.
JC: Is that a phase that every actor goes through?

GA: I don't know. I have run into many actors whose dream is to be on television.

JC: It's interesting that you say TV has picked up. It seems very strong in America in the '90s. The '80s weren't crash hot, but the '90s have seen a lot of quality drama and comedy. And yet, at the same time, the film industry in the U.S. seems to be having a hard time of it.

GA: It seems like the better drama and film is coming out of other countries and always has. I think that's because the industry in America has become so selfish, and it has in a sense peaked in an area of action films, and it can't go anywhere else. It's stuck. Out of Australia, New Zealand, England, with Almodovar doing stuff . . . There's so many wonderful foreign films coming in. The audience is taking a deep sigh of relief and going to see them for the first time because they're so tired of what America has to offer.

JC: When you saw the pilot script of *The X-Files*, what was it that stirred you? And don't just say the prospect of steady work.

GA: It had been about a year since I had worked. And that definitely influenced me. It was one of the first few television scripts that I had taken a look at. It was so different from anything that I had read, film or television wise. The relationship between Mulder and Scully was so interesting and compelling, their intellectual repartee. The whole dynamic and the tension between them was wonderful on paper. And the idea was brilliant. Everything. Certainly, when I was sitting at home reading that script, I didn't expect that this would be the result of me reading that script for the first time.

JC: Was Scully fully mapped out?

GA: I think Chris (Carter) is very particular about these characters and has a very strict formula of who these characters are. He helped in the beginning, through the audition process and throughout the shooting of the show, to guide me in that direction. He was very helpful at the beginning in describing to me his vision of this character. Her throughline is strong through every script. It's pretty obvious reading these scripts who these people are.

JC: He argued for you at network level, did he not?

GA: Yeah, he did.

JC: What was he seeing in you?

GA: I'm not sure exactly. There was something in me or in my performance I guess that he saw and said, This is the character that I wrote. I don't know exactly what that was. My answer before was that I tend to have a seriousness about me. I'm also incredibly goofy, but there is a seriousness about me, sometimes to a fault, that I think helped me to get the role. The character is written very seriously. She rarely cracks a smile. She is always very straightforward, very singlemindedly dedicated to her work. Maybe that came across in the audition.

JC: As an actor, could you feel her immediately?

GA: Yeah, I actually could. Sometimes it doesn't happen when you're reading a script. You have to search for it or fight for it in some way. Sometimes I think that's what deters actors from some scripts. The guiding point is when you read a script and something doesn't click. But something did. And I could feel her very strongly. I have fallen in love with this character, in many ways, straight from the beginning. I put it down and I said, god, I'd love to be involved in this.

I'd love to be a part of this process, to play this character. Then I took the steps to do that.

JC: What did you think it would be? It's such an unlikely show. You must have had every reason to believe it would just be a pilot or 13 episodes or maybe one season.

GA: I had no clue. Mostly because I was ignorant about television. I didn't know what a pilot was, what going to network was and what auditioning for network was. I didn't know and I didn't care up until then. I was excited when I got the role. And I assumed that I would be going up (to Vancouver) and shooting the three weeks of the pilot. I didn't know what it meant to be picked up or that things had seasons. I was very ignorant as far as television was concerned. And when I finally understood that, during the shooting process, I started to wish that it would continue, not knowing the ratios of what is picked up and what isn't. I didn't have a clue.

JC: Sounds like a blissful ignorance.

GA: Yes it was. And it still is. I'm still very ignorant as far as television is concerned. So I just assumed that it was going to be picked up, because it felt strong. But I had no idea what I was wishing for or talking about. It was just blind faith that it was going to be picked up. And it was.

JC: Was there a point, an incident, where you realized you were onto something, in terms of it being as successful as it has become?

GA: I don't really remember a specific point. I remember during the first year, being up here and shooting, we were in a vacuum, and a very difficult one. First of all, it was getting used to the hours and the rhythm of television. And it was hard to deal with the ups and downs, the emotional ups and downs, being away from home. All of that was getting in the way of experiencing the potential enjoyment of our success. We'd hear that the ratings were getting better. We'd hear that there was a cult following and all this stuff. I didn't really have any frame of reference, so it didn't mean anything to me. I would have been just as happy to . . . I was very happy that I had a job on something that I believed in and was gathering the success and respect. . . . But I would have been just as happy for it to end and to move on to something else.

JC: Was there a point then, at the end of that first season, where you went home, went shopping and thought, Why are all these people staring at me?

GA: That has really only happened in the last year. Yes, people would stop me and say hello, but it has now got to the extent that I basically cannot go anywhere without people stopping me. Except for Europe. I did some publicity in Europe last summer and maybe one person stopped me in the entire six weeks. Which was blissful.

JC: Did you ever have any interest in science fiction or TV of this variety?

GA: No, but I'm fascinated by the subject matter. When I was a kid I used to read the UFO section in *Omni* magazine and stuff like that, whenever it was lying around. But that was really the extent of it. It has not been something that I have studied or sought out in any way. I saw my first episode of *Star Trek* last year, one of the original episodes, which is the only way to go.

JC: Was *Close Encounters* a big film for you?

GA: It was actually. *Close Encounters* was for me. And the *Star Wars* trilogy. But not in a way where I thought, god, that's what I want to do or that is something I'm interested in. It was the enormity and the experience of them, the complete experience of getting lost in a film. And the excitement of that, the awe of that. I knew, and I still know, that I want to be involved in films that allow the audience to experience that kind of awe, whether it's from a big special-effects-related film or a smaller film where you sit back and get really taken by something.

JC: Do you think people get that kind of awe from *The X-Files?*

GA: Oh, I don't know. I think people get scared. They get freaked out. And are in a position to talk about it with people. . . . It's an important show because of the quality and the risks that are taken, but I don't know how life-changing it is. What's interesting though . . . I think the way it is life-changing is the response that the public has to the characters. These characters have become role models for young kids. And they're very positive role models. They're not role models who go out and shoot people up and get into sword fights. They're very honest, hardworking, straightforward, dedicated, clean individuals. That's excellent.

JC: So you took the part, turned around and got pregnant. Were you worried that they might let you go? Was it far enough into the program to be safe?

GA: No, it wasn't far enough in. It was halfway through the first season. It seemed like it was far enough in. It seemed like it had been going on forever, but in retrospect it was only halfway through the first season.

JC: How did you cope with 14 hours a day on set?

GA: There were different stages. The first stage was a lot of uneasiness and fear and frustration and not knowing how to be. It wasn't public information. It was something that only myself and some producers and the wardrobe people knew. The crew didn't know until I was quite a few months along. That was the hardest part. Once it was let out of the bag, it was much easier on an emotional level. Also, the crew helped out tremendously. They were very loving, very helpful, from experience and from sympathy. It was intense. I no longer felt like the person that they had hired to be this character.

JC: You felt like a fraud?

GA: When a woman gets pregnant, her hormones change and she becomes, for a short period of time, a different person. I mean, I'm different than I was before I was pregnant, but when I was pregnant, I was really different. Nothing about me felt familiar. So with that in mind and also the fact that I was [she laughs] six times my size, and that I had a baby kicking around inside my belly in the middle of scenes, it was a very strange, odd time.

JC: Would you do it again?

GA: I want to be pregnant again eventually, but not during this series. We're in the third season, so there might be a three- or four-year gap.

JC: The show used that pregnancy to write you out for an episode and use less of you in a few others. At that time, it explored more of David's character. Will Scully become more fleshed out in the third series?

GA: A tiny bit, yeah. Not to that degree. But yes, there have been a couple of episodes that reveal a bit more of Scully.

JC: The show works on the balance of the characters. We now know what drives Mulder. We also need to know what drives Scully.

GA: It's finally starting to feel like we are being perceived as partners. Granted, the first season was about us finding our way, finding who these characters were and adapting to life in Vancouver and 14-hour days. The second season, for me, was about coping with the pregnancy and post-pregnancy. Finally, this season feels like we're in it. Not only are we in it, but Scully is in it more than she was at the beginning. Everybody talks about how independent and strong they are, how they are considered as equals. But still, Scully was always five steps behind Mulder, always the last one to show up, always the one you didn't see. Finally in the third season, they're side by side.

JC: How much of their relationship is dependent on the no-sexual-tension rule?

GA: There isn't a no-sexual-tension ruling. There's nothing that says there should be no sexual tension. There's just not meant to be sex. It's only a platonic relationship, but we can toy around with the sexual tension as much as we want or as much as is appropriate for any scene.

JC: Do they fancy each other?

GA: Yes, in an odd way they do. I think they hugely respect each other and are incredibly intimate because of everything they have been through. I think they're both well aware of the boundaries that they need to keep in order to keep this working relationship going.

JC: They're very yin/yang. One skeptic, one believer. Do you embody either end?

GA: A bit of both, I'd say. It depends what the subject

matter is. I believe in ghosts, but if one actually appeared to me, it would scare the hell out of me. There are certain things that I believe in and certain things that I need to have proved.

JC: Has anything in two and a half seasons made you uneasy?

GA: Yeah, there have been a few episodes which have made me uneasy. . . . Anything that has to do with voodoo or possession or devil-related things.

JC: Why voodoo?

GA: It's very negative. There are other issues we deal with, paranormal situations, which are more spiritual than negative. Voodoo to me is purely about doing harm to other people. In terms of the aborigines, how do the general population in Australia feel about the culture and the spiritual practices of the aborigines . . . ? [I say a whole lot of stuff here that doesn't matter] I think there's going to be a day sometime in the not too far-off future, where we're all going to have . . . I keep having this image . . . to have to look back collectively at what we have done, and how we have not only destroyed the gifts that we have, but also we're going to realize collectively what we could have learned from the different cultures, from the American Indians, from the aborigines.

JC: What are the contemporary chords this program is hitting?

GA: You know, it's hard to pinpoint what it is. I think aside from the look of the show, the mood of the show, the special effects, the writing, the co-stars, everything, it seems to be incredibly timely right now. Why is it timely? Suddenly it has become OK if not trendy to believe in UFOs, at least in America. In other countries, they are taken for granted as being a reality. Suddenly it has become publicly OK to discuss them and believe in them. Also, it has become almost trendy to admit, discuss, lecture about one's distaste and frustration with the government, and the government's tendency toward secrecy and cover-ups.

JC: It seems to me that we're living in a time when all of the central pillars of society, the judicial system, government, religion, are no longer being seen as the answer. People have lost faith in all of them. And *The X-Files* kind of feeds into that, by saying look, there aren't any absolutes.

GA: Also, there is a very spiritual flavor to the show, whether we're dealing with flukeworms in the body or whatever. There is a spiritual throughline in one way or another. There is a search for meaning in it and I think that is primarily what the appeal is. The books that have become the most popular over the past few years. . . . *The Celestine Prophecy*, *Mutant Message from Down Under*, there was a book on angels . . . I think that people are searching desperately for some kind of answer, for some kind of hope, for some kind of respite to the norm, to the drudge, to the pain that they experience in everyday life. In some way, whether it is through escapism, or through some kind of spiritual or otherworldly connection, they're finding that in some odd juxtaposed way, from the show.

JC: One of the things the show does is refuse to resolve its storylines. It says the truth is out there, and then says the truth is changeable, manipulable. Maybe people find this comforting now. We don't get everything in our lives resolved, tied up neatly.

GA: And also, from a marketing standpoint, if you

don't close things up, it makes people question. It makes people verbalize their questions. And discussions are had. They're had that night, the next day. . . . You're at a table with someone who hasn't seen the show, you're talking about it, it gets passed. Because of the unresolved nature of it, it forces the show to become popular through hearsay, as well as through all the publicity.

JC: I think, in dramatic terms, that's the biggest risk the show has taken. It's often a drama without an ending. I don't think it has been recognized what a radical step that is.

GA: No. It hasn't and I'm not sure exactly if I myself have felt the weight of that risk because of my lack of knowledge of other television shows. Because I don't enjoy television very much, I have never really had a show that I have watched or followed. So I don't know. It has never occurred to me that these shows have endings, this one doesn't.

JC: Have you been on the convention circuit yet?

GA: No, there is one in January that I'm going to go to.

JC: How much of fandom are you privy to?

GA: Not much of it. I hear bits and pieces. I read the fan mail that I can and respond when I have time. I am aware of the degree of discussion that takes place on the Internet. But that's about it. I don't think I want to know.

JC: From the acting point of view, what is key to show? There are so many outlandish things going on. Is the job just making sure the characters stay believable?

GA: I think that Chris's take on these characters, and something that was injected into the scripts form the

beginning, was a dead seriousness about this information, about the paranormal, about the situations these two characters get put in. He completely took himself and these characters and his writing seriously, to the point where even in the notes between the lines, you would never hear a joke turned in on himself. Now there is a writer who is on his third episode for us, who has a sense of humor and is being allowed to put that into the script. But that is the first time. From the beginning, David and I, without actually talking about it, fell into the rhythm of trying to, knowing that we may be called upon to react time after time after time to odd, strange, peculiar, scary, freaky, bizarre situations, that we had to develop some way of being, some way of reacting, that could last that period of time, some way that we absolutely completely believed what we were doing and seeing, even with Scully being a skeptic. And whatever rhythm it was we fell into has worked.

JC: Is that the hardest part? Or is it the tech talk?

GA: There aren't really any hard, hard parts. There are a few aspects of shooting this series that collectively make it difficult, tiring, frustrating. For me those are the hours, the particular kind of dialogue that we share with each other and the other characters. In one-hour television, you have so little time to work on the scenes, to rehearse the scenes, to shoot the scenes, that you get into a rhythm of making choices that are good enough. Sometimes there is a luxury. . . . When I first started doing the show, it was so frustrating not to really feel like we had the scene. We know it, we have it, it's working. . . . Certainly some of them were written well enough for that possibility, but not having the luxury of time you get into a rhythm of making quick choices, and the frustrating part is doing a scene where you feel like you have made these choices already, you've done this, it's old, it's boring. And getting frustrated with that, just wanting to have the opportunity to explore other characters, to explore this in a different way, to do anything but say these same words, do these same actions, react the same way.

JC: Does that make it hard to watch yourself on TV?

GA: Occasionally. It makes it hard in my head, in imagining that the public is going to have a hard time or get bored or say god, she's still skeptical, didn't she see?

JC: She has to mature.

GA: Yep. And she has. Over time. Finally. She's getting to a point where she is seeing, she is beginning to believe, she is questioning her beliefs, struggling with them, growing up.

JC: What is the biggest joy of playing the part?

GA: I guess the joys are almost like stepping stones. Once in a while, a scene comes around in a script where you really have something to get into, to work on, to express another part of myself, another part of a character. Something more is revealed. I can come out of it feeling that I have done good work, that I have had something to say. Then we get back into the next X-file. So that's where the joy comes in, in feeling good about something that I have done. And also in working with this crew. I love this crew. That's been a pleasure. They really care about the show.

CBC RADIO REALTIME BROADCASTS WITH GILLIAN ANDERSON

Although she's done a number of radio interviews around the world, Anderson's first interview for CBC Radio in Vancouver set into motion some new experiences for her and the station. She returned three more times, acting as DJ in March and September of 1996.

What follows are the transcripts of her first two appearances, courtesy of the CBC and fans Mike Quigley and Victor Chan. We offer the set lists for her last two appearances, where Gillian played some of her favorite music.

Section 1:   November 19, 1994
Section 2:   September 16, 1995
Section 3:   March 16, 1996
Section 4:   September 21, 1996

SECTION 1

November 19, 1994: "The First Time" in Studio 4 CBC Vancouver (22 minutes).

Here is the official transcript of the Gillian Anderson interview. Many thanks to Vancouver's Mike Quigley for the work he did preparing the transcript:

This interview on the CBC's RealTime with Gillian Anderson in late November of 1994 ran about 21 minutes. The following is a transcription I did which was posted to the Usenet newsgroup alt.tv.x-files. The quotes are not always word-for-word.

Host Leora Kornfeld started asking about GA's new baby, born in Vancouver, and therefore half-Canadian, half-American. When asked why she went back to work so fast, GA says, "Because I was written into the next script," and the producers didn't give her much choice in the matter.

First phone guest is the president of an *X-Files* club at University of Western Ontario who gives GA an honorary membership in the club. She asks GA about her university experience, and which role she thought was most influential to her acting. GA says she went to DePaul Theater school at DePaul University in Chicago, where the whole curriculum was based around theater studies. The play that affected her the most was a comedy called *A Flea In Her Ear*, a farce, where she played a small role, a French maid. "It was good for me to explore the comedic side of acting."

When asked if she looks at Internet groups, GA says: "I am aware of them. I've only taken a look once or twice, with people that I log on with. I'm not a regular participant."

[LEORA KORNFELD] LK: Does it scare you? It must be terrible to have your life scrutinized.

[GILLIAN ANDERSON] GA: That's one reason I don't participate, because it's very personal stuff and in terms of the character I don't want to be influenced too much by people's opinions. I have to stick very closely to how I feel the character needs to be portrayed from episode to episode.

LK: How do people treat you when they run into you in Vancouver?

GA: Very calmly . . . I haven't been accosted by anyone. Everyone has been very polite. I haven't felt uncomfortable at any given time.

When asked to compare Vancouver to L.A. (where she is from), she says, "It's been so long since I've been in L.A.!" She says she doesn't get out much recently, because they shoot the show five days a week, and weekends are "family time."

Walter via e-mail asks if Mulder and Scully should be romantically involved.

GA: A lot of people have commented on that, but the show's not really about that. It's about the cases we are investigating and our professional relationship and it's occurred to the writers that if it was to go into any other direction it would distract from the main theme of the show. If we establish a romantic relationship, it would kind of go downhill.

LK: Was such a relationship a possibility earlier on in the show?

GA: I don't think so . . . they've been pretty concerned about keeping us platonic.

Someone told GA there was a debate on the Internet as to whether there was any sexual tension between the two characters. She comments that in the recent episodes, it's as strong as it was before she was "out of the picture."

Miranda on the phone in Vancouver says she's glad to see GA's character getting stronger in the most recent episode ("Firewalker") and asks how being a mom affects her work. Does it make her work seem less important?

GA: It's not less important, in terms of time I have to spend on the script, it has decreased, it's frustrating . . . I don't take it as seriously as I have taken it in the past. I'm not as obsessed as I was with it before. I'm still putting as much energy as I can into the show.

Evan from Manitoba asks if the "Feds" have ever shown up to stop the show.

GA: We visited the FBI at the beginning of this year, and they were very supportive. They let us know very clearly there were no such things as X-files. They were pretty determined that we note that. We have a lot of fans in the FBI. We've never been warned.

LK: Are you a sex symbol among FBI agents? Did you find your picture on a lot of fridges when you went to the FBI headquarters?

GA: No, I didn't see a single fridge.

Neil in Victoria (11 years old) asks if GA and David Duchovny are good friends off the screen.

GA: It's a lot of work to work with someone as intensely as we do on a daily basis. Our relationship shifts and changes, and on the weekends we don't hang out because we're sick of seeing each other all week!

There is discussion about DD being single, with a

girlfriend (who was in the vampire episode). LK comments that "a lot of hearts are broken."

Nicole in London, Ontario (member of Western *X-Files* Club) asks if any of the shows actually come from documented cases.

GA: A lot of the shows are based loosely on factual information. The writers read about scientific information and take bits and pieces and kind of formulate them into stories. Some information is factual, but in order to make an episode and make it playable on television it's pulled and tugged here and there to make it entertaining. There may be bits and pieces of factual information in each episode. Most of the stories are constructed for viewing audiences.

When asked how interested she was in the kind of materials portrayed on *The X-Files*:

GA: I've always been interested in it, it's been something that's been part of my mind and belief systems. I haven't read a lot of books or subscribed to a lot of magazines.

LK: Did that help you get the part?

GA: I don't think so. They didn't sit me down and ask me if I believe in this stuff before I got the audition.

Lynn in Calgary (fourth-year bio student) says she's interested in the scientific discussion on *The X-Files*. "How do you deal with the jargon?"

GA: Sometimes it's very hard to say this stuff and make it sound like I know what I'm talking about, because I don't. There's always a level at which I'm lost. It's fascinating, I can't tell you how much I hold in my brain after the scene . . . I probably forget everything that I supposedly learned. But I have a great deal of respect for someone who has to keep that stuff in their brain to use on a daily basis." GA adds: "At one point I was very interested in biology. Before I got interested in acting I was interested in marine biology a lot."

Doug in Calgary asks if the show is going to elaborate on Scully's abduction now that she is back.

GA: I was wondering that myself. I really don't know. It would certainly be an opportunity to do that.

LK asks if it was hard to be in a coma on the show.

GA: I was still blue from the caesarean section. They didn't have to use much makeup. During some of it I slept. It was only a few days after I got out of the hospital and it was an opportunity to get some rest.

LK comments that the show's producers really crack the whip.

GA: The show is doing very well. There was a lot of interest in Scully's disappearance and they wanted to keep the duo working together. I wasn't expecting that I would go back that early. But I'm very glad to be back at work.

LK: Were the producers less than thrilled to find out you were pregnant?

GA: I would say that. There was a lot of shooting from the neck up . . . a lot of very high angles and a lot of trenchcoats. There was a joke about the cameraman putting on a wide-angle lens.

LK: Have you got people coming up to you on the street and telling you their paranormal experiences and wild dreams?

GA: I haven't and I don't know if David has either. Why would anyone walk up to a skeptic? I think David perhaps has gotten more mail about people's individual experiences for that reason. In real life, David and

I . . . our opinions on the subject matter are opposite
from our characters'.
LK: So if you meet David on the street, should you
treat him like the skeptic he is?
GA: Yes.

SECTION 2

September 16, 1995: "Hello Gillian?"

*Gillian made broadcasting history on RealTime. This was the
first ever global celebrity call-in. It was broadcast around
the world in real time on the Internet courtesy of Progressive
Networks and their Live RealAudio server (42 minutes).
This transcript was prepared by "Cynical." He was very
faithful to the interview as broadcast:*

Leora Kornfeld hosted RealTime on CBC Stereo Radio
on September 16, 1995, with special guest Gillian
Anderson of *The X-Files*. The interview was broadcast
live at the CBC Vancouver station at around 7:15 p.m.
PST and was simulcast across the Internet using Progressive Network's RealAudio.
LK: Gillian Anderson is here to talk to me and to talk
to you and to take calls and e-mails. We're actually
simulcasting on the net and on the CBC Stereo network. This is wild. So, toll-free from within Canada,
1-800-563-2328; from anywhere else in the world it's
604-669-3733; e-mail is realtime@cbcstereo.com.
We've got a whole bunch of e-mail, we've got a whole
bunch of calls already so we're going to try to keep
them moving fast. The lines may be jammed so redial,

redial, and uh, Gillian . . . hello!

GA: Hi.

LK: Hi, how're you doing?

GA: I'm good.

LK: It's kind of weird [Gillian laughs] because the first thing Gillian and I were chatting during the song, I said, "Did you see a band called Quintron last night?"

GA: Yes, I did.

LK: Yeah.

GA: That's Mr. Quintron.

LK: It is Mr. Quintron? Explain what he does. See, I had a friend who was at the show who called me. "She's going to be on your show. Here, she's really here." I said, "No, no, it's not her — it's somebody else." And he held up the phone and it was just this bizarre organ music.

GA: Organ music, yes. Um, Mr. Quintron is an old friend of mine from Chicago and he was in town for the night playing at the Malcolm Lowry Room and we were there to witness it.

LK: And nobody bothered you, right?

GA: No. Nope. Nope.

LK: Nobody did that "you really look like that woman from *The X-Files*" to you?

GA: One person said, "You really look like the woman from *The X-Files*" to me and I said, "Thank you very much."

LK: And that was the end of that? [Both laugh] That was the end of that. Well, I have heard, because we're sort of getting into your musical past here. I've heard that you used to be a punk, that you had pink and purple and black hair, and all this kinda stuff.

GA: Ummm . . . I did.

LK: Yeah?

GA: I did.

LK: When was that?

GA: It was in high school and in college. I went through a stage. Although I don't necessarily feel like I've rid that part of myself yet. I mean if I weren't doing the show right now I'm not quite sure what color my hair would be [Leora laughs], so it's still inside of me somewhere.

LK: It's in there somewhere. What kind of bands were you into at that time?

GA: Oh, Circle Jerks, Dead Kennedys, I guess a little bit of Elvis Costello, um, I'm trying to think of . . .

LK: This is great, this is a whole new side of you.

GA: A whole new side . . .

LK: That's great. Well, we should take some calls 'cause we've got one from Australia right now. Mary, go ahead.

MARY: Hello?

GA: Hi . . . Australia!

MARY: Um, my friends from IRC told me that you'd be on so I thought, hey, I'll ring you. [Laughs]

GA: Well, you got lucky. [Laughs]

MARY: Yeah, very! I was just wondering: are you going to be coming to Australia anytime soon?

GA: I hope so. I have no idea when we will be shooting the show — until May at least. If I can get a job that takes me to Australia in the very short hiatus we have, I'd be very happy but I really don't know that far in advance.

LK: Thanks for the call, Mary.

MARY: Okay.

LK: It's exciting getting calls from Australia. We can

take another call right away. Why not? From Halifax, it's Alia? There you go, here's Gillian.

GA: Hi.

ALIA: Hi, I have a couple of questions. First, is your hair really that color or is that, like, not real.

GA: That's a big, big secret.

ALIA: Oh. [Gillian laughs]

LK: It looks real, though.

GA: It looks real.

LK: It looks very real.

GA: It does.

ALIA: Um, I had another question.

GA: Yes.

ALIA: Is the next season gonna be more like aliens or is it gonna be Mulder versus the FBI and all that stuff. Is it gonna be, like, bureaucratic or is it gonna be . . . ?

GA: I think it's a mixture of the two. The first two episodes at the top of the third season are Mulder and Scully versus the FBI and then it goes back and forth between FBI and aliens. Just . . .

ALIA: Oh, okay.

GA: . . . normal *X-Files* stuff.

LK: Thanks for the call.

ALIA: Bye.

LK: Got an e-mail here from Greg on the SaskNet in Saskatchewan. This is a good one. You'll like this question. "If you could be any of the aliens from the show, which one would you be?"

GA: Oh, gosh. Um, I guess I would have to be, uh, "Squeeze," just right off the top of my head. He didn't have any strange things protruding from his body or, um, slime. Well, I guess he did have slime, didn't he, but he could fit into lots of spaces and I guess it would have to be "Squeeze."

LK: Well, there. Good answer.

GA: Tooms, Eugene Tooms.

LK: There's a very interesting — it's sort of a conspiracy theory. I've been checking out all this Net stuff and everything about the alien autopsy that was shown on Fox a couple of weeks ago. Did you see it?

GA: No, I didn't see it. I think it was originally a German movie, wasn't it?

LK: That's what they were saying.

GA: It was shown in Germany first of all but it was a documentary made on the supposed alien that they found in Roswell. Uh, 1947, I think?

LK: '47, yeah, but now some people are saying: "Oh, this is just a really, really elaborate promo for the third season of *The X-Files*."

GA: Oh, dear.

LK: See, people [Gillian laughs] have very fertile imaginations.

GA: I was actually very intrigued in seeing it but I missed it. I just kind of assumed that it was for real.

LK: Do you think it's real?

GA: Yeaaah.

LK: I read an article that said they're monkeys. They were really monkeys. They didn't look like any monkeys I've ever seen.

GA: No, it's real . . .

LK: Okay, it's real. There, Scully says it's real [Gillian laughs], it's gotta be real. We're gonna go to the phones again. It's Afshan in Toronto. Hi, Afshan.

AFSHAN: Hi. Hi, Gillian. How are you?

GA: Nice name.

AFSHAN: Thanks. Um, first I'd like to say Happy Belated Birthday.

GA: Thank you very much.

AFSHAN: And, um, how has *The X-Files* heightened your career? And what, in terms of your acting career, will you be doing after *The X-Files* is over?

GA: How has it heightened my career? I guess it's put my face out there a lot more than it was beforehand, considering I wasn't working beforehand. So more people are seeing my work and hopefully it'll be easier in the future for me to get more work. See, your second question, in the future I don't know yet. They usually cast movies pretty close to the time that they start shooting them, and my next break isn't until May and then I have no idea when the show's gonna end. I'd like to move on and do features and independent films and theatre again, but who knows?

LK: Thanks for the call, Afshan. Good question. We've got a caller from St. Petersburg, Florida. It's Jennifer. Hi, Jennifer.

JEN: Hi.

LK: Do you have a question for Gillian?

JEN: Um, yeah. What was your favorite episode of *The X-Files*?

GA: Oh, boy. I have a few favorite episodes actually. One was "Beyond the Sea," one was "Irresistible," and then I think the first two in the third season are gonna be pretty hot and I haven't seen them yet but they might be part of my list too.

LK: Thanks for the call, Jennifer. Got an e-mail from Mary on the Net and she says, "Gillian, I love the show. I watch it every week. I also love your wardrobe and was wondering if you have a special designer or if you could let me know who does most of your clothes?"

GA: In Canada, there's a couple of designers. One is Fiso Verani who does some wonderful outfits for Scully. One is Jax. And then we have a lot of Armani, a lot of Maximara.

LK: Do you get to keep the stuff? Is it in your closet?

GA: You know, after wearing 'em zillions of times on the show, I never want to wear 'em again. There's some that I prefer and I'd like to borrow sometime but I don't think I could actually keep them in my closet.

LK: Don't want 'em around. We've got another call. It's Julie in Halifax. Hi, Julie.

JULIE: . . . I have sort of a two-part question.

GA: Okay.

JULIE: Being a skeptic, sort of, in the show, is Scully going to remain a skeptic? What sort of things are going to happen then? Second of all, in real life what sort of view do you have on supernatural things?

GA: In terms of Scully in the future, it's a very valid question and one that I'd be asking myself over and over again. She basically remains a skeptic through the show and I don't see that changing at all because there is a certain dramatic dynamic in that dichotomy between Mulder and Scully that keeps the show moving forward. She has become much more open-minded over the past couple of seasons and what I keep on relying on as an excuse is the fact that she does have a major history and background in the sciences and in medicine and even though she has witnessed some supernatural things it doesn't necessarily mean that she's going to automatically, sweepingly believe in everything supernatural and paranormal, so she's always gonna go back to trying to prove things from a scientific or medical standpoint. So that's that question. And to answer your second question, I'm not as skeptical as Scully is. I'm much more inclined to believe in life on other planets and people who bend spoons [Leora laughs] and catch things on fire and some of the stuff that we deal with. Not all of it, but some of it.

LK: Thanks for the call, Julie. Now, last year you were on the show and you had a brand-new baby. Little Piper was just, I think, eight weeks old. You did it on the phone. I know you're looking at me like, "I wasn't on this show before."

GA: I had a baby on the phone?

LK: No, no, you had a brand-new baby.

GA: I did have a brand new baby.

LK: And now, and now . . .

GA: She's now almost one year old.

LK: Almost one year old. So how's the juggling going?

GA: It's, um, it's juggling. It's fine. It's working out just fine. I'm blessed to be able to bring her on the set with me every day and she loves hanging around and being with the crew and she's got a big family over there and everybody plays with her and she makes everybody laugh and it's just fun. . . .

LK: She's *The X-Files* baby!

GA: She is.

LK: Does she have the little *X-Files* shirt and everything?

GA: No, she doesn't.

LK: No?

GA: She doesn't have a shirt yet. We have some but she has to grow into them.

LK: Yeah, and that'll happen soon. And, on the line

from Montreal, it's Bruce. Hi, Bruce.

BRUCE: Hi, how you doin'?

GA: Hi, Bruce.

BRUCE: Gillian, I just wanted to tell you I'm a big Circle Jerks and Dead Kennedys fan. [Gillian and Leora laugh] Um, I just want to ask you: exactly where are you from and how do you enjoy living in Vancouver while you're shooting the series?

GA: I was born in Chicago and grew up in London and Michigan, then moved around from Chicago to New York to Los Angeles blah blah blah blah blah. And now I'm up here. Um, and I do enjoy it. It gets frustrating when it rains and rains and rains and rains and rains and rains, and we shoot a lot outside in the rain, in the cold. I don't like that very much but other than that it's a beautiful, beautiful city.

LK: And they give you nice raincoats and wardrobe, right?

GA: Yes, they do, but rarely umbrellas. I think only twice in the entire season have we ever had umbrellas, even when it was raining.

LK: Hmmm . . . well, that's interesting. Thanks for the call, Bruce.

BRUCE: Thank you very much.

LK: And on to Ruby in Toronto. Hi, Ruby.

RUBY: Hi, Gillian.

GA: Hi, Ruby.

RUBY: I love you. You're great!

GA: Thank you. I love you, too. [Ruby laughs]

RUBY: I was wondering, what's your off-screen relationship with Mr. Duchovny like, in comparison to that of Mulder and Scully?

GA: Um, we have sex once a day, [Leora stifles laugh]

um, we eat off each other's feet . . . no. Um, let's see. What is our relationship like? We're friends. We don't usually socialize that much together. On the week-ends, we generally separate and do our own thing. But it's good. It's a good, down-to-earth, platonic relationship.

LK: There you go. Thanks for the call. He's with his dog, Blue. I always read about him and his dog, Blue.

GA: He is with his dog, Blue.

LK: Blue. What kinda dog?

GA: Ah, border collie. And I'm actually in the process of getting a dog who is actually blue. Will be a blue-colored dog.

LK: What kinda dogs are blue?

GA: So it'll be interesting. Ah, Neopolitan mastiffs are blue, some other dogs. Cane corsos are blue and, uh, weimaraners are bluish, you know?

LK: You're really gonna stick out on the streets though if you've got a blue dog.

GA: Well, it's not like blue, blue, blue, blue, blue.

LK: It's bluish.

GA: It's bluish.

LK: Bluish.

GA: Grayish-bluish.

LK: Got an e-mail here. Oh, yeah, now we're getting into it. Do you know about the G-A-T-B? Of course, you do. The Gillian Anderson Testosterone Brigade. This comes from Grim Reaper on the Net and he says, "I wanted to know if Gillian got the present the GATB sent her when Piper was born."

GA: Which one was that?

LK: Doesn't say! Did you get a lot of stuff?

GA: I've gotten a lot of presents. I'm sure that I did

get that. I remember, um, I wish I knew what it was 'cause I could say, "Well, yeah, it's sitting on the shelf. Or, yeah, it's in her little playpen-thingie." But I can't because you didn't tell me what it was. I'm sure I got it . . .

LK: And it was lovely.

GA: . . . and it was fabulous! [Laughs] No, I remember around the time that she was born sending a thank-you note to the GATB via somebody. Um, Jerry was his name? Terry somebody? I can't remember but I'm sure I got it and I'm sure I loved it to death. Thank you very much.

LK: The good ol' GATB. There's also the DDEB, the David Duchovny Estrogen Brigade. And, uh, these are just people on the Net. Do you spend a lot of time checking that stuff?

GA: I don't, I don't have a lot of time and it takes a lot of time to check that stuff. Um, I'd like to sometimes, but I don't.

LK: It's extremely time-consuming.

GA: I usually opt to play with my daughter.

LK: And you've got, what, 16-hour workdays as well.

GA: Yeah.

LK: On the line from Edmonton, it's Don. Hi, Don.

DON: Hi.

GA: Hi, Don.

DON: Hi, um, what I want to know is: will you be directing or writing any episodes this season?

GA: Um, probably not directing. I don't know about writing. Usually, what David does is he comes up with ideas and makes an outline or something for Chris and I'd be very interested in doing that as well. And then together they come up with an episode. And I've got

198

CBC
RADIO

a few ideas, but I haven't actually done that yet and I couldn't tell ya whether I'm actually gonna do it this season or not, but maybe!

LK: There! How's that for the middle? [Gillian laughs] Thanks, Don. On to Catherine, another caller from Australia. Wow! Hi, Catherine.

CAT: Hello?

GA: Hello?

CAT: Gillian?

GA: Yeah!

CAT: Oh, my God! Hi!

GA: Hi!

CAT: I'm talking to my idol! I idolize you so much. You're the best actress.

GA: Thank you very much.

CAT: I love *The X-Files*. I watch it every week. Oh, um . . . oh my God!

GA: What season are you in? Are you presently in the second season?

CAT: Just finished second season.

GA: So you have to wait another few months till the third.

CAT: I know, I'm really depressed. [Laughs]

GA: Oh, I'm sorry! [Laughs]

LK: Do you have a question, Catherine?

CAT: Oh, that's okay. Oh, wow, this is great, thank you.

LK: Do you have a question, Catherine?

CAT: Um, yeah, I wanna know how you maintain such a [static] acting under so much pressure from everyone and so much grueling hours and everything. I just wondered how you do it.

GA: I, ah, ohhh boy. I don't know. I guess you just kind of have to as much as you may not want to at any given time. There's enough producers around and people around to remind you of why you're there and what it's really all about.

CAT: Yeah, um. Oh, wow. Um, how's your baby?

GA: She's wonderful, thank you very much.

CAT: Is she? Ohhh.

GA: Yeah, she's almost a year.

CAT: I thought she has a great life and everything with you.

GA: I hope so. She seems to be very happy.

LK: Thanks for the call, Catherine. Australia, twice. How 'bout that? And on to Ottawa. Samantha? Hi, Samantha.

SAM: Hi, there.

GA: Hi.

SAM: We were just wondering: do you realize what a good role model you are for young girls? Such a strong female character?

GA: Um, I think that that first started to hit me somewhere in the middle of the first season when a lot of young girls would write to me and tell me that. I think it's probably one of the most wonderful things that could come out of this job. Because of all of Scully's positive attributes: her perseverance in her work, her perseverance in studying, she's in pursuit of justice, and truth, and honesty and she's strong and intelligent and independent and capable, and those all are wonderful things to try and achieve in one's life and so I think it's *excellent* that a lot of young girls are attracted to that. I've many young women actually writing to me, saying that they have now decided that they want to become FBI agents [Leora laughs] when they grow up and I think that's fantastic.

CBC

RADIO

LK: And you can encourage them. Thanks for the call, Samantha. I have to say, Gillian, we've got a stack of e-mails about just that thing, what a positive role model the Scully character is, because there aren't a lot of positive female role models on TV.

GA: No, there aren't.

LK: It's a big responsibility, though.

GA: Um, it used to be. When it first started to hit me I felt the weight of the responsibility, but it's just become part of the whole thing, now and it's excellent. I'll say that word one more time. It's excellent.

LK: Exccccellent, there you go. Ah, it's B.J. in Sarasota, Florida. Hi.

B.J.: Hi, there.

GA: Hi, B.J.

B.J.: I'm a very big fan. Our whole family loves to sit and watch the show. Um, I was wondering: were you prepared or did you expect the success to be as good as it is and to have many fans and T-shirts [Gillian laughs] and Internet, live broadcasts? Is it overwhelming?

GA: It's, um, it's not overwhelming anymore. It was. I'm not sure if I completely realize how big the show has gotten yet and it's probably good that I haven't realized that. There was a transitional stage about the time that I was pregnant which may have only had to do with hormones, I don't know, but when I did start to get a little freaked by it all. I don't think any of us realized that it was to become as big as it has become. Especially not Chris Carter. I mean, for Chris, it's completely a dream come true and he deserves all of it.

LK: He's the creator, producer, writes a lot of episodes.

GA: He's the man. He's the main man.

LK: And he is also the godfather of your daughter?

GA: Yes, he is. He is the godfather of Piper and he just finished directing an episode, number five, which is, I don't know how he does that because he's also, you know, in post-production for three other episodes and writing five other episodes and doing all that kind of stuff.

LK: And he surfs too, doesn't he?

GA: He used to surf. [Laughs] He doesn't surf in Vancouver very much.

LK: Yeah, but thanks for the call, B.J. We are broadcasting across Canada on the CBC Stereo Network and around the world on the Internet thanks to Progressive Networks, RealAudio. That's why we're gettin' calls from Florida, Australia, and all over the place. Actually, two from Florida and two from Australia. Got some e-mails from California, too, so it's pretty, pretty exciting. Another e-mail question here. Funny, we were just talking about Chris Carter. This comes from Wallace on the JaxNet and he says, "How much creative freedom do Chris Carter and the producers give you in developing your character?"

GA: Not much. At the beginning, Chris had a very clear, specific idea of who these characters were and made sure that we stuck to it as much as possible. I mean, when we first got these jobs we were up here and shooting right away so there wasn't really a lot of time to think about or come up with, um, brilliant characters. It was just something that kind of happened over time in front of millions of people on the air and I think at least for myself, it wasn't until somewhere through the second season when I really started to feel comfortable with Scully and then I got pregnant and didn't feel comfortable [Leora laughs] with Scully at *all*. And so, the beginning of the third season is feeling comfortable with Scully again. I think that most of the time we are guided by the scripts. It's very specific in the scripts, just from the dialogue and the side-notes, how we react to certain situations and it's very story-driven more than character-driven this show is and so it's pretty cut and dried how it's gonna go. I don't know in the future where our characters are gonna go. It's probably gonna remain pretty much by the book. So far it seems to be working.

LK: It seems to be working extremely well. That's the thing. Do you ever stop and think, y'know, I'm here doing my best, the writers are doing their best and, y'know, it's a good show but has this gotten out of hand? Do you ever think that?

GA: Well, yeah. There are times when I wish that it would stop, y'know, but I wish that something would happen and I wouldn't have to work 16 hours back-to-back anymore but, you know, then I have a good day and the work is good and the script is good and it's a pleasure to work on and everything goes smoothly and I change my mind. It's just like life, you know? I mean, I think everyone faces that from time to time, showing up at work, really wishing that they didn't have to do it. The blessing would be to be in a situation where you're doing exactly what you want to do and also have your own freedom around it. That's something to search for.

LK: Yeah. And we have another call. This is Noreen in Toronto. Hi, Noreen.

NOREEN: Hi, Gillian. How are you?

GA: Good.

NOREEN: Um, I just want to know how you got this part. Like, I know you've done theater acting before but how did you get this part and what did you have to do to get it?

GA: You mean who did I have to sleep with to get it? [Leora laughs]

NOREEN: Well . . .

LK: She didn't ask that!

GA: No, it was just . . . I was living in Los Angeles and going to a lot of auditions and eventually this one came along and it seemed, at the beginning, to be just like any other audition. I went in for the casting director and then got called back for Chris Carter and a couple other producers and the director of the pilot and then got called back again and then went to network, which is an L.A. thing which is terrifying, where you go in front of all of the network producers and practice how to have a heart attack and then they cast you or they cast somebody else. And they just happened to cast me and so it was one of those kind of things where I was in the right place at the right time and did the best that I could do and they said, "Okay! You're the one now." My turn!

LK: And it has been your turn. Thanks for the call, Noreen. Another call from Australia. It's Kylie. Hello, Kylie.

KYLIE: Hello, there. Oh, my God, I'm your biggest fan, I swear. You're my idol!

LK: They love you in Australia!

GA: Hi, Kylie! How are you?

KYLIE: Um, I'm good.

GA: Good!

KYLIE: Um, how are you?

GA: I'm excellent!

LK: Kylie, is there a doctor near you? [Laughs]

KYLIE: Um, okay. Um, I was just wondering what do you think of all your fans? Like, do you ever get scared of them, you know?

GA: I don't get scared of them. I mean, once in a while, I get some strange letters. Most of the letters though that we get are wonderful and incredibly flattering and sweet and positive and congratulatory. It's not scary at all.

KYLIE: Okay . . .

LK: Thanks for the call. You can breathe again, Kylie. Breathe, breathe.

KYLIE: Okay . . . bye.

LK: Thank you. [Laughs]

GA: Bye! Too bad these interviews are so short.

LK: I know . . . . You can stay for a couple hours. You want to?

GA: Okay.

LK: Unless you have something else planned.

GA: Awright, let's stay a couple hours.

LK: Okay, we can spin some tunes, we can play some Dead Kennedys, it'll be a great time. [Gillian laughs] I've got an e-mail here from New Zealand. This is from Gordon and he says, "On Anne Rice's *Exit to Eden* . . .

GA: Oh, no!!

LK: . . . how did you do so many voice variations?" What is he talking about?

GA: Gawd! I did a booktape once as a favor to . . . well, not as a favor — I needed the money desperately but it was a friend of mine who was producing and

recording booktapes for Random House, I think it
was, in New York, and I was back and I auditioned for
it and ended up getting it and it was *Exit to Eden* which
has recently become a film. It's an Anne Rice, um, or
Anne Rampling, is her name, for her sexy books, and
it was something where we had like two days to read.
It was myself and a guy and I was reading like half of
it, and he was reading the second half of it, and it's
based on the novel *Exit to Eden*, which is not a comedy
like the movie. It's a very serious, very actually somewhat romantic book and you know, after doing one
read-through, realizing that we had to do all of the
voices, some French, some Southern, male, female,
all this stuff! [Leora laughs] I was like, "Whaaat did I
just get myself into?!" And you know, it was like a
matter of like, "Okay, now we have to record it." So
we sat in the studio for a couple of hours and just, you
know, I just "wung" it, even though that's not a word,
is it?

LK: Now you know what I'm going to ask you. Yeah,
no you've got to give me, give me some Southern . . .

GA: No, thank you.

LK: But this guy says, he says, "Simply it's amazing
what you can do with your voice." So he thought you
did a great job.

GA: Oh, wow! Well, thank you very much.

LK: Yeah, he says, "Did it all come naturally?

GA: Um . . .

LK: Took a lot of work, I bet.

GA: It's . . . well, there wasn't any time to work on
it. It was mostly [laughs] just diving in headfirst and
hoping that I didn't completely embarrass myself.

LK: And is this thing still out there?

GA: It is still out there and obviously people [laughs] are buying it.

LK: In New Zealand, too!

GA: Ohhh, boy.

LK: See, that's what happens. I know, you can't escape. We're just going to take a couple more questions. Uh, Timothy in Michigan. Hi.

TIM: Hi.

GA: Where in Michigan?

TIM: Well, uh, just outside Detroit.

GA: Mmm . . .

TIM: Yeah.

GA: . . . yummy!

TIM: I know you said that you and David have nothing going on, but how about Scully and Mulder? Is there anything planned for the next season?

GA: Um, I don't know much about the future season. The writers may have something planned. I doubt it though.

TIM: Okay.

GA: I've heard Chris Carter say over and over again that he wants the relationship to remain platonic and, um, I think both David and I agree that that's the right direction to go.

TIM: Oh, it would be an interesting change. [Laughs]

LK: Yeah, thanks for the call, Timothy. And on to Jeff in Calgary. Hi, Jeff.

JEFF: Hi, there.

GA: Hi, Jeff.

JEFF: I'm afraid I'm not Australian. [Gillian and Leora laugh]

GA: It's okay.

LK: It's okay, we'll let you through.

JEFF: I was wondering, my friends and I have noticed from the first and second season that your appearance seems to have changed a bit. [Gillian laughs] There's more of an emphasis on your femininity now and I was just wondering if you agree, and if you agree, if you mind at all.

GA: Between the first and second season?

JEFF: Yeah, once the show got popular, it's like they had to have a beautiful woman up front.

GA: Well, I . . .

JEFF: Not that you weren't before, but . . . [Laughs]

GA: Well, I became pregnant and I gained about 52 pounds. [Laughs]

LK: Are you serious?

GA: Yeah, 52 pounds. I packed it on there for a bit. Um, but, I don't know what to say, Jeff. [Jeff laughs] I don't know if they have, I don't know. I didn't notice that. I don't think that the wardrobe has changed any. My skirts haven't gotten shorter or anything like that. My hair might have changed a little bit. Certainly from the pilot my hair changed. You know, from looking like my mother to [Leora laughs] looking like not my mother.

LK: But, uh, good question. Thank you. I also read — this is more Internet stuff — people on the Net said they didn't like your hair all of the second season and then they said *you* didn't like your hair all of the second season.

GA: I didn't. You know, and a lot of women will say this, that when they're pregnant, they just want to shave it all off. That's just something that happens and I, every day, just wanted to shave my head, and I couldn't [Laughs] because I was on the show but it just became annoying, it was this thing that was just stuck on top of my head [Leora laughs] and I just couldn't stand it. But now that's over.

LK: Now we're gonna have just wonderfully manageable Scully hair for the third season.

GA: Hopefully. I like it when it looks like, you know, a real person's hair. You know, when it gets messy and, um, looks real.

LK: We're taking just a couple more calls. Anne-Marie in Toronto, hi.

A.M.: How are you?

GA: I'm good. How are you?

A.M.: Oh, very excited to talk to someone from a show that I've just become a very big fan of.

GA: Well, thank you.

A.M.: I was afraid to watch it in the past because I had a discussion with my brother about your show and you mentioned earlier that you don't have much control over your position — that it's very story-driven. I was wondering whether it was based on factual information or not.

GA: Um, I have heard the writers say before that what they usually do is come up with an idea, whether it stems from something that they've read in a book or a magazine or a newspaper or something that they've heard. What they're looking for is to come up with a whole idea that can encompass the characters and the throughline of the show that we've already established. Um, and sometimes that involves tapping into stuff that has been reported to be real, stuff that has been written about as being real in the past, but I guess as Chris Carter says, most of the storylines generally fall within the realm of extreme possibility.

LK: I like that — extreme possibility. Thanks, Anne-Marie. Uh, we're going to squeeze in one more e-mail. This is from Virginia on the Net. And Virginia says, "Rumors have been spreading for weeks about an *X-Files* movie. Can you supply us with any concrete information about it?"

GA: Oh, boy. I don't know about this *X-Files* movie thing. I've also read that there's going to be a movie in 1997. Um, I honestly don't know who's gonna star in that movie because I don't think David and I are going to have time to do it and I have no idea when Chris Carter is gonna have the opportunity to write a feature film, let alone try and direct and produce it in between seasons. It's hugely ambitious for the schedules that we're all working under right now. It sounds wonderful but, you know, I also question the validity of having a feature come out while the show is still running. It seems like it would be much more exciting to have a feature out when the series is no longer on anymore and you don't have Friday nights to tune into a new episode. So, um . . .

LK: The *Star Trek*-type thing.

GA: Yeah.

LK: Yeah.

GA: So I don't know what their plans are with it. Um, so, sorry.

LK: Who knows?

GA: That's it — who knows?

LK: Who knows?

GA: Who knows what's gonna happen?

LK: It is RealTime Anderson who plays, you know, Dana Scully on *The X-Files*. We have got time for two more calls. Sarah in Boston. Hi, Sarah.

SARAH: Hi, um, I just wanted to say that I'm a really big fan . . .

GA: Thank you.

SARAH: . . . of *The X-Files*. Um, I know everybody's said that but I am [Gillian laughs] and, um . . .

GA: But they lied, and you are. [Sarah and Leora laugh]

SARAH: Yeah, um, well, not that they lie. Okay!

GA: Okay.

SARAH: Um, well, now all of a sudden I just can't think of anything to say.

[Gillian laughs]

GA: That's so funny.

LK: No questions? That's okay.

GA: That's okay.

LK: You got to talk to Gillian and that was fun, right?

SARAH: Yeah, that was fun.

LK: Thanks for calling, Sarah.

GA: Thank you.

SARAH: Okay, bye.

GA: Bye.

LK: And our final call is Nichola in Montreal. Hi.

NICHOLA: Hi.

GA: Hi.

NICHOLA: Hi. I wrote down my question.

GA: Good!

LK: Good thing. [Nichola laughs] Good thing.

NICHOLA: Um, I think that someone said earlier that you, that Dana Scully rather, is a great role model for . . .

LK: Mm hm.

NICHOLA: . . . women. My only problem actually with her character . . .

GA: Mm hm.

NICHOLA: . . . is that she seems to, uh, need to be rescued by Mulder very frequently and she has this problem with blood lately [laughs] and bodies. I'm curious how she got through med school if she had this , , ,

GA: She has a problem with blood? When did that come up?

NICHOLA: Well, for example, in the show, um . . .

GA: "Irresistible"?

NICHOLA: I don't even know the name . . . [Laughs]

GA: There was one episode in particular where Scully has a bit of a freakout, but it's an accumulation of her abduction and her father dying and everything else that she hasn't really been talking about which has accumulated in her freaking out. A guy, um, cutting women's hair and, uh . . .

NICHOLA: Yeah, right. That one.

GA: . . . taking their fingernails out when they're dead.

NICHOLA: And then the one with the bugs.

GA: The bugs?

LK: You ate a bug, didn't you?

GA: Which one were the bugs?

NICHOLA: The green bugs.

GA: That was first season. The green bugs.

LK: Oh, the green bugs. Okay.

GA: Um, I don't know if it's necessarily Scully needing to be rescued or the writers needing to see her being rescued by a man.

NICHOLA: Well, that was more the impression I got and I'm wondering if they were going to be changing that perspective.

GA: Um, it changes now and again. I mean sometimes Scully rescues Mulder's life and, uh, [laughs] rescues his life? Sometimes Scully rescues Mulder, you know, but I wouldn't mind seeing that a bit more myself. I'll put in a good word for you.

LK: How's that? Thanks a lot, Nichola.

NICHOLA: Thank you.

GA: Bye.

LK: Gillian Anderson of *The X-Files* has been my guest and this has been a first for us, possibly international broadcasting history. Did you know that? To do the simulcast on the Net and do interaction from around the world. So . . .

GA: You mean no one across the entire world has ever done this before?

LK: Apparently not. Isn't that exciting?

GA: Bum bum bum!

LK: Go home and tell the daughter. Well, thank you very much. [Gillian laughs] We were originally gonna do 15 minutes and now it's, like, almost an hour later. Thanks so much. You're gonna do about 15 minutes on the IRC . . .

GA: That's correct.

LK: . . . and people can find out how to do that. That's computer chat. Send us an e-mail. We'll tell you how. Realtime@cbcstereo.com. So, third season of *The X-Files*, Friday, Fox Network. You can't tell us what's gonna happen, can you?

GA: Um, we live, we almost die, we chase monsters and . . . we live.

LK: There. Thanks so much, Gillian! Here, I've got some music I think you'll like.

GA: Okay.

LK: Do you like the Foo Fighters?

GA: I've never heard of them.

LK: Dave Grohl from Nirvana? It's his new band.

GA: Oh, really?

LK: Yeah, this is for you. X-static. [Song is broadcast]

SECTION 3

March 16, 1996: "DJ for a Day" — On her previous visit in September, Gillian had expressed an interest in being able to play DJ for a while. She was serious and spent hours on the phone with story producer Loc Dao getting music set for the show (1 hour, 39 minutes).

Here is her set list:

SET 1

"Russian Roulette" — Lords of the New Church
James/Chimes
Killer Lords (IRS X2 0777 7 13178 28)
CD, cut 3 . . . cue to :02
3:36 Cold/Fade

"Save Me" — Joan Armatrading
Joan Armatrading (A&M CD3228)
CD, cut 5
3:25 Cold/Fade

"Time Waits for No One" — Rolling Stones
Jagger/Richards
It's Only Rock & Roll (Rolling Stones CK40493)
CD, cut 5
6:13 Fades

Callers: Tracey in Winnipeg; Reem in Windsor, Ontario;
Kevin in Boston; Naomi in Vancouver

SET 2

"This Is a Call" — Foo Fighters
Grohl
Foo Fighters (Capitol C2 7243 8 34027 2 4)
CD, cut 1
3:52 Cold . . . tight to next track

"California" — Rusty
Rusty — MAPL
Fluke (Handsome Boy hbcd0003)
CD, cut 6
4:21 Cold/Decay

"Goodbye" — Emmy Lou Harris
Earle
Wrecking Ball (Elektra CD61854)
CD, cut 2
4:43 Cold/Fade

Callers: Gina in Toronto; Mary in San Francisco;
Mike in Montreal; Steve in London, Ontario;
Poe in Thorold, Ontario; Rebecca in Guelph, Ontario;
Mike in Calgary; Anne in Australia

SET 3

"Add It Up" — Violent Femmes
Gano
Violent Femmes (Slash 92 38451)
12" vinyl, side 1, cut 4 — 33 RPM
4:40 Cold

"Not My Idea" — Garbage
Garbage
Garbage (ALMO AMSSD 80004)
CD, cut 5
3:36 Fades

"Fade Into You" — Mazzy Star
Sandoval/Roback

So Tonight I Might See (EMI C2 0777 7 98253 2 5)
CD, cut 1
4:35 Fades

Callers: Terry in Auckland, New Zealand;
Mike in Rustin, Louisiana; Sasha in Vancouver;
Victor in Edmonton; Liz in Vancouver

SET 4

"Hand in My Pocket" — Alanis Morissette
Morissette/Ballard — MAL
Jagged Little Pill (Maverick CDW 45901)
CD, cut 4
3:31 Cold/Fade

"Life Insurance" — Spookey Ruben
Ruben — MAPL
Modes of Transportation, Vol. 1 (TVT TVT 5410-2)
CD, cut 13
:03
4:54 Cold/Decay

"The Gospel According to Darkness" —
Jane Siberry
Siberry — MAPL
When I Was a Boy (WEA/Reprise CD 26824)
CD, cut 7
:07
4:43 Cold/Decay

SECTION 4

September 21, 1996: "DJ Gillian Returns" — Anderson produced another two-hour show where she played music, took calls, and answered e-mail.

Here is her set list:

SET   1

"Who Will Save Your Soul" — Jewel
Kilcher5
Pieces of You (Atlantic 82700-2)
CD, cut 1
:07
3:40 Fades

"Leave" — REM
REM
New Adventures in Hi-Fi (Warner Bros. CDW 46320)
CD, cut 6
1:33
7:15 Cold

"Samba Pa Ti" — Santana
Santana
Santana's Greatest Hits (Columbia VCK 33050)
CD, cut 4
Ins.
4:20 Fades

Callers: Naomi in Vancouver; Reechee in Toronto;
Angela in Portola, California; Kim in Ottawa;
Vince in Montreal; Tracey in Winnipeg;
Miriam in Cheshire, Connecticut; e-mail

SET   2

"San Andreas Fault" — Natalie Merchant
Merchant
Tigerlily (Elektra CD61745)
CD, cut 1
:00
3:31 Fades

"Standing Outside a Broken Phone Booth with
Money in My Hand" — Primitive Radio Gods
O'Connor

Rocket (Ergo/Columbia CK 67600)
CD, cut 3
:20
5:25 Fades

"Give Me One Reason" — Tracy Chapman
Chapman
New Beginning (Elektra CD 61850)
CD, cut 9
:32
4:20 Cold/Fade

Callers: Princess in Lubbock, Texas;
Jeff in Detroit; c.j. in Vancouver; Gard in Burnaby;
Dave in Edmonton; Tony in Ottawa;
Gillian's Kitchen w/ Rosemary (GA's mom); After
the Kitchen; let Gillian do the phone sell and ID

SET 3

"Goodbye" — Emmy Lou Harris
Earle
Wrecking Ball (Elektra CD61854)
CD, cut 2
:40
4:43 Cold/Fade

"Ready or Not" — Fugees
Jean/Michel/Hill/Hart/Bell
The Score (Ruffhouse/Columbia CK 67147)
CD, cut 3
:10
3:40 Fades . . . must be out by 3:46

"Goodbye Sweet Pumpkinhead" — Jane Siberry
Siberry — MAPL
Maria (WEA/Reprise CD 45915)
CD, cut 7
:13
4:22 Cold/fade
Gillian does ID, backsell, pluto sell

Callers: Maristella in Bellingham; Martin in Stockholm,
Sweden; Francesca in Rome, Italy; Ross in Edmonton;
Jeremy in St. Catharines, Ontario; Jennifer in Vancouver;
Kelly in Rhode Island; e-mails

SET 4

"Elsewhere" — Sarah McLachlan
McLachlan — MAPL
Fumbling Towards Ecstasy (Nettwerk w 2 3 0 0 8 1)
CD, cut 6
:0 8
4 : 2 8 Fades

"Maggie May" — Rod Stewart
Stewart / Quittenton
Vintage (Mercury 3 1 4 5 1 8 0 9 7-2)
CD, cut 8
: 1 4
5 : 0 6 Fades

"Fly Away" — Poe
Poe
Hello (Atlantic CD 9 2 6 0 5)
CD, cut 1 1
: 0 0
3 : 3 5 Fades

Callers: Jackie in Winnipeg;
Tara in Madison, Wisconsin.

X-FILES EPISODE GUIDES

SEASON ONE (1993–94)

1.00 Pilot

ORIGINAL AIR DATE: September 10, 1993
WRITTEN BY: Chris Carter
DIRECTED BY: Robert Mandel
CAST: David Duchovny as Special Agent Fox Mulder
                  Gillian Anderson as Special Agent Dana Scully
GUEST CAST: Cliff Deyoung as Dr. Jay Nemm
                  Sarah Koskoff as Theresa Nemman
                  Leon Russom as Detective Miles
                  Zachary Ansley as Billy Miles
                  William B. Davis as Cigarette-Smoking Man

In this premier episode we meet FBI Special Agents Dana Scully, a medical doctor with a specialty in physics, and Fox "Spooky" Mulder, a talented but distrusted FBI fixture, well-known for his psychological profiles of serial killers. Their first case together involves a girl found dead in the woods with no discernible cause beyond two tiny marks on her back, a high-school class particularly prone to dying in this manner, and a coma victim who is somehow at the center of it all.

The ideas here are well thought out and interesting. Presenting heroes that are FBI agents (as opposed to scrawny little computer hackers or Kolchak-style gumshoes) creates a very useful sense of the government as a less-than-cohesive and dangerous place to be. The quality is in the details; implants in people's heads, corpses that do not appear to be human, a coma victim with dirt on his feet. All of this leaves the audience with a heightened sense of paranoia, culminating in the now familiar final shot of the ordinary-looking Cigarette-Smoking Man (a man with no name or speaking lines) filing the only remaining evidence in an ordinary-looking vault.

1.01 Deep Throat

ORIGINAL AIR DATE: September 17, 1993
WRITTEN BY: Chris Carter
DIRECTED BY: Daniel Sackheim
GUEST CAST: Jerry Hardin as Deep Throat
Charles Cioffi as Chief Blevins
Michael Bryan French as Paul Mossinger
Andrew Johnston as Col. Robert Budahas
Seth Green as Emil
Lalainia Lindejerg as Zoe
Vince Metcalfe as Kissell
Gabrielle Rose as Mrs. Anita Budahas
Monica Parker as Ladonna
Doc Harris as Mr. McLennen
Sheila Moore as Verla McLennen
John Cuthbert as Commanding Officer
Brian Furlong as Lead Officer
Michael Puttonen as Motel Manager

Scully and Mulder investigate the report of a missing test pilot, despite being warned off the case by a shadowy "Deep Throat"-styled character, and, along the way, discover that Ellen's Air Force Base seems to be the home to a craft with remarkable abilities. In his burning need to know, Mulder breaks into the base and sees the thing with his own eyes (as does the audience), but he is arrested, his memory erased, and Scully must bargain for his return.

Scully plays knight-with-shining-gun to Mulder's damsel-in-distress. Just as the first episode ended with Scully's confusion and bewilderment, in this one it is Mulder who cannot fathom what has happened to him. Scully, instead, is back on her feet. We are also introduced to the shadowy, watchful figure of "Deep Throat," front-man (or mole?) for a profoundly neat government conspiracy. As Chris Carter and Co. give us another plot-rich story, this is still one of the series' best episodes as it establishes nearly all of the major themes (in terms of character, plot, and ideas) that will be explored over the coming seasons.

The episode exposes the audience to the general conspiracy themes of the abuse of military power, government cover-up, illegal surveillance of the agents, the control of information (this includes even Mulder's withholding of information from Scully throughout the series), and the violation or theft of memory (this theme will be played with many variations over the seasons). The episode also establishes many of the character and relationship patterns: Mulder and Scully's bickering and banter, Scully's willingness (true scientific open-mindedness) to entertain and hold up to the light of reason Mulder's most outlandish assertions and theories, her quick insights and resourceful-

ness, and her powerful loyalty to her partner (interesting, considering how new the partnership is) which even at this early stage outweighs her otherwise evident respect for authority.

Visual elements and recurring events of the series are established early also, particularly, the bright white light which regularly accompanies a UFO, and abduction images which be refrained repeatedly throughout the series. There are the delightful scenes with the stoned teenagers (who will return in different incarnations), the ominous surveillance of Mulder and Scully through the restaurant window (another image that will gain power over the seasons), and the humorous set-up of Mulder as distinctly "un-cool."

The most powerful of all these conceits lies in the final scene between Deep Throat and Mulder. Deep Throat is eager to establish himself as mentor and guide but it just as easy to read his conversation with Mulder as a *test* of the efficacy of the "memory wipe" Mulder has undergone. The moment is made more chilling by the realization that this theft of memory is the ultimate violation for Mulder who has made "the truth" his quest.

1.02 Squeeze

ORIGINAL AIR DATE: September 24, 1993
WRITTEN BY: Glen Morgan and James Wong
DIRECTED BY: Harry Longstreet
GUEST CAST: Doug Hutchison as Eugene Victor Tooms
            Donal Logue as Agent Tom Colton
            Henry Beckman as Detective Frank Briggs
            Kevin McNulty as Fuller

Terence Kelly as George Usher
Colleen Winton as Lie Detector Technician
James Bell as Johnson
Gary Hetherington as Kennedy
Rob Morton as Kramer
Paul Joyce as Mr. Werner

Scully's professional reputation and her belief in Mulder are put to the test in this episode, when a former classmate, Tom Colton, asks her to help him solve a strange case: a man has been killed inside his locked office, within a secure building, his liver torn out, apparently by hand. Based on previous X-files that date back to the 1960s and 1930s, Mulder forms the theory that the killer is a century-old genetic mutant who requires five human livers before he can return to his 30-year hibernation.

This macabre "locked-room" mystery introduces one of *The X-Files'* greatest villains: Eugene Victor Tooms. Hutchison plays his slithery, vicious character like he could just taste a sequel. We also learn a little about FBI politics. If we didn't believe Mulder when he said he was the black sheep of the FBI, we do now. Agent Colton is nothing if not a favor-seeker, and he obviously sees any association with Mulder as professional suicide. Scully's face-off with Colton is an early sign of her mettle, her sense of fairness, and her disgust with machismo. The sense of foreboding in this one is pretty powerful, as is the chemistry between the two agents. The scene in the car is as close as these two will come (until the fourth season) to a connection of *that* kind.

This is also another in a series of X-Files nebbish-killers (see: "Irresistible," "Clyde Bruckman's Final Repose," "D.P.O.," and "Unruhe" for more nerds who kill.)

1.03 Conduit

ORIGINAL AIR DATE: October 1, 1993
WRITTEN BY: Alex Gansa, Howard Gordon
DIRECTED BY: Daniel Sackheim
GUEST CAST: Carrie Snodgrass as Darlene Morris
Joel Palmer as Kevin Morris
Charles Cioffi as Section Chief Scott Blevins
Taunya Dee as Ruby Morris
Michael Cavanaugh as Sheriff
Shelly Owens as Tessa
Don Thompson as Holtzman
Don Gibb as Kip
Akiko Morison as Leza Atsumi
Anthony Harrison as 4th Man
Glen Roald as M.E. Worker
Mauricio Mercado as the Coroner

Scully and Mulder travel to Lake Okobogee where a local teen has been abducted by aliens, her mother claims, though no one believes her, but the case begins to look like no more than a disastrous teen love-triangle. Except for the fact that the mother herself claims to have had a close encounter when she was a teen (no one believed her then

either), and that the girl's brother is receiving messages from the television which turn out to be coded transmissions from a Defense satellite.

This is a creepy, varied episode with the appearance of science, but a backbone of pure magic. The coded transmissions turning out to be a pixilated image of the girl, is a nice sleight of hand because of what we *thought* they were, but when applied to the logic of the case, it makes little sense. It sort of suggests the presence of an unfathomable alien code, which conveniently excuses illogic. The appearance of white wolves, melted sand, and a girl's bodily trauma pointing to prolonged weightlessness, are potent images of nature abused by an outside force, but would have little meaning, say, to the skeptical Scully. In fact, for most of the episode, Scully can make little sense of things, even when presented with hard medical evidence.

Professionally, Scully's position is awkward from the beginning. She is overtly reminded of her role as watchdog by Blevins and asked to account for Mulder's latest idiocy — a thing which is meant to deepen the gulf between agents and FBI brass. Her loyalty to him is further beleaguered by his ridiculous source for the case, and the embarrassment of his possible neurosis on the subject of his sister. The question of whether Mulder's little obsession will destroy Scully's reputation (or in later seasons her health) is present already, in this scene in Blevins' office. Scully's decision (apparently point-blank) to stand by her partner in public but question him privately is one she will make many times. Her obvious belief that the teen's estranged father, or her boyfriend are behind it all is far more plausible than the reality. But the reality is Mulder's in this episode. This is the first time the scientific data backs up Mulder's theory, and Anderson's performance makes clear the implications of this for her character. It's interestingly voyeuristic when she listens to the tapes of his hypno-regression therapy (as well as reminiscent of the video-watching scene in "Young at Heart"). Mulder's subconscious is an integral part of the plot, and yet that subconscious is so powerful that it seems to be plugged into reality. We are also led to see Kevin as a stand-in for Mulder — a loyal little boy, mystified by his sister's disappearance, believing faithfully that if he works hard enough she will return.

1.04 The Jersey Devil

ORIGINAL AIR DATE: October 8, 1993
WRITTEN BY: Chris Carter
DIRECTED BY: Joe Napolitano
GUEST CAST: Michael Macrae as Ranger Peter Brullet
Gregory Sierra as Dr. Diamond
Wayne Tippit as Detective Thompson
Claire Stansfield as The Jersey Devil
Jill Teed as Glenna
Tamsin Kelsey as Ellen
Andrew Airlie as Rob
Bill Dow as Dad
Hrothgar Mathews as Jack
Jayme Knox as Mom
Scott Swanson as 1st Officer
Sean O'Byrne as 2nd Officer
David Lewis as Young Officer
D. Neil Monk as SWAT Team Officer

Scully brings a story to Mulder's attention: a man found dead in the Jersey woods, partially eaten by what must be another human. Mulder believes it is the "Jersey Devil," an enduring urban myth of a Yeti-like creature living unseen in the woods.

This episode is almost all Scully's, from the appearance of her "godson," to her first date, to her reluctant (unspoken) decision to leave a potential personal life behind. In fact, "normalcy" takes a beating in the form of a wretchedly dull man who cannot stop talking about children, his failed marriage, and the fact that Scully will surely sympathize when she, inevitably, ends up like him. In this light, crazy old Mulder looks attractive. And speaking of attractive, there is some beautiful camera work here, but it seems only to hypnotize the director. Shot after shot, our agents creep uneventfully through back alleys and damp warehouses, discussing evolution and the human condition. The final shot of a beast-baby is on a par with the final shot in "Quagmire," a silly afterthought.

With such archetypal subject matter (so many good horror movies are based on urban myths), this episode is an unexpected misfire. The problem for Carter, obviously, was how to avoid campiness, how to present a hairy, naked actor as a powerful image. The stately Claire Stansfield, who stands over six feet, appeared oddly unimposing and hunched while tiptoeing around in the buff. Dr. Diamond, a supposed expert on human evolution, actually says the Devil will be afraid of heights, like all primates (which is why you *never* see a monkey in a tree, right?). What with the suggestion of an entire nuclear beast-family, Scully's bemused foray into kids' birthday parties and dates, and Mulder's eventful night on the bum, this episode is a confused treatise on domesticity.

1.05 Shadows

ORIGINAL AIR DATE: October 22, 1993
WRITTEN BY: Glen Morgan, James Wong
DIRECTED BY: Michael Katleman
GUEST CAST: Lisa Waltz as Lauren Kyte
Barry Primus as Robert Dorland
Lorena Gale as Ellen Bledsoe
Veena Sood as Ms. Saunders
Deryl Hayes as Webster
Kelli Fox as Pathologist
Tom Pickett as the Cop
Tom Heaton as Groundskeeper
Janie Woods-Morris as Ms. Lange
Nora McLellan as Jane Morris
Anna Ferguson as Ms. Winn

A pretty young secretary, Lauren Kyte, is attacked at an automated teller machine and her two assailants, members of a Middle East terrorist group, are found later, their throats crushed from the inside, leading Mulder to suspect psychokinesis as the weapon of choice. Scully and Mulder discover that Lauren is protected by the ghost of her boss — the head of a company doing contract work for the Department of Defense who was murdered by his secret-peddling slimeball of a business partner — and like all ghosts, this one wants to be avenged.

Passable special effects and international intrigue cannot raise this predictable episode out of its lethargy. For this we can blame Fox executives who exhorted Morgan and Wong to let their talent go into remission and write a poltergeist story, one with a character who was "relatable," which is execu-speak for sympathetic. But Kyte, the paralyzed drip of a secretary who knows too much, makes the Lone Gunman look good. You'd prefer to spend an hour trapped in an elevator with Frohike's libido than this poor creature and her melancholy. And it is irritating to see Scully (twice!) stuck in see-no-evil-land, so she misses all the paranormal fun. In the next to last scene, she is outside a locked room struggling impotently with the doorknob while Mulder ignores her shouting. Humph!

1.06 Ghost in the Machine

ORIGINAL AIR DATE: October 29, 1993
WRITTEN BY: Howard Gordon, Alex Gansa
DIRECTED BY: Jerrold Freedman
GUEST CAST: Wayne Duvall as Agent Jerry Lamana
Gillian Barber as Agent Nancy Spiller
Rob Labelle as Steven Wilcz
Jerry Hardin as Deep Throat
Blu Mankuma as Claude Peterson
Marc Baur as Man in Suit
Bill Finck as Sandwich Man
Theodore Thomas as Clyde
Tom Butler as Benjamin Drake

Brad Wilczek is the owner and creator of COS (Central Operating System), a super-computer so complex that it becomes self-aware and starts murdering people. Investigating the murders, Scully and Mulder must fight their way past every office worker's nightmare: falling elevators, malicious environmental controls, sadistic security devices.

Bill Gates meets the Exorcist in this static-free ball of cyber-fluff. The idea here is that, like all self-aware things, COS will naturally be moved to start killing (huh?). It's a tip of the hat to some pretty good films like "2001" and "Demon Seed," though these films are now laughable in their depiction of computers. Even Morgan and Wong agreed: "It was a completely unsuccessful episode. Well, it pretty much sucked." However, Carter continues to give television a much-needed powerful female presence in the person of Agent Scully. It's a satisfying sight to see the resourceful Scully *not* whining for help, but instead disabling a hungry rotating fan by shooting the power cable to bits while hanging by one arm — a good chance for Anderson to do some macho styling. But could it be more predictable that the Bill Gates bore-alike gets snapped up to share a cell with the rest of the X-files abductees? Or that Mulder never apologizes to Scully for, once again, leaving her on the wrong side of a locked door? Humph again!

1.07 Ice

ORIGINAL AIR DATE: November 5, 1993
WRITTEN BY: Glen Morgan, James Wong
DIRECTED BY: David Nutter
GUEST CAST: Xander Berkeley as Dr. Hodge
Felicity Huffman as Dr. Nancy Da Silva
Steve Hynter as Dr. Denny Murphy
Jeff Kober as Bear
Ken Kirzinger as Richter
Sonny Surwiec as Campbell

Scully and Mulder are sent to Alaska to find out what happened to the members of the Ice Core Project team, whose most recent transmission via satellite showed a demented scientist, armed with a handgun, staggering to the camera to warn people away. Investigating, Scully discovers the men were carrying a worm-like parasite whose by-product, adrenaline, drowned out rational thought; but when she also discovers that the investigation team is at risk, she knows she must isolate the cause of infection and quarantine anyone found to be carrying the worm — and Mulder, always a panicky guy, looks to be the most likely subject.

A new twist to the "cure kills the patient" trope with Scully acting as the *only* person figuring things out, but also acting as an unwitting danger to Mulder. The episode is rife with questions of identity, from the last transmission of the Ice Core Project team, to the paranoid little ID-flashing scene before the investigative team takes off in the plane, to the moment when Scully and Mulder hold guns on each other and enact a strange debate on authenticity. Is this the real Mulder, or a panicky automaton begging for its continued existence? Scully's acceptance of responsibility for Mulder is the first step toward closeness, and their gentle inspection of one another for signs of infection, feeds the sexual tension between them while somehow also diffusing it. This is a tense, claustrophobic episode and is another installment in the Chris Carter canon of infection/infestation paranoia stories. (See "Darkness Falls," "Firewalker," and "F. Emasculata," for stories of unwitting contagion, and "Zero Sum" for deliberate contamination.)

1.08 Space

ORIGINAL AIR DATE: November 12, 1993
WRITTEN BY: Chris Carter
DIRECTED BY: William Graham
GUEST CAST: Ed Lauter as Lt. Col. Marcus Aurelius Belt
Susanna Thompson as Michelle Generoo
Tom MacBeath as the Scientist
Terry David Mulligan as Mission Controller
Tyronne L'Hirondelle as Databank Scientist

Norma Wick as the Reporter
Alf Humphreys as 2nd Controller
David Cameron as Young Scientist
French Tickner as Preacher
Paul Desroches as Paramedic

The agents are approached by a scientist at NASA, *Michelle Generoo, who has received an anonymous x-ray proving that the space shuttle is somehow being sabotaged, and that, although the damage is obviously deliberate, no human could have accomplished it. Col. Marcus Aurelius Belt, Mission Director for* NASA *and himself a retired astronaut, is dismissive of their concerns; but when he goes home and lies down for a nap, we see that he is somehow invaded by a spectral entity, one which has been with him since a routine space walk in his early career.*

This episode was being written at the same time as Chris Carter and crew were launching *The X-Files*, so he can be forgiven for this stinker. Proceeding from the odd assumption that the "face" found on the Martian topography fools anyone here on earth, this universally reviled episode was stitched together from real NASA footage that Chris Carter bought cheap. One wonders why two little FBI agents are allowed to loiter on the floor at mission control, but who cares when there is so much else to be amazed at. The "face" emerging from Belt's face couldn't look sillier, and the floating specter is far too Peter Pan-ish. What is the finger thing Mulder is trying at the end? (Try that next time someone you know is in pain — see what you get.) Why is Generoo so snuggly with Mulder? Isn't she engaged? Worst of all, it is rotten to see Scully, a medical doctor, wait helplessly for the paramedics to arrive while Belt convulses and makes faces.

As an esoteric aside, Marcus Aurelius Antoninus, Roman Emperor (AD 121–80) was the originator of the philosophy of "Stoicism" which holds, among other things, that thought is an ethereal form of matter, which might explain the intellectual origins of our little floating friend.

1.09 Fallen Angel

ORIGINAL AIR DATE: November 19, 1993
WRITTEN BY: Alex Gansa, Howard Gordon
DIRECTED BY: Larry Shaw
GUEST CAST: Frederick Coffin as Chief Joseph McGrath
Jerry Hardin as Deep Throat
Marshall Bell as Commander Calvin Henderson
Scott Bellis as Max Fenig
Alvin Sanders as Deputy Wright
Sheila Patterson as Gina Watkins
Tony Pantages as Lt. Fraser
Jane MacDougall as Laura Dalton
Bret Stait as Corp. Taylor
Freda Perry as Mrs. Wright
Michael Rogers as Lt. Griffin
William McDonald as Dr. Oppenheim
Kimberly Unger as Karen Koretz

Tipped off to a UFO *crash in the woods, Mulder manages to witness a covert clean-up operation before he gets picked up and kept in a cell with another* UFO *seeker, Max Fenig; he must wait until a crabby Scully turns up to take him home for a good old fashioned reaming out, and, true to form, Mulder bucks her every effort and keeps her working on the mystery with him. Meanwhile, an unseen survivor from the crash is searching for something, irradicating any soldier who gets in the way, and Mulder begins to suspect that Max, who at first appears to be just another socially runty Ufologist, may be a kind of homing beacon, a lost-and-found for extraterrestrials.*

After the wretched "Space" this one looked like a ripping good yarn, despite the fact that Scully might just as well not have been there. Claustrophobic and actually very sad, especially on the subject of Max's painful, obsessive little life, this episode is like "E.B.E." in that it seems to bring lots of disclosure — but not quite. It also treats us to a mixed bag of special effects: the Predator-like alien is all right, but the fish-eye lens trick is old; the wreckage of the craft seen only in glimpses has the grand, cinematic feel of "2001"; the photos of fake-looking latex scars behind people's ears is standard *X-Files* fare. This episode also introduces us to one of *The X-Files'* most charming guest stars, Canada's Scott Bellis, as Max. There is something about Bellis that makes Max seem real, sympathetic, and even familiar, despite his odd occupation and his maladies. Sadly, this is another episode where Scully can do little more than pull weakly on Mulder's leash. He pays no attention to her. Even when his little escapade buys her eight hours of horrifying volunteer work in an Emergency room, the fact seems barely to register. Any of the toughness we usually associate with Scully's character is there in this episode only because Anderson *put* it there, not because the writers did.

1.10 Eve

ORIGINAL AIR DATE: December 10, 1993
WRITTEN BY: Kenneth Biller, Chris Brancato
DIRECTED BY: Fred Gerber
GUEST CAST: Harriet Harris as Sally Kendrick/Eve
Erika Kreivins as Cindy Reardon
Sabrina Kreivins as Teena Simmons
Jerry Hardin as Deep Throat
George Touliatos as Dr. Katz
Janet Hodgkinson as the Waitress
Tasha Simms as Ellen Reardon
Tina Gilbertson as Donna Watkins
Christine Upright-Letain as Ms. Wells
Gordon Tipple as the Detective
Garry Davey as Hunter
Joe Maffei as Guard #1
Maria Herrera as Guard #2
Robert Lewis as the Officer

Teena and Cindy are twins (the product of a cloning experiment which originally produced psychotic geniuses during the Litchfield experiments of the 1950's) and they are brought together, from opposite ends of the country, by Mulder and Scully's

*investigation into the simultaneous deaths by ex-sanguination of each of the girls'
"fathers." The true parentage of the twins lies in the experiments of the one of the
Litchfield clones (Eve) who, in seeking to correct the errors of her progenitors, has created
greater monsters in these two homicidal girls.*

This episode holds many delights, the first of which is red-herring of the blood
loss (what the heck did the twins do with liters and liters of their fathers'
blood?) and the "red lightning" Teena reports to Mulder at the scene of the
first murder. It's a great tease for the audience who by now, like Mulder, is
ready to see aliens in every dark corner. And it is good to see Mulder blow it
for once.

We also get what will become an increasingly rare treat (a domestic moment
of sorts): a scene with Mulder and Scully in a roadside diner, paying a visit to
a restroom and buying drinks for themselves and their young charges, Teena
and Cindy. With more than a nod to "The Bad Seed" this becomes a highly
suspenseful sequence as the twins try to kill off Mulder and Scully by slipping
digitalis — their poison of preference — into the agents' sodas.

Harriet Harris, as Eve, is wonderful, particularly as Eve 6 — locked away
in a mental institution she twitches and snaps her way through a classically
gothic scene. The use of Deep Throat merely for the purposes of exposition
is awkward. But in light of the subsequent and ominous storylines of the "arc"
dealing with cloning and the creation of alien-human hybrids the exploitation
of such a powerful and ambiguously motivated character seems less forced
than on first viewing. Overall, this is a successful, suspenseful stand-alone
episode.

1.11 Fire

ORIGINAL AIR DATE: December 17, 1993
WRITTEN BY: Chris Carter
DIRECTED BY: Larry Shaw
GUEST CAST: Mark Sheppard as Bob the Caretaker/Cecil L'Ively
Amanda Pays as Phoebe Green
Dan Lett as Sir Malcolm Marsden
Duncan Fraser as Beatty
Lynda Boyd as Bar Patron
Laurie Paton as Lady Malcolm
Phil Hayes as Driver #1
Christopher Gray as Jimmie
Alan Robertson as Gray-Haired Man
Keegan MacIntosh as Michael

*Several members of British Parliament have died by spontaneous combustion and
authorities believe Lord Marsden, who is traveling to the U.S. on diplomatic business,
is the next intended victim because Lord Marsden's wife has recently received a love
letter, which is the killer's signature. While Mulder is busy with a Scotland Yard operative,
Phoebe Green, a charming, manipulative, and self-serving woman from Mulder's past,
Scully must do her best to find a killer who can not only control fire, but can survive it.*

Scully's patience is sorely tried in this episode by the appearance of Phoebe
Green. Green is a coquettish sadist who victimizes Mulder because she can.

It is a particularly negative female creation here, perhaps meant to contrast Scully's own personality, and, as if spurred on by the challenge, Scully practically solves the case on her own. The scene where she walks in on Mulder and Phoebe getting amorous goes a long way to making the Brit look like a purely evil force who may be enabling the killer either consciously or unconsciously. But this is dealt with at the end — and it's a bit of a disappointment. Even Mulder thinks of the woman as an ill wind, and he'd know!

The star here is the special effects, especially when combined with Mark Sheppard's depiction of the nasty, prowling little Cecil. His bizarre parlor trick in the bar, the glee with which he exposes his "gift" to people he knows will never live to tell, and his merciless pursuit of Mulder through flaming hallways, are impressive even on TV where it seems practically everybody is running through a burning building. Although we are given to believe that Mulder has a phobia about fire, it doesn't do much beyond serving as a plot device that gets Mulder in awkward positions, or it gets him out of the way. Of Mulder's many peccadilloes, this one is the least telling.

1.12 Beyond the Sea

ORIGINAL AIR DATE: January 7, 1994
WRITTEN BY: Glen Morgan, James Wong
DIRECTED BY: David Nutter
GUEST CAST: Brad Dourif as Luther Lee Boggs
Don Davis as Captain William Scully
Sheila Larken as Margaret Scully
Fred Henderson as Agent Thomas
Lisa Vultaggio as Liz Hawley
Chad Willet as Jim Summers
Lawrence King as Lucas Jackson Henry
Don MacKay as Warden Joseph Cash
Katherynn Chisholm as the Nurse
Randy Lee as the Paramedic
Len Rose as ER Doctor

Seeking a reduction of his sentence to life imprisonment, Luther Lee Boggs (a serial killer awaiting execution after Mulder's profile led to his capture and conviction) claims to have information that could save the life of two students who have been kidnapped and tortured and will be killed within days, following the pattern of a similar crime a year earlier. Mulder refuses to accept that the death row prisoner is channeling spirits, believing instead that Boggs is working with an accomplice on the outside and is orchestrating a trap to exact his revenge on Mulder; but Scully, whose father has just died, leaving emotional matters unresolved between them, is less willing to dismiss Boggs's claims, particularly after he hums the song played at her father's funeral and addresses her as Starbuck (her father's pet name for her — hers for him was Ahab).

For the first time the roles of "believer" and "skeptic" are exchanged with this episode and Scully opens herself up to "extreme possibilities" after she sees a vision of her dead father. This reversal of roles came out of writers Morgan and Wong's desire to offer Scully the chance to take the emotional lead in an episode and give Gillian Anderson the raw material for what became an outstanding and layered performance. Up to this point in the series the emphasis has been on Mulder's quest and establishing the trust implicit in the agents' partnership, but with this episode Scully establishes her credentials as both an agent and as a person. Morgan and Wong have finally brought Scully to the fore and Anderson is more than ready for the challenge of the highly charged scenes with Boggs (Brad Dourif in a brilliant, searing, out-there performance) and the subtle intimacies of family tensions and unresolved emotional pain. Scully, for her part, is ready and able to close the agents' case without her partner and excels even with the extreme pressures of her father's death, her visions, and her injured partner. Morgan and Wong establish, once and for all, Scully's equal standing with Mulder.

This episode marks the first appearance of Don Davis as William Scully and Sheila Larkin as Margaret Scully, who would re-appear in the second season when Scully is abducted and then returns. And although their scenes are short, the actors bring Scully's family life into sharp focus and provide a stark contrast to Mulder's parents when they finally appear in second season's "Colony"/"End Game." Although there are unspoken emotions between Scully and her father, the opening scene is one of warmth and caring. Scully's need for parental approval, hinted at in the pilot, is further developed by the writers, and her "father figure" issues, which are examined in more detail in season four, are given wider scope as Scully seeks to "please" Mulder by opening herself up to "extreme possibilities." Anderson shines as she communicates the growing complexities in Scully's relationship with Mulder. This episode has remained to this day the first season favorite for both Anderson and *X-Files* creator Chris Carter.

1.13 Genderbender

ORIGINAL AIR DATE: January 21, 1994
WRITTEN BY: Larry Barber, Paul Barber
DIRECTED BY: Rob Bowman
GUEST CAST: Brent Hinkley as Brother Andrew
David Thomson as Brother Oakley
Kate Twa as Marty (female)
Peter Stebbings as Marty (male)
Mitchell Kosterman as Detective Horton
Michele Goodger as Sister Abigail
Aundrea MacDonald as Pretty Woman
John R. Taylor as Husband
Grai Carrington as Tall Man
Tony Morelli as the Cop
Lesley Ewen as Agent #1
Nicholas Lea as Michael
Paul Batten as Brother Wilton
Doug Abrahams as Agent #2

Love is the drug, and some people are overdosing; the substance of choice, it seems, is pheromones (a sex hormone secreted by many animals and insects to attract mates, but only debatably present in the human world). Clues lead Scully and Mulder to Massachusetts, where they encounter a puritanistic cult called The Kindred (modeled

on the Amish in a cruel act of Freudian finger-pointing) who mine white clay from
which they make their famous pottery — but what else do they do down there in the
hive-like catacombs?

This is a fun, rain-soaked episode which uses the loneliness of the British
Columbia woods to positive advantage. The story seems, at first, to be about
Mulder but quickly turns into a Scully-fest. It's Scully who drives Mulder to
pursue the mystery, driven perhaps by those debatably present hormones. It's
Scully who asks all the right questions, like why there are no kids (hey, it's TV,
they *cost* too much!). And it's an *X-Files* first to see the chaste agent get hot
and swoony in the embrace of the ambiguously-motivated Andrew (played
with cookie-sneaking innocence by Brent Hinkley). It might interest some to
know that Saint Andrew, whose very name means "manly'," was said to have
been crucified on a cross that was — you guessed it — X-shaped! Several
welcome sights in this one: the appearance of Nicholas Lea (the intriguing
Alex Krycek in later episodes) as the lone survivor (how appropriate!) of the
killings, and the sight of our agents standing in the middle of a crop circle.
It had to happen, didn't it?

1.14 Lazarus

ORIGINAL AIR DATE: February 4, 1994
WRITTEN BY: Alex Gansa, Howard Gordon
DIRECTED BY: David Nutter
GUEST CAST: Christopher Allport as Agent Jack Willis
      Jason Schombing as Warren James Dupre
      Cec Verrell as Lula Philips
      Callum Keith Rennie as Tommy
      Peter Kelamis as O'Dell
      Jay Brazeau as Professor Varnes
      Jackson Davies as Agent Bruskin
      Lisa Bunting as Doctor #1
      Russel Hamilton as Officer Daniels
      Brenda Crichlow as the Reporter
      Alexander Boynton as the Clean Cut Man
      Mark Saunders as Doctor #2

In a sting operation that goes wrong, Scully's ex-lover (and her instructor at the FBI
academy) is shot by bank robber Warren Dupre before Scully coolly dispatches Dupre.
At the hospital, the two men die simultaneously, but, through Scully's heroic efforts,
Willis' body is brought back to life — with Dupre at the helm.

An interesting creep-fest that feels longer than its allotted time. Many treats
here. In a series of parallel scenes, we see Mulder's determination to find and
rescue Scully, his professionalism and control weighed against the fatal flaw in
Dupre's blind and violent love for Lula. The bank robbery gone wrong is one
of the strongest teasers of the season and Anderson's taut performance is
worth a rewind and a second watch. In fact, the scenes between Scully and
Willis are warm and intimate and cast light on Scully's earthiness (and her
weakness for father-figures). The added touch of Dupre's left-handedness and
Willis's diabetes are truly inspired and open debate on what constitutes a

person's physical being. But the kicker is Dupre/Willis's first encounter with Scully and the flash of realization that this is the woman who killed him. However, the endless enumerations of how Scully froze her butt off in a cabin with Willis, punctuated by "shut ups" from the inner Dupre, is painful and finally dull. Her bewilderment in the final scene makes her unable to see Mulder's care for her, all of which widens the gulf between them. This is a good one; but why did the watch have to stop when the old man died? One wonders what more beyond a shotgun blast is expected to stop a watch? After an hour of extreme possibility, it's too little, too late.

1.15 Young at Heart

ORIGINAL AIR DATE: February 11, 1994
WRITTEN BY: Scott Kauffer, Chris Carter
DIRECTED BY: Michael Lange
GUEST CAST: Dick Anthony Williams as Reggie Purdue
Alan Boyce as Young John Barnett
David Peterson as Old John Barnett
Graham Jarvis as NIH Doctor
William B. Davis as Cigarette-Smoking Man
Merrilyn Gann as the Prosecutor
Jerry Hardin as Deep Throat
Robin Mossley as Dr. Joe Ridley
Gordon Tipple as Joe Crandall
Courtney Arciaga as Progeria Victim
Robin Douglas as Computer Specialist
Christine Estabrook as Agent Hendrson

Bad-ass bogeyman, John Barnett, seems to have come back from the dead to taunt Mulder, the man responsible for his arrest many years ago, during which a hostage and a young FBI agent were killed because Mulder acted "by the book." A now-older and far wilder Fox Mulder is being stalked by Barnett — who by all accounts, died four years earlier in prison — and everyone close to him, including Reggie Purdue (his former supervisor at the FBI), and Scully, are targets.

Following in the tradition of movies like *The Fly*, "Young at Heart" is a very Mulder-heavy hour, with glimpses into how the character has changed, both as the result of growing older and by deliberate decision.

The idea that getting younger is the ultimate disguise is fairly innovative, and will be reversed in the fourth season's "Synchrony." The *X-Files* casting people managed to get actors who really looked like the same man at different ages, but Alan Boyce's slacker-boy delivery is a bit ponderous; far more icky and malevolent is David Peterson's rheumy gaze. Mulder's guilt could have been more powerfully portrayed (perhaps a shaky duck into the washroom to weep into a towel?) but instead, we get Purdue, who should be royally disgusted with this former pip-squeak, trying to recall Mulder to his days as a brilliant FBI prodigy. We even get Mulder scolding Scully for not taking it seriously enough, like it was her error in judgment, not his. Scully herself seems rapt by the news of Mulder's shame, and seems to forget that, as someone who relies on Mulder, her *own* life might be similarly threatened.

But Scully's role here is not all dopey. After all, her counter-theory involving an accomplice of Barnett's is far more plausible, really, than the truth. Perhaps the best scenes here figure Scully acting as bait for Barnett. Anderson's natural physicality brings a realistic flair to the stunts, and we see just a little of her comedic ability coming into play when she comes out of her gorgeous swoon.

1.16 E.B.E.

ORIGINAL AIR DATE: February 18, 1994
WRITTEN BY: Glen Morgan, James Wong
DIRECTED BY: William Graham
GUEST CAST: Jerry Hardin as Deep Throat
Allan Lysell as Chief Rivers
Peter Lacroix as Ranheim/Druse
Bruce Harwood as Byers
Dean Haglund as Langly
Tom Braidwood as Frohike

Mulder and Scully investigate the site of a supposed "close encounter," but after a local police sheriff releases the truck and the driver nervously refuses to cooperate with the FBI investigation, the agents' suspicions are aroused (these suspicions turn to paranoia when Scully makes the chilling discovery of a listening device in her pen). Further paranoia develops when a UFO picture supplied by Deep Throat turns out to be a fake and the cross-country truck chase turns out to be a diversion, exposing Deep Throat as an untrustworthy ally and perhaps an enemy to the truth.

Mulder and Scully's verbal sparring is at its best, as is the balance of humour and tension in Morgan and Wong's excellent script. The deepening bond between the agents is also evident when Scully's insight and compassion lead her to warn Mulder that others, like Deep Throat, may turn Mulder's own passion for the truth against him. The writers keep us guessing where the truth ends and the lies begin as Deep Throat is exposed in his first *apparent* betrayal of Mulder's trust.

This episode also marks the introduction of the publishers of *The Lone Gunman*: Byers, Frohike, and Langley. This trio, who raises paranoia to an art form, is one of the writers' greatest inventions; in this episode, as in subsequent ones, they prove to be steadfast allies to Mulder and Scully. Great humour lies in the fact that Mulder's ideas connecting UFOs with the Gulf War Syndrome are weird even for these guys. (Ironically, in fourth season episodes "Tunguska" and "Terma" Mulder's theories pan out). The scene is also memorable as it marks the beginning of Frohike's infatuation with Scully. It is finally with the help of this and other fringe groups, such as MUFON and NICAP, that Mulder locates the EBE by tracking UFO sightings along the route of the truck carrying the real crash survivor, emphasizing the series' themes of mistrust of authority and the power of the individual and the personal.

This episode is also Deep Throat's back story. But in spite of his revealing tale of international conspiracy and the execution of recovered extraterrestrial biological entities, we are left, like Mulder, wondering which lie to believe.

1.17 Miracle Man

ORIGINAL AIR DATE: March 18, 1994
WRITTEN BY: Howard Gordon, Chris Carter
DIRECTED BY: Michael Lange
GUEST CAST: R.D. Call as Sheriff Daniels
Scott Bairstow as Samuel Hartley
George Gerdes as Reverend Cal Hartley
Dennis Lipscomb as Leonard Vance
Campbell Lane as Margaret's Father
Chilton Crane as Margaret Hohman
Howard Storey as Fire Chief
Lisa Ann Beley as Beatrice Salinger
Alex Doduk as Young Samuel
Walter Marsh as the Judge
Iris Quinn Bernard as Lillian Daniels
Roger Haskett as Deputy Tyson

A young faith healer practices the laying-on of hands in a Tennessee revival tent and comes up with a stunning track record; spontaneous regeneration of nerve tissue, remission of cancer; but Scully is called in to give her medical opinion (and asks Mulder to tag along) because the boy's shows have taken a macabre turn and people are dying at his very touch. Convinced that the Lord has judged and punished him for pride by removing his "gift," Samuel Hartley refuses to help himself — still, he can tell, just by looking at Mulder, that his pain is centered on a missing sister.

The acting is the high point of this solid, melancho inquiry into the efficacy of faith, with Anderson and Duchovny nearly overshadowed by some fine guest stars. Scott Bairstow, as the doomed Samuel Hartley, brings a glowering, juvenile wrath to what could be an act-by-numbers role, and the (apparently natural) dark rings under his eyes seem to speak volumes about "the burden of greatness." Two other actors do a fine job of reversing expectation: the kindly "father," Reverend Hartley seeming at first to be a slave-driving huckster, and the "doubting Thomas" sheriff revealing himself to be a rotten swine. Neither were expected nor telegraphed — what a relief! Scully, though Catholic herself, must cool Mulder's jets as he dives head first into the Book of Revelations — a position which will be reversed in the third season episode "Revelations." Even though this is the usual fare for the two agents (Mulder leaping to conclusions, Scully arguing reason) the context changes things enough to keep it interesting. Finally, the writers cleverly find a way to resolve the plot so that *both* world views are served. Good entertainment.

1.18 Shapes

ORIGINAL AIR DATE: April 1, 1994
WRITTEN BY: Marilyn Osborn
DIRECTED BY: David Nutter
GUEST CAST: Ty Miller as Lyle Parker
Michael Horse as Sheriff Charley Tskany
Donnelly Rhodes as Jim Parker

EPISODE GUIDES

Dwight Mcfee as David Gates
Paul McLean as Dr. Josephs
Renae Morriseau as Gwen Goodensnake
Jimmy Herman as Ish

The FBI is called in when a rancher, Parker, shoots into the dark at what he thinks is a large animal in his corral, only to discover the body of a young Native boy; unable to account for why he couldn't see a human at such close range, the rancher also has difficulty explaining away his on-going battle over boundaries with a neighboring Native reservation. Mulder, meanwhile, finds strange tracks in the mud and forms a theory involving a mythic monster common to many Native cultures which resembles the European "werewolf."

Not one of the best. Network executives meddled again and asked Morgan and Wong for a monster story, and this is what we get. Native people are the only ones who don't come off as fools here. Ish's ridiculous ghost story of seeing the "Manitou" (they're even sitting around cross-legged like a bunch of boys at camp!) is barely saved by the sandy-voiced, ultra-cool Jimmy Herman. The most passably written characters are Gwen Goodensnake and the local sheriff, played by the stolid and sympathetic Michael Horse (of *Twin Peaks* fame). But Mulder and Scully look wildly out of place in this one, tiptoeing around in the mud in their Armani trench coats, or driving the mains streets of the "Rez" in their Hertz car. They sit in the car at Goodensnake's funeral, like a couple of lovers on a hillside watching the twinkling lights of town and Scully only steps out to pay her respects when driven from the car by Mulder's twaddle about werewolves.

We get treated to the usual shorthand tricks of "gee the lights must be out, so we'll have to crawl around in the dark" and Scully's phone being out of range "due to the mountains." Please! Worst of all, Scully can't hear Lyle Parker roaring and busting up the bathroom as he transforms into the "Manitou," a ravening monster, lusting for blood, and later tells Mulder she thought it was a mountain lion. Despite the best efforts of the leads, perhaps the only thing that worked here was the corner-of-the-eye shot of Jim Parker getting shredded by the monster — a strangely savage moment.

1.19 **Darkness Falls**

ORIGINAL AIR DATE: April 15, 1994
WRITTEN BY: Chris Carter
DIRECTED BY: Joe Napolitano
GUEST CAST: Jason Beghe as Larry Moore
Tom O'Rourke as Steve Humphreys
Titus Welliver as Doug Spinney
Barry Greene as Perkins
David Hay as Clean-Suited Man
Ken Tremblett as Dyer

Mulder and Scully investigate the disappearance of 30 loggers in a Washington state forest who have recently been dogged by a small group of militant environmentalists, and the logging company believes his men have met with foul play at the hands of the environmentalists. But Mulder has an X-file on a crew who disappeared without a trace from the same area in 1934, and it's not long before Scully and Mulder, amid the bickering of their companions, discover an old-growth tree stump whose inner rings reveal the presence of an unusual breed of wood mites which are dormant in the light but deadly in the darkness, when they swarm and feed on their prey.

In the tradition of stories like "Ice," where our heroes are trapped, isolated and under attack by a deadly and ancient parasite, comes "Darkness Falls." The story proceeds with all the classic suspense-story obstacles. As the representative of big business and the company who has sanctioned the cutting of old-growth trees, Humphreys, of course, is the first to die. Disbelieving the stories of "killer bugs," and with a disrespect and disregard for Mother Nature he hikes down the mountain to fix the jeep; he, of course, has left the keys behind and is soon under attack. The group in the camp, left with only one working light bulb, wait out a sleepless night, with a generator running on fumes. It's a classic fear of the dark story. However, why no one thinks to light a fire in a forest full of trees is a mystery in itself.

As in "Ice," Scully and Mulder are tested by the fight for survival. Mulder makes one of his classic unilateral decisions when he lets Spinney, the environmentalist (would a nature lover lie?), leave the camp with the promise he will return the next day to pick everyone up in his own jeep which is only two valleys away. The real treat here is to see Scully confront Mulder with the stupidity of his actions which have left them with barely enough fuel to keep the generator going. We also see Scully in a rare "freak-out" when she realizes she is covered with bugs, however inert they may be in the light. This behavior would seem wholly uncharacteristic if it weren't a teaser for the final horror of seeing Mulder and Scully under attack, arms flailing, trapped inside the jeep as night falls. "Darkness Falls" is a good episode that succeeds despite the plot holes one could drive a logging truck through.

1.20 Tooms

ORIGINAL AIR DATE: April 22, 1994
WRITTEN BY: Glen Morgan, James Wong
DIRECTED BY: David Nutter
GUEST CAST: Doug Hutchison as Eugene Victor Tooms
　　　　　　　Paul Ben Victor as Dr. Aaron Monte
　　　　　　　Mitch Pileggi as Assistant Director Walter Skinner
　　　　　　　William B. Davis as Cigarette-Smoking Man
　　　　　　　Timothy Webber as Detective Talbot
　　　　　　　Frank C. Turner as Dr. Collins
　　　　　　　Gillian Carfra as Christine Ranford
　　　　　　　Pat Bermel as Frank Ranford
　　　　　　　Jan D'Arcy as Judge Kann
　　　　　　　Jerry Wasserman as Dr. Plith
　　　　　　　Mikal Dughi as Dr. Karetzky
　　　　　　　Glynis Davies as Nelson
　　　　　　　Steve Adams as Myers
　　　　　　　Andre Daniels as Arlan Green
　　　　　　　Catherine Lough as Dr. Richmond
　　　　　　　Henry Beckman as Detective Frank Briggs

Genetic mutant Eugene Victor Tooms (first seen in "Squeeze") is released from a psychiatric institution, despite the near-ranting objections of Agent Mulder: Tooms, Mulder says, still needs one more victim to reach his quota. In an attempt to stave off the inevitable, Mulder follows Tooms everywhere and impedes his attempts to find a new victim, while Scully gets "reeled in" by a boss we've not met before, Assistant Director Walter Skinner.

We never forgot him and, apparently, neither did Chris Carter. More memorable even than "Fallen Angel's" Max Fenig and the fourth season's shape-shifting alien known only as "The Pilot," Tooms is one of the best creations in *The X-Files* canon, especially as played with reptilian stillness by Doug Hutchison. Now that the audience knows about Tooms, he seems like a force of nature. The added power of a good back-story has given the writers, and Hutchison, something to work with, so this is a powerful, humorous, scary episode. And David Nutter's direction is downright clever, too. Many shots are from Tooms' tunnel-vision perspective as he searches for a victim (most of whom seem to be wearing blue trench coats, for some reason). Through the use of slow-motion and unsubtle lighting, the director presents us with a parade of trusting do-gooders and innocent passers-by, who seem to float like sugarplums before Tooms' eyes. And there is humor here which was lacking from "Squeeze," as evinced by the finger-licking shot near the beginning and the fact that Mulder keeps popping up like a nagging chaperone. Hutchison's final appearance in the buff (insisted upon by Hutchison himself — he couldn't see Tooms as *clothed* in that scene) was a good choice for its animal baseness, and the series of rapid-fire, claustrophobic shots culminate in the welcome sight of Scully's hand reaching out to Mulder like a lifeline.

Besides the welcome return of one of the great villains, this episode marks the first appearance of Assistant Director Walter Skinner. With Cigarette-Smoking Man hanging over him like a vulture, Pileggi manages, in a mere cameo, to impress himself all over this episode. Far from being a ventriloquist's dummy for the conspiracy, we get the impression that Skinner is offering his agents a way to avoid the bear trap he himself is in. His criticism of Scully at the beginning is mirrored by her retort to him later that he can trust her *just* as much as she trusts him. Yes sir, that sound you hear is Scully blowing a raspberry at you.

1.21 Born Again

ORIGINAL AIR DATE: April 29, 1994
WRITTEN BY: Alex Gansa, Howard Gordon
DIRECTED BY: Jerrold Freedman
GUEST CAST: Brian Markinson as Tony Fiore
    Mimi Lieber as Anita Fiore
    Maggie Wheeler as Detective Sharon Lazard
    Andre Libman as Michelle Bishop
    Dey Young as Judy Bishop
    Leslie Carlson as Dr. Spitz
    P. Lynn Johnson as Dr. Sheila Braun
    Peter Lapres as Harry Linhart
    Richard Sali as Felder
    Dwight Koss as Detective Barbala

Detective Barbala is thrown out the window of a Buffalo police station, with the only witness being a 9-year-old girl named Michelle Bishop, and even though Barbala was a self-satisfied, lazy goof, his death is deemed suicide — despite the fact that the girl claims to have seen another man in the room with them. When the composite sketch turns out to be a murdered policeman, Charlie Morris, and when Michelle's psychiatrist gives the agents a doll mutilated by Michelle in the exact way Morris was killed (a gangland-style assassination) Mulder suspects the girl is Morris reincarnated, and that she has psychokinetic abilities.

Despite the interesting gamble of depicting a vengeful older man in the body of a 9-year-old girl (Andrea Libman is unnervingly blank as the host to a murderous spirit) and despite the inventive bit about getting a psychic image off a video tape, this episode is a merely competent hour's entertainment. How does Mulder know this is an image of Morris' last sight on earth? Why not a cherished memory? For that matter, why not a problem with the film? Why does Michelle dispatch the rest of Morris' betrayers with ferocious violence, while she seems content to smash glass objects for ages while Fiore cowers? And finally, why does the inner spirit leave Michelle at all; which is it, reincarnation or just possession?

1.22 **Roland**

ORIGINAL AIR DATE: May 6, 1994
WRITTEN BY: Chris Ruppenthal
DIRECTED BY: David Nutter
GUEST CAST: Zeljko Ivanek as Roland Fuller
Garry Davey as Keats
James Sloyan as Dr. Nollette
Matthew Walker as Dr. Surnow
Dave Hurtubise as Barrington
Sue Mathew as Lisa Dole
Micole Mercurio as Mrs. Stodie
Kerry Sandomirsky as Tracy

The much-maligned mentally handicapped Roland gets his own back on his surly scientist boss when he slices and dices him in the college's experimental high speed wind tunnel; but how is it that Roland, who cannot remember his 3-digit pass number, can operate the sophisticated computer-controlled device? It turns out Roland has an accomplice or, more to the point, Roland is the unwilling accomplice to his deceased but cryogenically frozen genius twin brother: Dr. Arthur Grable is miffed that his lesser colleagues are continuing his groundbreaking work and taking all the credit so, with the help of Roland's body, he is dispatching them by day and completing his work by night.

The episode has some fun moments. There is the deliciously gruesome head-shattering scene where Dr. Keats is dunked in liquid nitrogen and drops to the floor (the gag is extended later when we see the taped outline of the torso and little Xs marking the locations of the cranial shards). Mulder and Scully figure out the mystery of the who and the how just in time to prevent the death of the research team's last member but it is Scully who has the insight (or skepticism) to call on Roland (and not Dr. Grable) to override the wind tunnel's controls to save the last scientist. It is a revealing moment for Scully who sets aside the supernatural and relies on Roland's humanity to save a life.

There is some classic Mulder-Scully banter. Scully gets in some sarcastic shots but a favorite has to be Scully leading a lost Mulder to the college security office in a cleverly edited "off-camera" moment. We see the pair through a security camera monitor and it is this *cinema verité* technique that sells the joke.

This episode, a twist on the "evil twin" theme or "back-from-the-dead-to-wreak-havoc" plot-line (perhaps a little too soon after "Born Again"), succeeds mostly because of Zeljko Ivanek's feeling performance as the tormented Roland.

1.23 The Erlenmeyer Flask

ORIGINAL AIR DATE: May 13, 1994
WRITTEN BY: Chris Carter
DIRECTED BY: R.W. Goodwin
GUEST CAST: Simon Webb as Dr. Secare
Jerry Hardin as Deep Throat
Ken Kramer as Dr. Berube
Lindsey Ginter as the Crew-Cut Man
Anne Desalvo as Dr. Carpenter
William B. Davis as Cigarette-Smoking Man
Jaylene Hamilton as the Reporter
Jim Leard as Captain Roy Lacerio
Phillip MacKenzie as the Medic
Mike Mitchell as the Cop
John Payne as the Guard

In his panic to escape, a fugitive fleeing from the police rushes off the edge of a pier and apparently drowns — all because of a moving violation. Deep Throat urges, cajoles, and finally begs Scully and Mulder to follow this seemingly pointless case, and in the end, the agents uncover proof of government experiments (successful, apparently) involving alien DNA, alien-human hybridization, and a clean-up operation in which all evidence, including the "fugitive," is being erased.

You can forgive the ferocious pace here, and the fact that it could (should?) have been a two-parter, because the pay-off is so high. Bringing us full circle with the pilot, this season finale carries some of the sweeping material *The X-Files* will grapple with for the next three seasons. The centerpiece in the *X-Files* image gallery (so far, at least) has to be the scene where Mulder discovers the storage facility full of floating bodies (an image quite like the one we will see in the fourth season's "Memento Mori"). This is not only unexpected but mesmerizing: the shots go on so long that it actually looks like those actors are in no need of air.

Anderson has a lot to do in this one, taking Scully from irritated fatigue with Mulder's nonsense, to a gradual layering of surprise, shock, and, in the scenes in the high-containment facility, controlled terror. The camerawork is great here as Scully is asked for a code word and her eyes slip from locked door, to the guard's impassive eyes, to a glowing red alarm button. Jerry

Hardin's Deep Throat is heartbreaking, in his rising panic and urgency to achieve . . . what? In the end, Deep Throat remains a delightful puzzle to us; his motives are hidden, the "truth" he seeks is debatable, and his rage for control, especially over the ever-independent Scully, is barely contained. Finally, there is his cryptic warning to her (interesting that she, alone, hears this famous phrase) which could easily refer to himself.

SEASON TWO (1994–95)

2.01 Little Green Men

ORIGINAL AIR DATE: September 16, 1994
WRITTEN BY: Glen Morgan, James Wong
DIRECTED BY: David Nutter
GUEST CAST: Raymond J. Barry as Senator Richard Matheson
William B. Davis as Cigarette-Smoking Man
Mike Gomez as Jorge Concepcion
Mitch Pileggi as Assistant Director Walter Skinner
Vanessa Morley as Samantha (age 8)
Marcus Turner as Fox Mulder (age 12)
Les Carlson as Dr. Troisky
Fulvio Cecere as the Aide
Deryl Hayes as Agent Morris
Dwight McFee as the Commander
Lisa Anne Beley as the Student
Gary Hetherington as Lewin
Bob Wilde as Rand

Following the assassination of Deep Throat and the official closing of the X-files, Mulder is assigned to one pointless, vulgar case after another, while Scully is sent to teach at the Quantico training centre until a message reaches Mulder from his contact in the U.S. Congress, and he is sent to an abandoned SETI site in Puerto Rico that has received a burst of ordered extraterrestrial radio signals — intelligent contact. The information could help Mulder get the evidence he needs, as well as strengthen his fading memory of Samantha's abduction, it could even bring about reinstatement of the X-files — if he can get it before a secret UFO retrieval team erases everybody and everything.

Another in a tired series of "Mulder turns his back on Scully," "Mulder ditches Scully and sneaks off," "Scully uses her wits to find and save Mulder." Their painful meeting in the FBI parking garage (despite any power it might borrow from its similarity to the tense scenes in "All the President's Men") is a well-written, well-acted illumination of their different personalities. Scully is worried and solicitous; Mulder despairing and angry. His rough dismissal of her attempt to regroup *could* speak to a frustration at losing the X-files and her; then again, it *might* be all about the X-files.

In effect, this continues the ongoing *X-Files* debate over whether the truth is worth dying for. (See "The Blessing Way" and the final episodes of season four for more musings on how deadly the truth can be). The story is meant to be Mulder's exile in the desert, the moment when despair and questioning is replaced by a reason to go on, but it only works to a degree. The set is almost a character in itself, the SETI building is much like the dingy sets in "Ice" and "Dod Kalm" and is a counterpoint to the clean, bright threat of sets like "The Erlenmeyer Flask" and "Nisei." Fear, *The X-Files* team tells us, can be found in either world and so can the truth. Despite it being a kind of closed-room drama, we don't get a sense of claustrophobia until it is necessary, when Mulder is crammed against the back door in terror.

In the end, however, there is not enough here to fully scare or elate us. Mulder's rambling into a tape recorder is a letter to Scully and a lame way to let non-fans know why they should care. It's called exposition and all writers are ashamed when they resort to it. On top of that, it's pointless. If he gets out alive, he can tell her; if not, the "black ops" will surely destroy the tape. The character of Jorge, while meant to give us a taste of Mulder's relative comfort in scary situations, is a little too childlike, and his final moment of frozen terror strains credibility. Worst of all, Scully must play camp counselor to the kid lost in the woods again, and virtually drag the man out by his ear — at which point, guess who gets to drive?

2.02 The Host

ORIGINAL AIR DATE: September 23, 1994
WRITTEN BY: Chris Carter
DIRECTED BY: Daniel Sackheim
GUEST CAST: Darin Morgan as Flukeman
Marc Baur as Agent Brisentine
Mitch Pileggi as Assistant Director Walter Skinner
Matthew Bennet as First Workman
Freddy Andreiuci as Detective Norman
Don MacKay as Charlie
Hrothgar Matthews as Man on Phone
Gabrielle Rose as Dr. Zenzola
Ron Sauve as the Foreman
Dmitri Boudrine as the Russian Engineer
Raoul Ganee as Dmitri
William MacDonald as Federal Marshal

Mulder is dragged away from a moronic wire-tapping assignment to go slogging through the New Jersey sewers and wonders bitterly why he's working at the FBI. Despite a voice on the phone telling him not to give up, Mulder is ready to give up; but Scully convinces him to let her help, and together they pursue what looks to be a genetic mutant looking for a host so it can reproduce.

In *The X-Files* canon, you can find all manner of urban myth. The only staple missing is the Willard-style, giant rat episode. Not surprising, then, that Carter would cross alligators in the sewers with Chernobyl paranoia, and come up with this concept: a human mutated by radiation into a monster-worm.

Moody and creepy, with too many good ganders at the beast, this episode is well-shot but goofy. Despite the fact that we get our first glimpse of Mulder's endangered and feral informer, X, and that this is the debut of the brilliant Darin Morgan (author of arguably the best *X-Files* episodes), this episode just doesn't "have legs." Morgan's physical misery in the worm suit is palpable as he squints and snarls and tries to hide. Why Mulder gets the cryptic message from X, or what any of it has to do with the greater importance of *The X-Files* is confusing, except as a first taste of X's inscrutability. Scully's worry over Mulder's loss of faith and his wordless relief at her caring is the deepest thing here. Still, with the ick-factor as high as it is, Scully's coolness is again impressive as she works on putrefying corpses and pounces on horrid little fluke worms with pincers. Ever brave, our Scully.

2.03 Blood

ORIGINAL AIR DATE: September 30, 1994
TELEPLAY BY: Glen Morgan, James Wong
STORY BY: Darin Morgan
DIRECTED BY: David Nutter
GUEST CAST: William Sanderson as Ed Funsch

John Cygan as Sheriff Spencer
George Touliatos as Larry Winter
Kimberly Ashlyn Gere as Mrs. McRoberts
Andre Daniels as Harry McNally
Tom Braidwood as Frohike
Dean Haglund as Langly
Bruce Harwood as Byers
John Harris as Taber
Gerry Rousseau as the Mechanic
William MacKenzie as the Bus Driver
Diana Stevan as Mrs. Adams
David Fredricks as the Security Guard
Kathleen Duborg as the Mother
B.J. Harrison as the Clerk

*Mulder investigates a series of "spree" killings in the town Franklin and he is at a loss
to explain their cause because of their very random and senseless nature but he does
recognize a common element at each crime scene: the destruction of a electronic device.
He seeks help from Scully who analyzes and quickly identifies the chemical and its effect
on the brain and behaviour but when the poison is linked to secret night-time crop
spraying, Mulder suspects a government conspiracy.*

Morgan & Wong are in top form for this episode. The Lone Gunmen return
to give us a history lesson on the evils of DDT and the government that lied
about its use. This fuels the government conspiracy angle. Frohike is still in
the early, lecherous stage of his Scully-lust, keeping the agent's presence felt
even in her relative absence (as a pregnant Anderson awaited the birth of her
daughter).

William Sanderson is an absolute gem as Edward Funsch, a twitchy, nondes-
cript loser who literally goes "postie" under the influence of the experimental
pesticide being secretly sprayed on local cherry and apple orchards. The hour
tracks Funsch's psychological disintegration as the laid-off postal worker starts
receiving messages from digital displays of all sorts: first a zip code input
device, later TV screens, a digital sign, a remote control, and even his own
digital watch. The episode plays on modern fears of powerlessness in the face
of the escalating presence and intrusion of technology into our lives. It is a
more elemental fear of blood (heightened to an extreme paranoid state by the
poison in his blood stream), though, that leads Funsch, finally, to take a gun
and re-enact the 1960s sniper horror at the University of Texas. Director
David Nutter lets Sanderson fly in the tower scene as the actor explores
Funsch's desperation, fear, frustration, horror, anger, and new-found power.

The story is full of delightful little details. The writers "wink" as a readout
for an engine diagnostic program ominously blinks "NEXT" after we see one
murder and await another. Mulder, having been exposed to the pesticide, sees
"DO IT" on a hospital TV screen — this turns out to be an ad for a gym and
a clever play upon the expectations of the audience. But the best is truly saved
for last when Mulder picks up his cell phone, dials Scully's number, hears a
digital screech on the line and the display reads "ALL DONE, BYE BYE." It is
one of the series's scariest moments.

2.04 Sleepless

ORIGINAL AIR DATE: October 7, 1994
WRITTEN BY: Howard Gordon
DIRECTED BY: Rob Bowman
GUEST CAST: Nicholas Lea as Agent Alex Krycek
Tony Todd as Augustus Cole
Mitch Pileggi as Assistant Director Skinner
Steven Williams as X
Jonathan Gries as Sal Matola
William B. Davis as Cigarette-Smoking Man
Mitch Kosterman as Detective Horton
Don Thompson as Henry Willig
David Adams as Doctor Girardi
Michael Puttonen as Dr. Pilsson
Anna Hagan as Doctor Charyn
Paul Bittante as the Team Leader
Claude De Martino as Doctor Grissom

A renowned doctor, a specialist in sleep disorders, calls 911 about a fire, but is found dead later in his untouched apartment, a spent fire extinguisher at his side. The case is officially Krycek's, but Mulder tags along and even has Scully do the autopsy, and, when a second death is discovered, this time with "internal" bullet wounds, Mulder and Krycek discover more links in the chain; Charles Augustus Cole and a Marine training center on Paris Island where all three were involved in sleep eradication experiments.

Who better than a writer on a TV show deadline to tell us about insomnia? Proceeding from a number of recently revealed stories about Cold War attempts to build the 'ultimate soldier,' this episode is a somber epistle to the monster's inner guilt. Laced with Christian notions, like martyrdom, judgment, and redemption, this story is told from the perspective of the abominations themselves. In fact, the creators of the monsters in question are peripheral to the story. We see them very briefly, suffering for their sins, but we have never met them before and so have no serious feelings for them. Instead, they slip away to join a rogues gallery of other *X-Files* creeps who deliberately messed with nature.

In his first step into the light, Mulder's informant X, proves to be an unwholesome change from the parental care bestowed by Deep Throat. Steven Williams brings a feline quality to X, as if the man will spring to protect himself at any moment. This guy doesn't want to be here, and yet he is here; so what motivates him? It suggests various intriguing possibilities about Mulder's quest, or his job, or perhaps there's an unknown factor at work.

Fans also got their first taste, in this episode, of the Krycek Uncertainty Principle. The boyish charm has now been revealed to conceal something far more complex. He's smarter than he looks. Scully and Mulder's relationship seems to have risen intact from the no man's land it has been sent to. Their banter, as written, is just playful, but in Anderson and Duchovny's hands it takes on a yearning quality so intense it briefly stops the action altogether.

Finally, Tony Todd is like the specter at the feast here. His towering physique and obvious gentility, as well as the eyes that look wept-out, make him a very affecting villain — if a villain he is. This must be the only *X-Files* episode where the multiple murderer is not only justified, but vaguely saintly.

2.05 Duane Barry

ORIGINAL AIR DATE: October 14, 1994
WRITTEN BY: Chris Carter
DIRECTED BY: Chris Carter
GUEST CAST: Steve Railsback as Duane Barry
C.C.H. Pounder as Agent Kazdin
Nicholas Lea as Alex Krycek
Frank C. Turner as Dr. Hakkie
William B. Davis as Cigarette-Smoking Man
Stephen E. Miller as the Tactical Commander
Fred Henderson as Agent Rich
Barbara Pollard as Gwen
Sarah Strange as Kimberly
Robert Lewis as the Officer
Michael Dobson as Marksman #2
Tosca Baggoo as the Clerk
Tim Dixon as Bob
Prince Maryland as Agent Janus
John Sampson as Marksmon #1

Duane Barry, an ex-FBI agent who claims to be a repeat abductee, has taken his psychiatrist and the employees of a travel agency hostage as he attempts to make his way to the spot where he was first taken. Barry's assertions to a captive Mulder are first explained away by Scully who uncovers Barry's medical history of delusions, and then are supported, when doctors extract metal implants from Barry's gums, sinuses, and abdomen. After Scully discovers a bar-code style pattern etched into one of the implants, the first hour of this three-part story concludes with the shocking abduction of Agent Scully from her home, by Barry.

This episode marks Chris Carter's directorial debut. The story, also penned by Carter, gives us Mulder as a hostage not only to Barry but to Barry's increasingly credible tale. The plot makes several 180s and Steve Railsback (in a casting coup for the show) gives us a powerful and hypnotic performance as Duane Barry. Duchovny is marvelous as he draws the audience along through the maze of his reactions to Barry's tale. The two actors are at full power and their scenes are some of the most memorable of the series.

Visually stunning, the episode is a catalogue of alien abduction horrors. The scenes in the travel agency are truly claustrophobic, the atmosphere of paranoia is heightened by the images of invasion and voyeurism (telescopic drill bits, laser drills, miniature cameras, laser sights, etc.) and marvelous editing brings the hostage scene to a dramatic conclusion. Duchovny does a great job as he exposes the depth of Mulder's obsession. There are some lighter moments too: (the wonderful) C.C.H. Pounder gives the eager-to-please Krycek her coffee order (which he is later seen delivering), and Scully is seen in the grocery store buying pickles and ice cream!

One of the best episodes of the series, "Duane Barry," and its conclusion "Ascension" and "One Breath," breaks all the rules of series television as Carter and his staff sought a creative solution to the problem of Anderson's pregnancy with this, the first installment, of Scully's so-called "mythology arc."

2.06 Ascension

ORIGINAL AIR DATE: October 21, 1994
WRITTEN BY: Paul Brown
DIRECTED BY: Michael Lange
GUEST CAST: Steve Railsback as Duane Barry
Nicholas Lea as Alex Krycek
William B. Davis as Cigarette-Smoking Man
Sheila Larken as Margaret Scully
Mitch Pileggi as Assistant Director Walter Skinner
Steven Williams as X
Merideth Bain Woodward as Doctor Ruth Slaughter
Peter Lacroix as Dwight
Steve Makaj as the Patrolman
Robyn Douglass as the Video Technician
Bobby L. Stewart as the Deputy

"Ascension" picks up the story of Scully's abduction as a crime scene unit catalogues and photographs the blood, hair, fingerprints, and broken glass of Scully's apartment. Videotape from a murdered patrolman's vehicle gives Mulder proof that Scully is still alive and the lead that takes him, and Krycek, to Skyland Mountain where, in an impressive sequence, Mulder uses a tram to climb to the summit but, hindered by the duplicitous Krycek, arrives too late to prevent Scully's disappearance.

Writer Paul Brown keeps the audience guessing as to the true identity of Scully's abductors for, while Barry insists the aliens have taken her in his place, we only see a white light not unlike that of the helicopter which arrives moments later. The scene echoes the one in "Deep Throat" where a military helicopter chases Mulder and his partner away from a "UFO light-show."

The episode tries hard to keep up the pace of "Duane Barry" and that is a difficult challenge which it does not meet. But there are some treats as Krycek is finally revealed to be the ambitious protégé of Cancer Man. Nicholas Lea also has a nice moment in an ad-libbed bit of business when he smoothes back his hair after attacking the tram operator. Sheila Larkin returns as Dana's mother and she and Duchovny do fine work in the final scene which reveals the deeper, personal cost of Scully's disappearance. But the audience is left, like Mulder, with more unanswered questions. Who led Barry to Scully and why? Who has taken her and why? Did Scully have hard and damning evidence of alien technology in the implant or was she taken to prevent further involvement with Mulder's work? These are questions that will propel the series forward for seasons to come.

2.07 3

ORIGINAL AIR DATE: November 4, 1994
WRITTEN BY: Chris Ruppenthal, Glen Morgan, James Wong
DIRECTED BY: David Nutter
GUEST CAST: Frank Military as The Son/John
Perrey Reeves as Kristen Kilar
Frank Ferrucci as Detective Nettles

Tom McBeath as Detective Munson
Gustavo Moreno as The Father
Justina Vail as The Unholy Spirit
Malcom Stewart as Commander Carver
Ken Kramer as Doctor Browning
Roger Allford as Garrett Lore
Richard Yee as David Yung
Brad Loree as the Fireman
John Tierney as Doctor Jacobs
David Livingstone as the Guard
Guyle Frazier as the Officer

With Scully gone, Mulder buries himself in the recently opened X-files, the most recent of which involves a businessman murdered in his outdoor hot tub, drained of all his blood in what looks like a vampiristic ritual, the oddest feature being bloody Helter-Skelter-like writing on the walls. Mulder must follow his instincts, and he delves into a world of pleasure clubs where he meets the mysterious and melancholy Kristen — a woman who is being shadowed by two other vampires who want her to become one of them, and the only way to do this, they say, is for her to kill Mulder.

Opting to go the "Lost Boys" route rather than the less hip, far scarier "Nosferatu" route, Carter and team bring us another tired genre piece. Morgan and Wong have made their names on making the ordinary seem terrifying, the touchstones of American society corrupted and out of control — they bring us a distinctly new kind of paranoia. Why they chose to bring us a vampire piece is a mystery (although the answer may lie in the problem of churning out 22 episodes, minimum, a year). Vampire lore, at this point, is a bore, muscle-bound as it is in rules and dogma (you know: a vampire can't be killed unless *blah*, when the sun rises all vampires *blah*, to test if someone is a vampire you have to show them *blah-blah-blah*). It all reminds one of a folk cure for warts. And this story is no different. Kristen's final act of retribution is a twist based on the logic, vampire logic that is, of who can kill whom and when and how. Her act ties it all up in a neat bundle.

But there is something short-form about the way the material is approached. These are writers who can pull something new out of thin air, but perhaps it is harder to do when dealing with such well-worn material. There's the arcane nonsense of the loaf of bloody bread, the sunlight as death-ray trope, and (most yawn-worthy) the "oops, I nicked my *neck* while shaving!" scene. Although the first crime scene is grimly reminiscent of the Manson

murders, and although it is interesting to see Mulder get foolishly involved in Scully's absence (as if this was a rebound relationship!), and despite the surprise that "John" is not delusional (as well as the *gross* scene of the coroner fooling with his skin) this is a let-down and a bore. Even for those of us who like a good vampire yarn, "3" is hardly inspired. It's just a passable example of the genre; a kind of vampire-by-numbers.

2.08 One Breath

ORIGINAL AIR DATE: November 11, 1994
WRITTEN BY: Glen Morgan, James Wong
DIRECTED BY: R.W. Goodwin
GUEST CAST: Sheila Larken as Margaret Scully
Melinda McGraw as Melissa Scully
Tom Braidwood as Frohike
Jay Brazeau as Dr. Daly
Mitch Pileggi as Assistant Director Walter Skinner
Dean Haglund as Langly
Bruce Harwood as Byers
Nicola Cavendish as Nurse Owens
Steven Williams as X
Don Davis as Captain William Scully
William B. Davis as Cigarette-Smoking Man
Lorena Gale as Nurse Wilkins
Ryan Michael as Overcoat Man
Tegan Moss as Young Dana Scully

Scully inexplicably re-appears, in the middle of the night, in the intensive care unit of a Washington hospital in a deep coma where, removed from life support, as per the instructions of her living will, she floats between the worlds of the living and the dead. She is guided through a journey of self-discovery by the loving figure of Nurse Owens as she struggles with the decision to live or die; Mulder embarks on a much darker journey of his own as he burns with the need for revenge and rages to find the answers to the questions of how Scully came to be returned, who brought her back, who took her, and why.

"One Breath" is a delight. And though it would seem to be a Scully story, centered on her return, it is as much Mulder's story. The so-called "mythology arc" lives up to its name as the two agents take the mythic "hero's journey" from darkness into light and, particularly for Mulder, to self-knowledge. Mulder's journey is peopled with some of his usual "guides" in the persons of the Lone Gunmen (the appearance of Frohike, in a bow tie, bearing flowers, at Scully's bedside is a very sweet moment, particularly in light of his more libidinous attentions of the past) and "The Thinker" who determine the true extent to which Scully's immune system has been decimated. Even the Gunmen's usual schoolboy enthusiasm for conspiracy theories is diminished in light of the cost Scully has paid. Mulder is further "guided" by X, who shows him "the way" in the shocking, cold-blooded execution of a man clearly working for "them." X's form of justice is swift and deliberate and terminal, and we see for the first time how little X is like his first season predecessor,

Deep Throat. Scully's quest, by contrast to Mulder's, is literally light-filled as she is reunited with the spirit of her dead father, at last. Don Davis gives a moving performance as William Scully, a man who offers his daughter back to the world of the living in spite of his keen and painful need to finally tell her of his love for her.

Mulder also wrestles with the "mythic obstacles" of guilt (what if he knew the potential consequences of their work but never told Scully?) and temptation (when Mulder confronts the devil, in the person of Cigarette-Smoking Man, in his lair). He suffers a crisis of faith (when, deriving no strength from his decision not to join the "game" and blow Cigarette-Smoking Man's head off, he hands in his resignation) but gets a second chance from Skinner (who takes over as guide and tells Mulder the tale of *his* loss of faith in the jungles of Vietnam). Finally Mulder reaches a crossroads (when Melissa, Scully's sister, shines a light on the choices he is making and challenges him to see Scully through her death) and a resolution. Duchovny turns in a lovely performance as a man hollowed out by fatigue, frustration, grief, and rage who finally breaks down, holding out empty hands in a final gesture of release, amidst the debris of his apartment, which has been ransacked by the kidnappers while he held a vigil at Scully's bedside through the night.

There is a beautifully conceived sequence when Scully miraculously awakes from the coma. The sun-filled forest of Scully's "limbo" is slowly filled up and, eventually, replaced by the objects, noise, and activity of this world's Intensive Care Unit. It is the partners' abiding faith in each other that lead them both back to life.

Morgan & Wong have created, in this exquisite script, a brilliant solution to the problem created by Scully's disappearance and an opportunity for Duchovny to shine equal to the opportunity offered Anderson in "Beyond the Sea." Between the script, the photography by John Bartley, and the performances of the regular players as well as the guest actors (particularly Sheila Larken as Margaret Scully) this hour is still one of the series's very best.

2.09 Firewalker

ORIGINAL AIR DATE: November 18, 1994
WRITTEN BY: Howard Gordon
DIRECTED BY: David Nutter
GUEST CAST: Bradley Whitford as Doctor Daniel Trepkos
David Lewis as Vosberg
Tuck Milligan as Doctor Adam Pierce
Leland Oirser as Jason Ludwig
Torben Rolfsen as the Technician
Shawnee Smith as Jesse O'Neil
Hiro Kanagawa as Peter Tanaka
David Kaye as Reporter

Firewalker, an expensive probe used to study the conditions inside volcanoes, has sent back images of a dead team member, briefly glimpsed before an unseen hand comes up and destroys the video camera. The two agents investigate Dr. Trepkos, the moody genius behind the Firewalker project, who has gone postie and begun killing his colleagues.

This episode marks Scully's return to duty and Anderson's first physical challenge after a very short maternity leave. Her comment to Mulder that he should lay off worrying about her is obviously an aside to fans who thought she'd quit the show. Despite the thrilling repellence of the foot-long spore and the fact that Scully handily saves herself (Mulder only arrives in time to make comforting noises), this is a dull hour's entertainment.

Hopelessly derivative (see "Ice," "Darkness Falls," and "Dod Kalm," never mind movies like *Alien* and the woeful *Congo*) the hoary plot also sports a few holes. Why did the first spore-spewing victim run away, while the second craved Scully with a zombie-like lust? Why do vulcanologists think that the temperature in the cave is hostile to human life, when any Canadian will tell you 130 degrees Fahrenheit is just a real hot day downtown? (Now, Celsius is another matter.) And if it *is* that hot, how can Trepkos stand the heat long enough to do his dirty work? Worst of all, why does Mulder fudge the facts at the end, Scully acquiescing like a little girl? Because Trepkos is crazy as an outhouse owl, just like Mulder? Piffle.

2.10 Red Museum

ORIGINAL AIR DATE: December 9, 1994
WRITTEN BY: Chris Carter
DIRECTED BY: Win Phelps
GUEST CAST: Gillian Barber as Beth Kane
Steve Eastin as Sherrif Mazeroski
Lindsey Ginter as the Crew-Cut Man
Mark Rolston as Richard Odin
Paul Sand as Gerd Thomas
Bob Frazer as Gary Kane
Robert Clothier as the Old Man
Elisabeth Rosen as Katie
Crystal Verge as the Woman Reading Words
Cameron Labine as Rick
Tony Sampson as Brad
Gerry Naim as the 1st Man
Brian McGugan as the 1st Officer

When a boy leaves home for a few minutes and is found the next day, drugged and terrified, wandering by the highway in his underwear with the words "He Is One" scrawled on his back, local suspicion falls on a vegetarian cult, The Church of the Red Museum, whose leader, Richard Odin, is a disbarred medical doctor. But, after the kindly local doctor is found in the wreckage of a plane crash, with lots of money in his briefcase, and a vial that turns out to contain — hang on to your seat — "purity control," it looks like certain local children may have been part of an experiment involving alien DNA.

This one is loaded with goodies, not least of which is the return of "purity control," which first made its insinuation of eugenics in "The Erlenmeyer Flask." The implications of Scully's remembrance of the Crew Cut Man, and her realization of what they have stumbled across is beautifully related in her fervent whispering-match with Mulder, as if the two agents' suddenly realized

they were standing on ground zero. That Odin was a red herring, his role understood too late, and that Crew Cut Man dies unidentified, continues *The X-Files* motif of "you just missed it" where information is cruelly withdrawn. (In fact, when information is given in *The X-Files*, it is usually suspect.) Finally, compared to other episodes with the same scary notion of regular people used as guinea pigs (like "Blood," "Wetwired," and "Zero Sum") this one has some narrative back story, refuses to get cute (like the last shot in "Blood"), and seems most plausible.

2.11 Excelsius Dei

ORIGINAL AIR DATE: December 16, 1994
WRITTEN BY: Paul Brown
DIRECTED BY: Steven Surjik
GUEST CAST: Frances Bay as Dorothy
Teryl Rothery as Nurse Michelle Charters
Eric Christmas as Stan Phillips
David Fresco as Hal Arden
Sab Shimono as Gung Bittuen
Tasha Simms as Laura Kelly

Just for a change, Scully initiates this investigation into a nurse's allegations that she was raped; the twist to this one: the rapist was an unseen spirit that the nurse, nevertheless, insists was one of her aged patients, Hal Arden. Mulder plays nay-sayer this time as the two agents face ghosts, confused old folks, and a secretive orderly who has been handing out a really popular herbal remedy to his impossibly sprightly charges.

A heavy-handed treatise on the way we treat our elders that borrows from the heavy-handed movie *Awakenings*. Some fine acting here, especially from Christmas and Fresco as the salty old boys who just can't say no to drugs. (Note yet another example of referential casting in Christmas' case — he had a memorable cameo in *Harold and Maude* as the priest who was revolted by the idea of intergenerational sex.) And the sad-faced Sab Shimono, as Malaysian orderly Gung Bittouen, brings real charm to his minimal role.

It is also very telling that it is Scully who can see the human element in the case, and pushes her partner to see things her way, despite Mulder's yawning indifference to an X-file that cannot be followed *as* an X-file — in other words, a case that's not about him or his quest.

The shot of 500 pounds of water bursting from a door is rare footage for a TV show, and the image of Gung's mushroom patch is high gothic in its gnarliness. But overall this is a dreary, soggy episode and our agents seem to be getting little accomplished. Scully spends most of her time running from one emergency to another. The pacing is the problem, with near-drownings, heart attacks, and ghostly overpopulation all happening in the same five minutes. And then there is the confusion over what caused the ghosts in the first place. Does Gung's herbal medicine cure Alzheimer's, reverse aging, or anger ghosts? Why do the ghosts depart when Stan is revived? Of course, our agents debate the question of tripping out with the spirit world, but it seems too little, too late, and is at war with the haunted-house atmosphere of the horrible old building. And why, with so many people in wheelchairs, is Scully one of two people with a medical degree in the place?

2.12 Aubrey

ORIGINAL AIR DATE: January 6, 1995
WRITTEN BY: Sara Charno
DIRECTED BY: Rob Bowman
GUEST CAST: Deborah Strang as Detective B.J. Morrow
Morgan Woodward as Old Harry Cokely
Terry O'Quinn as Lt. Brian Tillman
Joy Coghill as Mrs. Ruby Thibodeaux
Robyn Driscoll as Detective Joe Darnell
Peter Fleming as Officer #1
Sarah Jane Redmond as Young Mom
Emanuel Hajek as Young Cokely

A detective, B. J. Morrow, has been having disturbing and bloody dreams, but her dreams have become waking nightmares when she finds herself in the middle of a field one night digging up the bones of a U.S. Marshall who was working to solve a series of murder/rapes in 1942 that left the female victims dead, with the word "sister" cut into their chests. Now it appears Aubrey, Missouri, has a killer on the loose with the same

M.O., *and Mulder believes the clues to the killer's identity now and in 1942 lie buried in Morrow's dreams.*

"Aubrey" is a great straight-ahead suspenseful murder mystery with a nice helping of the supernatural thrown in. The familiar Carter theme that the truth of our present can be found in the clues of our past finds its expression herein the person of Morrow who, despite following in the footsteps of her adoptive father to become a police detective, has inherited her rapist-grandfather's murderous genes and is carrying on his crimes of 50 years ago.

There is another nice nod to the continuity between the past and present: Sam Chaney and his partner, Tim Ledbetter (the 1942 victims), are direct professional antecedents to Mulder and Scully. As partners they spent much of their free time investigating "stranger killings" and their methods became the foundation for Mulder's present-day profiling of serial killers.

Bowman's direction gives the episode its unique feel. Mulder and Scully are true outsiders to this small community and most of the best moments lie in the little details and personal moments: the agents in the background while B.J. deciphers "brother" from the cuts on the ribs of Chaney's skeleton, Scully's observation that B.J. and Tillman are lovers and B.J. is pregnant. It's a beautiful looking episode as well as it moves between the 1940's period sequences of Morrow's dreams and the current horrors of her visions (especially Cokely's appearance in the mirror of Morrow's bedroom).

This episode is creepy and scary. Deborah Strang, as B.J., is strong and sells the intricate plot developments from start to finish. Morgan Woodward, a well known screen-villain, is wonderful as Cokely. Terry O'Quinn plays Tillman, B.J.'s lieutenant and lover, with presence and gravity, and will later join Chris Carter as part of the regular cast of *Millennium*.

2.13 Irresistible

ORIGINAL AIR DATE: January 13, 1995
WRITTEN BY: Chris Carter
DIRECTED BY: David Nutter
GUEST CAST: Nick Chinlund as Donnie Pfaster
Robert Thurston as Jackson Toews
Bruce Weitz as Agent Moe Bocks
Denalda Williams as Marilyn
Christine Willes as Karen Kossoff
Denna Milligan as Satin
Glynis Davies as Ellen
Tim Progosh as Mr. Fiebling
Dwight McFee as the Suspect
Maggie O'Hara as the Young Woman
Kathleen Duborg as the Prostitute
Mark Saunders as Agent Busch
Ciara Hunter as the Coed

When three graves are disturbed simply to harvest the dead women's hair and fingernails, Mulder believes the perpetrator is a fetishist who, in his urgency, may escalate and turn to killing in order to satisfy his desires. Despite her sometimes gruesome job, Scully is deeply disturbed by these crimes, enough that she visits the FBI psychiatrist; but because of her job, Scully attracts the fetishist's attention and she finds herself his next intended victim.

Almost entirely devoted to Scully's inner fears, this monster story is another one where the audience knows all and must hang on to their seats as the agents catch up. Five short episodes after her abduction and near-death, Scully is given yet another rough ride, not least from her own repressed memory. In Anderson's able hands, she is a secretive wreck. Her hard-won weep at the end is so far from being the usual TV fare as to be a clinic in how to do that kind of scene. Nick Chinlund is another wonderful *X-Files* guest star. His meek stillness as Donny Pfaster is belied by his physical size and strength, so he gives off a unique sense of threat. His fixation on the trappings of femininity (hair and nails) is mixed with an even dose of male aggression (calling Scully "girlie-girl") all of which adds up to one scary package. Pfaster's three-time transformation into a monster (once in the funeral home, once in Scully's dream, and finally in Pfaster's house before the over-stressed Scully's eyes) indicates that this episode isn't just about a crime, but about victimhood itself.

2.14 Die Hand Die Verletzt

ORIGINAL AIR DATE: January 27, 1995
WRITTEN BY: Glen Morgan, James Wong
DIRECTED BY: Kim Manners
GUEST CAST: Susan Blommaert as Mrs. Phyllis Paddock
          Dan Butler as Jim Ausbury
          Heather McComb as Shannon Ausbury
          P. Lynn Johnson as Deborah Brown
          Shawn Johnston as Pete Calcagni
          Travis MacDonald as Dave Duran
          Michelle Goodger as Barbara Ausbury
          Larry Musser as Sheriff John Oakes
          Franky Czinege as Jerry Thomas
          Laura Harris as Andrea
          Doug Abrahams as Paul Vitaris

Trouble starts when two teenage boys and their dates perform an ancient ritual in the woods but instead of getting lucky, the boys call up a spirit without a sense of humor. Mulder and Scully are drawn in because the local sheriff fears that cultists are to blame when one of the teens is killed, but little do they know that Satan is doing a little housecleaning: four devil-worshipping PTA members have let their faith slip.

This was Morgan & Wong's final script before they left *The X-Files* for *Space: Above and Beyond* and it's another gem. From the very beginning, with the teaser in which the yet-to-be-revealed Satanists debate the appropriateness of mounting a production of *Jesus Christ Superstar*, the writers have their tongues planted firmly in their cheeks in this funny and scary episode. There are some grotesque and frightening moments mixed in for good measure, culminating in the nail-biting finale in which our bound heroes witness the murder-suicide of their captors. Mulder and Scully become unwitting dupes as they stumble along, always three steps behind the devil (in the person of Mrs. Paddock). The devil may not have a sense of humor when it comes to lapsed faith but she sure is polite (she leaves a note of thanks on the blackboard for the bewildered agents when her work is complete).

Hilarious and creepy this episode features great photography (and of course, there is a power outage when the devilish Mrs. Paddock really hits her stride) and an evocative score from Mark Snow. There are also some *great* moments from the special effects and make-up teams: a dissected pig that re-animates, Paddock's snake eyes and tongue movements, frogs that descend from the skies landing on Scully and Mulder (this apparently was a scene drawn from *X-Files* staff writer Sara Charno's real-life experience with a "toad-rain"), and water that drains counter-clockwise in a water fountain.

Susan Blommaert offers the perfect blend of menace and mockery as Paddock, and Heather McComb as Shannon has to be one of the best criers on TV (she's also appeared recently in *Millenium* and *Profiler*). The scene in which she describes her molestation is deeply disturbing and sends a chill through the otherwise darkly humorous episode.

2.15 Fresh Bones

ORIGINAL AIR DATE: February 3, 1995
WRITTEN BY: Howard Gordon
DIRECTED BY: Rob Bowman
GUEST CAST: Kevin Conway as Private McAlpin
Daniel Benzali as Colonel Wharton
Katya Gardner as Robin McAlpin
Matt Hill as Private Harry Dunham
Jamil Walker Smith as Chester Bonaparte
Bruce Young as Pierre Bauvais
Roger Cross as Private Kittel
Steven Williams as X
Callum Keith Rennie as the Groundskeeper
Peter Kelamis as Lt. Foyle
Adrien Malebranche as the Skinny Man

Scully believes! — well, just for a moment, anyway, in this creepy tale of voodoo-involved deaths in a detainment camp for Haitian refugees. When the agents investigate the apparent suicide of a Marine at the request of his widow they discover the camp commander has been misusing sacred ceremonies for his own benefit.

The episode is another creepy stand-alone. The highlight of the episode has to be an intensely frightening (and gross) sequence in which Scully believes she sees liquid oozing out of a wound in her hand. When fingers, then an entire man, emerge from the opening, and with no hope of escape or defense she reaches for a "protective charm," we are offered one of those rare moments where Scully sets aside reason for instinct. It's an astounding suspension of disbelief for her and it's an experience that sadly goes unexamined as the story's focus shifts to a face-off of "black" magic against "white" magic. Even Mulder is unfazed by the voodoo-induced pain that stops him in his tracks.

Despite a strong supporting cast, particularly Daniel Benzali (who went on to star in the first season of *Murder One*), Bruce Young as Pierre Beauvais, and the charming Jamil Walker Smith as Chester Bonaparte, this is an uneven and heavy-handed, preachy episode.

2.16 Colony

ORIGINAL AIR DATE: February 10, 1995
WRITTEN BY: Chris Carter
STORY BY: David Duchovny, Chris Carter
DIRECTED BY: Nick Marck
GUEST CAST: Brian Thompson as the Pilot
Dana Gladstone as Dr. Landon Prince/Gregor
Megan Leitch as Samantha Mulder
Peter Donat as William Mulder
Tom Butler as CIA Agent Chapel
David L. Gordon as the FBI Agent
Andrew Johnston as Agent Weiss
Tim Henry as the Federal Marshall
Michael McDonald as the M.P.
Mitch Pileggi as Assistant Director Walter Skinner
Capper McIntyre as the Jailer
Bonnie Hay as the Field Doctor
Rebecca Toolan as Mulder's Mother
James Leard as Sgt. Al Dixon
Linden Banks as The Reverend Sistrunk
Kim Restell as the Newspaper Clerk
Richard Sargent as the Captain
Ken Roberts as the Proprietor
Michael Rogers as the 1st Crewman
Oliver Becker as the 2nd Doctor

Mulder's missing sister, now a grown woman, turns up and begs Mulder to help her "family," a group of clones posing as fertility doctors who she says are unofficially here to foil the official plan to colonize the earth. Rocked by this news, and unable to help Scully, who is also stunned by the things she sees in the doctors' research facility, Mulder is far from convinced — until a shape-shifting bounty hunter looking for Samantha turns up at Scully's door.

This two-parter about authenticity and faith has a neat circular plot, beginning where it leaves off, with Mulder paying dearly for his obsessions and Scully trying to find a safe course through the disaster. In fact, the two agents spend much of this episode separated, each at risk from their respective alien shadows, at risk *because* they are separated. And the show ends with a cliff-hanger that is an unexpected twist on the overriding and paranoid message: trust and ye shall pay.

The motif of suspect identity is infused into this episode. The gradual unveiling of identical doctors takes our agents from thinking in terms of an individual, to thinking they are after twins, to finally identifying these men as clones; spatially separate but identical — the ultimate identity puzzle. Samantha has such an outrageous story to tell that she is marked immediately as a possible phony. Even Mulder is reluctant to give himself over to the very thing he has always wanted (which suggests a psychological need for the quest itself). But frankly, to both Mulder and the audience it seems too convenient. Added to this is the casting of Megan Leitch, a reddish-blonde. We have always seen Samantha as a dark-haired girl and so we are visually cued to think she is not quite right. There is also the shape-shifting alien bounty hunter (identified in the credits only as "The Pilot") who is the happiest of criminals — one which is unidentifiable. He has a terminator-like quality to him, a calm that says he'll win — in fact, he flattens everything in his path. Brian Thompson's physique and Scandinavian looks are reminiscent of Schwarzenegger, but his face appears to be half-baked, as if this shape-shifter puts no effort into his own image.

Finally, Mulder's identity gets a boost when we meet his family for the first time. Notice that the icy Bill Mulder appears at first to be Cigarette-Smoking Man, his cigarette glowing in the dark. At first, even Mulder isn't sure who he is. Notice, too, that he seems none too happy about Samantha's return.

2.17 End Game

ORIGINAL AIR DATE: February 17, 1995
WRITTEN BY: Frank Spotnitz
DIRECTED BY: Rob Bowman
GUEST CAST: Brian Thompson as the Pilot
Dana Gladstone as Doctor Prince/Gregor
Megan Leitch as Samantha Mulder
Peter Donat as William Mulder
Colin Cunningham as Lt. Wilmer
Mitch Pileggi as Assistant Director Walter Skinner
Steven Williams as X
Garry Davey as the Captain
Andrew Johnston as Special Agent Weiss
Allan Lysell as Able Gardner
J.B. Bivens as the Sharpshooter
Oliver Becker as the 2nd Doctor
Beatrice Zeilinger as the Paramedic
Bonnie Hay as the Field Doctor

The two-parter continues, getting icier as we go, with the Pilot taking Scully hostage and using her as bait to get Samantha. With that accomplished and the rest of the clones dead, The Pilot returns to his point of entry, the Arctic Circle, with Mulder in hot pursuit — and only through the intervention of Skinner can Scully locate and save her partner from the consequences of his need to know the truth.

Loaded to the gills with new information and turning up the volume on the "myth arc," this episode is about faith, as usual, but ends with one of the most emblematic Scully voice-overs ever, affirming *her* faith in the redemptive power of pure science. Although these two episodes are largely about Mulder, Scully isn't forgotten along the way. Her battle with the mighty shape-shifter is shorter but more ferocious than Mulder's. After her ordeal is over, we see how harrowing her time with the Pilot has been, and our knowledge of this is due entirely to a fleeting expression on Anderson's face. Her resourcefulness and tenacity are highlighted as she breaks Mulder's secret codes, summons his evil helper, and even begs Skinner for help — all in an attempt to pull him back from the brink he has willingly gone to. Mulder's vulnerability is patent. He would again be dead if not for Scully (and if not for the intervention of Skinner who literally knocks heads with X).

There are many ground-shakers in this complex plot, but there are tiny tremors, as well. Mulder's agony at having to tell his father that he has allowed Samantha's abduction highlights his guilt at having allowed it the first time, and Duchovny's body-language is great here. He does "defeat" very well. But why does Bill Mulder refuse to refer to her as "your sister," opting instead for "Samantha," as if he knew that she wasn't who she claimed to be?

2.18 Fearful Symmetry

ORIGINAL AIR DATE: February 24, 1995
WRITTEN BY: Steve De Jarnatt
DIRECTED BY: James Whitmore Jr.
GUEST CAST: Charles Andre as Ray Floyd
Jack Rader as Ed Meecham
Jayne Atkinson as Willa Ambrose
Lance Guest as Kyle Lang
Bruce Harwood as Byers
Tom Braidwood as Frohike
Dean Haglund as Langly
Garvin Cross as the Red Head Kid
Tom Glass as the Trucker
Jody St. Michael as Sophie

An invisible elephant rampages through town, unseen until it charges a truck and dies, leading Scully and Mulder to investigate a zoo where no births have ever been carried to term and animals have been disappearing and then reappearing outside the zoo perimeter. Mulder theorizes that aliens are abducting the animals and trying to create a kind of Noah's Ark, but the agents also find themselves embroiled in an administrative power-struggle that has reached the point of violence.

"What immortal hand or eye/Could frame thy fearful symmetry?" Certainly one of William Blake's odder rhyme schemes and one of *The X-Files'* worst flunk-outs. The Noah's Ark motif ties in with Samantha's suspiciously pat statement later (in "Colony") that the aliens are saving us from ourselves. It's also an intriguing idea — that humans aren't even near the zenith of creation, in fact they are barely worth preserving when compared to animals. It's also an idea that is patently funny — that the aliens have lost their aim and are dumping freaked out zoo animals all over the place — a humor that could have been made more of. Instead, this is a very melancholy episode, even upsetting (especially in the jarring image of an exhausted, dying elephant at the side of a suburban road, as if by being in the wrong place, this animal would be destroyed).

But there is much silliness here, too. If the aliens have been at this work for a while, why did they stop when two little FBI agents turn up? When was the last time people killed for a job — especially when the cops are around? And finally, what was Mulder thinking, trying to "interview" a gorilla? Well, at least we got to see some pretty animals, not least of which were our favorite menagerie, The Lone Gunmen. Frohike's continued interest in Scully is one of the things that provide a backdrop for Scully and Mulder's sometimes flat presence in the overriding story.

2.19 Dod Kalm

ORIGINAL AIR DATE: March 10, 1995
STORY BY: Howard Gordon
TELEPLAY BY: Howard Gordon, Alex Gansa
DIRECTED BY: Rob Bowman
GUEST CAST: John Savage as Henry Trondheim
Mar Anderson as Halverson
Dmitry Chepovetsky as Lt. Harper
David Cubitt as Captain Barclay
Vladamir Kulich as Olafsson
Claire Riley as Doctor Laskos
Stephen Dimopolous as Ionesco
John McConnach as the Sailor
Bob Metcalfe as the Nurse
Kelly Irving as Burke

Somewhere off the coast of Norway, a rogue group of marines, refusing to end up like the "others," seizes a lifeboat and abandons ship, but the next night, they are found by a Canadian fishing boat, floating stranded in the mist, every man now obviously dying — of old age. Scully and Mulder's investigation uncovers reports of temporal anomalies in the area, a local fishing population that won't fish the area, and finally we see them stranded on the same ship, aging rapidly, and Scully, the scientist, must deduce the answer to it all before they run out of time.

"Water, water everywhere and not a drop to drink!" This is "The Ancient Mariner" done *X-Files* style, with both agents standing in as the pushy outsiders who don't understand the "lore," and the albatross being Mulder's quest. A claustrophobic, gray-green nightmare utilizing any number of basic human fears to set the audience off, this one is stylish and gothic. The corroding hulk of the USS Arden, filled as it is with the desiccated corpses of Marines, is a kind of floating crypt, complete with a seemingly unnatural crypt-dweller (Olafsson). It even has the standard key to escape: faith and goodness. In this case, it is Scully's faith and goodness. Her calm in the face of death is unexpected, even though it stems from her intimate knowledge of "the other shore" (interesting, too, that the border between life and death in "One Breath" was depicted as a boat floating on water). It is also Scully's personality, her habit of making notes of her scientific observations, that saves them.

The acting is pretty good in this one. John Savage as Trondheim is an apt choice; not only is he good, with his familiar worried-yet-tough face, he also starred in a movie called "White Squall" involving a disabled ship called "The Albatross." The makeup, however, is as awful as it always is when they try to make young people look old, and there is a little bit of the old rabbit-from-a-hat problem in the final scene when our two leads come back as pretty and latex-free as in the credits. Much more refreshing was the final scene in "Darkness Falls" where the agents are clearly still wracked by their ordeal, two frail creatures whose bodies have been under attack.

2.20 Humbug

ORIGINAL AIR DATE: March 31, 1995
WRITTEN BY: Darin Morgan
DIRECTED BY: Kim Manners
GUEST CAST: Jim Rose as Dr. Blockhead
The Enigma as The Conundrum
Michael Anderson as Mr. Nutt
Wayne Grace as Sheriff Hamilton
Vincent Schiavelli as Lanny
George Tipple as Hepcat Helm
Alex Diakun as the Curator
John Payne as Jerald Glazebrook
Alvin Law as the Reverend
Blair Slater as Glazebrook Child (older)
Devin Walker as Glazebrook Child (younger)
Debis Simpson as the waiter

Scully and Mulder are drawn into the investigation of a bloody murder of a circus performer when Mulder ties the death of the "Alligator Man" to a string of similar killings across several states — all the victims share a horrendous wound to the abdomen. The apprehension of the criminal, though, becomes as elusive as his identity has been and it is finally the audience, not the agents, that knows that circus people "take care of their own" as the diminutive killer meets his end as a late night snack for the Conundrum — a gaff who will literally eat anything.

The teaser for this episode doesn't quite prepare us for the hour to come. Darin Morgan has written a true original — a funny *X-Files* episode. In a hilarious, absurd, and touching story Morgan presents a town populated for the most part by circus freaks, geeks, and gaffs. Although Mulder's police work brings the agents to town, this is where Mulder's contribution to crime-solving ends. We get to watch the pair bumble along displaying prejudices (at a loss for suspects they question even the sheriff when Scully discovers he used to be Jim-Jim the Dog-faced boy) and ineptitude at nearly every turn. All expectation is turned on its head. The audience is offered the welcome sight of Mulder clued out to the very end. It is Scully who figures out the killer's identity and has to explain it to Mulder.

This hour is a true delight. It is filled with brilliant self-referential gags and peopled with astutely observant "philosophers." Witness Mr. Nutt's acute appraisal of Mulder, the Blockhead's observations on "freaks" of nature, and Lanny's (played with great pathos by Vincent Schiavelli) touching description of his new life away from the "indignities" of circus life in which he now carries peoples' luggage for them. Where else can you see Scully eat a bug?

It is also a show about appearances, about looking and not seeing — particularly in the cleverly shot sequence in the Museum of Curiosities, that allows us to see and not see the disfigured curator through rippled glass and distorted mirror reflections. Arguably the most telling scene occurs when Lanny, who, in his half-open dressing gown, wakes Scully early one morning, affording her a view of the unusual twin Leonard. Scully, similarly disheveled, offers Lanny an equally fascinating glimpse of the curve of her breast. The scene is both funny and sad and it is the balance of these impulses that inform all of Morgan's *X-Files* scripts to come.

2.21 The Calusari

ORIGINAL AIR DATE: April 4, 1995
WRITTEN BY: Sara Charno
DIRECTED BY: Mike Vejar
GUEST CAST: Joel Palmer as Charlie/Michael Holvey
Lilyan Chauvin as Golda
Helene Clarkson as Maggie Holvey
Ric Reid as Steve Holvey
Oliver and Jeremy Isaac Wildsmith as Teddy Holvey
Christine Willes as Agent Kosseff
Bill Dow as Doctor Charles Burk
Kay E. Kuter as the Head Calusari
Jacqueline Dandeneau as Nurse Castor
Bill Croft as Calusari #2
Campbell Lane as Calusari #3
George Josef as Calusari #4

Mulder pursues the case of the death of a toddler when photographic evidence leads him to suspect the boy was led to his fate by a ghost, but after a visit to the child's home and a look at the children's medical records Scully suspects an abusive home environment and a case of "Munchausen by proxy" (whereby a parent induces illness in a child to gain attention). Well, it turns out Mulder is closer to the truth: Charlie, the toddler's brother, is shadowed by the murderous Michael, the spirit of his twin who died at birth.

Carter and Co. break one of television's major taboos when they kill off two-year-old Teddy Holvey at the hands of his jealous brother Charlie/Michael. It's a daring move but for the most part the rest of the story does not live up to its billing. The real conflict in this story takes place across generations and across cultures, between the boys' parents and their Romanian grandmother who holds fast to superstition. The story disintegrates into a TV version of *The Exorcist* when the Calusari (keepers of the old ways) are brought in to rid the house and Charlie of evil. There is a grim exorcism scene with all the attendant dripping walls, floating beds, rotted teeth, and hellish voices.

Even the open-ended conclusion in which Mulder is warned to be on guard against the Evil One is hokey and we are further punished by Mulder's final moralizing voice-over. Worse still, Scully experiences Michael's poltergeist-style power first-hand as she is tossed around like a rag doll. It's one of those episodes that tests to the absolute limit the audience's tolerance for Scully as non-believer, particularly after the beating she takes at the hands of a disembodied spirit. There is no reward in this episode in terms of scares or humor (not even the opportunity to finally hear Scully refer to ghosties and beasties).

2.22 F. Emasculata

ORIGINAL AIR DATE: April 28, 1995
WRITTEN BY: Chris Carter, Howard Gordon
DIRECTED BY: Rob Bowman
GUEST CAST: Charles Martin Smith as Dr. Osbourne
John Tench as Steve (prisoner)

Angelo Vacco as Angelo Garza
Morris Panych as Dr. Simon Auerbach
John Pyper-Ferguson as Paul (prisoner)
Dean Norris as U.S. Marshal Tapia
Mitch Pileggi as Assistant Director Walter Skinner
William B. Davis as Cigarette-Smoking Man
Lynda Boyd as Elizabeth
Alvin Sanders as the Bus Driver
Kim Kondrashoff as Bobby Torrence
Chilton Crane as Mother at Bus Station
Bill Rowat as Doctor Torrence
Jude Zachary as Winston

Scully and Mulder are called in to aid federal marshals in their pursuit of two escaped convicts, but it is Scully who uncovers the real cause for commotion at the prison. A lethal and infectious micro-organism has been unleashed on an unsuspecting prison population and it is likely that the escapees have been exposed, so Mulder races the clock to track down the contagious prisoners.

The gross-out factor is dialed up to 10 in this action story with a dark underbelly. It's a story about power and the control of information. And this is a Scully story at its best. She is operating in her area of expertise and we are treated to the sight of her bullying her way into the quarantined area. Anderson gets to stretch here; she has a great scene as she awaits the results of tests that will tell her whether or not she is infected by the contagion. She is the picture of controlled fear and weary relief. Scully also uncovers the linchpin of the cover-up, the "postal error" that sent the package carrying the infected material to the prison instead of to a scientist working for Pink Pharmaceuticals. It is Scully, for once, who exposes the intricate plan that has purposefully placed the agents in a lethal situation to discredit and maybe even kill them. And it is Scully who advocates the control of information about the contagion's public health risk.

The debate over whether or not the truth should be exposed is a classic *X-Files* trope and one that is explored from several angles. Cigarette-Smoking Man and Scully share points of view but for opposing reasons. But it is the dying girlfriend of one of the prisoners who offers the most telling argument, perhaps of the whole series. Why *should she* tell the truth when the government won't? This argument over the control of information and, therefore, power underlies all of the government conspiracy episodes and will take on a new colors in season three's "Talitha Cumi."

2.23 Soft Light

ORIGINAL AIR DATE: May 5, 1995
WRITTEN BY: Vince Gilligan
DIRECTED BY: Jim Contner
GUEST CAST: Tony Shalhoub as Doctor Chester Banton
Kevin McNulty as Doctor Davey
Kate Twa as Detective Ryan
Nathaniel Deveaux as Detective Barron

Steven Williams as X
Guyle Frazier as Barney
Forbes Angus as the Government Scientist
Donna Yamamoto as the Night Nurse
Robert Rozen as the Doctor
Steve Bacic as the 2nd Officer
Craig Brunanski as the Security Guard

Jung meets Oppenheimer in this sci-fi tale of a scientist who transforms his shadow into a lethal "black hole" during an accident in a particle accelerator.

When Scully's help is requested by former student Kelly Ryan, now a detective on her first case, in solving a string of missing persons cases we get to glimpse a new side of the agent: Scully as mentor. The theme of women trying to survive "the boy's club," however laudable, is awkwardly handled as it functions merely as a plot device. The episode never explores the obstacles in Scully's professional career to which she alludes nor her relationship with a female colleague, either of which could have made for truly interesting fare.

Steven Williams gets the chance to fly a bit, revealing more of X's dark side and hidden agendas. The indifference he shows as we see Dr. Banton's final fate as government guinea pig just makes a chilling scene all the more moving. Tony Shalhoub's performance as the fragile Banton serves as the perfect counterpoint to the hardened X. The interesting special effects take center stage in "Soft Light," unfortunately at the expense of the story.

2.24 Our Town

ORIGINAL AIR DATE: May 12, 1995
WRITTEN BY: Frank Spotnitz
DIRECTED BY: Rob Bowman
GUEST CAST: John Milford as Walter Chaco
Caroline Kava as Doris Kearns
Gary Grubbs as Sheriff Tom Arens
Robin Mossley as Dr. Randolph
John MacLaren as George Kearns
Hrothgar Mathews as the Mental Patient
Gabrielle Miller as Paula Gray
Timothy Webber as Jess Harold
Robert Moloney as the Worker
Carrie Cain Sparks as the Maid

A federal food inspector (who suffers from a very rare disease), goes missing in Arkansas and, when a local teen goes nuts and is shot by the local police chief, Scully discovers that the girl suffers from the same rare disease — the odds make it impossible that this is a coincidence: one person must have ingested the other. In the end, the agents uncover a cult of creeps retaining their youth through cannibalism, but, due to the madness they all share (thanks to the sickly government inspector), cohesion in the group is eroding and a normally cautious group of people are looking at the FBI agents and seeing — dinner!

A funny and very wicked episode with its fair share of humor. Continuing in the 'pandora's box' motif, where one small mistake could lead to a national public safety threat (see: "Darkness Falls," "Ice," or "F. Emasculata" for more) Carter and company give us another diverting episode full of gross jokes. Scully prancing in with a *huge* bucket of Chaco Chicken is hilarious, under the circumstances, but is also reminiscent of her eager munching of bar-be-cued ribs in "Red Museum" and — let's face it — her beetle-eating scene in "Humbug." It seems she's afraid of nothing.

Even the ending, which is eye-rollingly bad (Mulder is distinctly uninspiring as he flat-foots it across a field to save Scully from the cheap horror flick she seems stuck in), could actually be a nod to all the *bad* movies we love to hate. (After all, the makers of *Mystery Science Theater 3000* made a living doing that.) The foray into how chicken is prepared in North America, though a red herring, is barely perceived as one, so repellent is the information. In fact, Scully's discovery that chickens are fed other chickens is basically a fore-shadowing of the horrible truth. However, the masked executioner is a ridiculous creation, even as he raises his medieval axe and hangs there as if waiting for a commercial break. At the first sight of the local police chief, one asks why he happily dragged the river and produced all those bones for the FBI agents in the first place when he could have lied? Just good people, perhaps.

2.25 Anasazi

ORIGINAL AIR DATE: May 19, 1995
WRITTEN BY: Chris Carter
STORY BY: David Duchovny, Chris Carter
DIRECTED BY: R.W. Goodwin
GUEST CAST: Byron Chief Moon as the Father
Bernie Coulson as The Thinker
Peter Donat as William Mulder
Nicholas Lea as Agent Alex Krycek
Mitch Pileggi as Assistant Director Walter Skinner
Paul McLean as Agent Kautz
Floyd "Red Crow" Westerman as Albert Hosteen
Renae Morriseau as Josephine Doane
Auriello Dinunzio as Antonio
William B. Davis as Cigarette-Smoking Man
Dean Haglund as Langly
Tom Braidwood as Frohike
Bruce Harwood as Byers
Michael David Simms as the Senior Agent
Ken Camroux as the 2nd Senior Agent
Mitch Davies as the Stealth Man

Mulder goes mad in this first installment when he is handed what may be the definitive proof of the existence of extraterrestrials only to find that it is encoded — but Scully recognizes the code as Navajo and discovers that the documents include the words "merchandise," "tests" and, incredibly, her own name! What follows is revelation upon twist in a complex plot which figures Scully actually shooting Mulder, Krycek killing Bill Mulder (an old friend of Cigarette-Smoking Man, we discover), a family of Navajo men who may know everything, and a boxcar buried in the desert filled with bodies which are not apparently human.

A breathless joyride through the 'myth arc' with a cliff-hanger that is a beautiful visual tie-in with the next season's first shot of fire roaring out of the boxcar where, moments before, Mulder stood. Though focusing on Mulder, this episode is all about Scully, her acceptance of responsibility for her partner, her resourcefulness, and her loyalty. If not for Scully's careful handling of her insane partner, Mulder, as isolated as he is from his fellow man, might have been destroyed. In fact, one wonders why "they" didn't think of it before. Tied to history by the inclusion of WWII Navajo "code-talkers" (Navajo, with its complex vowel system and emphasis on puns was impossible for the Japanese to decode) and the discussion of real-life Nazi scientists allowed into the U.S. to continue their ghastly work, this episode brings a strong element of plausibility to its wild subject matter: secrecy and alien hybridization. It also deepens Scully's back story through the innocent mention that she recognizes the code as Navajo because her father showed it to her when she was young (interesting for anyone who wonders if Bill Scully might have a role in the conspiracy).

SEASON THREE (1995–1996)

3.01 Blessing Way

ORIGINAL AIR DATE: September 22, 1995
WRITTEN BY: Chris Carter
DIRECTED BY: R.W. Goodwin
GUEST CAST: Floyd "Red Crow" Westerman as Albert Hosteen
            Tim Michael as Albert's son
            Dakota House as Eric Hosteen
            Mitch Davies as the Camouflage Man
            William B. Davis as Cigarette-Smoking Man
            Michael David Simms as the Senior Agent
            Mitch Pileggi as Assistant Director Walter Skinner
            Don Williams as the 1st Elder
            Stanly Walsh as the 2nd Elder
            John Moore as the 3rd Elder
            John Neville as Well-Manicured Man
            Sheila Larken as Margaret Scully
            Melinda McGraw as Melissa Scully
            Tom Braidwood as Frohike
            Peter Donat as William Mulder
            Jerry Hardin as Deep Throat
            Benita Ha as the Tour Guide

Ernie Foort as the Security Guard
Forbes Angus as the M.D.
Alf Humphreys as Dr. Pomerantz
Rebecca Toolan as Mrs. Mulder
Nicholas Lea as Agent Alex Krycek
Lenno Britos as the Hispanic Man
Ian Victor as the Minister

Mulder, somehow alive after Cigarette-Smoking Man and his goons sanitize the boxcar where he was standing with a firebomb, is taken in by the Hosteen family and given "the Blessing Way" healing ceremony, and as he hangs between life and death he is visited by ghosts who exhort him to continue to pursue the truth. Scully, meanwhile, is suspended from duty and must enter the FBI building through the front doors where, passing through a metal detector, she discovers an implant in her neck that turns out to be a kind of microchip processor.

We continue with the second installment as the plot thickens almost to the point of strangulation. What we get is a barrage of new information and terrifying repercussions. Scully's abduction comes back to haunt her in the form of a microchip in her neck, but this is only the tip of a horrifying iceberg that will carry *The X-Files* writers through the fourth season and beyond, binding Scully inexorably to Mulder's quest. Memory is the central image here. Albert Hosteen's poetic voice-over in the first shot, about the common nature of memory and fire, makes it clear what this three-parter is *about* and, in a way, what the *The X-Files* in general are *about*. But the notion of memory is given a clunky dissertation during Mulder's Blessing Way healing ceremony. In a series of oddly dull scenes (which contrast Scully's moving and eerie counterpart in "One Breath"), Mulder floats like a pine airwick in a starry sky while ghosts of the past come to convince him to live. Despite hard work from Hardin and Donat, Deep Throat and Bill Mulder's speeches are torpid and posturing. As with many such speeches on this show, one wonders where the periods went as sentences run together and trip over one another.

3.02 Paper Clip

ORIGINAL AIR DATE: September 29, 1995
WRITTEN BY: Chris Carter
DIRECTED BY: Rob Bowman
GUEST CAST: Mitch Pileggi as Assistant Director Walter Skinner
Sheila Larken as Margaret Scully
Robert Lewis as the E.R. Doctor
Melinda McGraw as Melissa Scully
Bruce Harwood as Byers
Tom Braidwood as Frohike
Dean Haglund as Langly
William B. Davis as Cigarette-Smoking Man
John Neville as the Well Manicured Man
Don Williams as the 1st Elder
Stanley Walsh as the 2nd Elder
John Moore as the 3rd Elder
Walter Gotell as Klemper

Martin Evans as Factotum
Peta Brookstone as the I.C.U. Nurse
Floyd "Red Crow" Westerman as Albert Hosteen
Nicholas Lea as Agent Alex Krycek
Lenno Britos as the Hispanic Man
Rebecca Toolan as Mrs. Mulder

With Mulder alive and the DAT *tape safely in Skinner's possession, Scully and Mulder are given clues by an elderly Nazi, Victor Klemper, that lead them to an abandoned mine containing filing cabinets full of medical information for an untold number of*

people — including Scully, Samantha and Mulder himself. But Skinner is ambushed by Krycek and his boys, and the DAT tape is stolen, leaving him nothing to bargain with Cigarette-Smoking Man for Scully and Mulder's jobs — until Skinner produces his trump card: Albert Hosteen and twenty other Navajo men have memorized the contents of the tape.

Memory, so beleaguered in the past two installments, finds retribution in this final episode. The guarded, mystical world of Navajo belief is used to good effect here with the reference to the Navajo "code-talkers"; their reliance on memorization, and mistrust of history. Albert Hosteen's moving soliloquy hammers in the on-going idea that the ever-threatened truth exists in memory as surely as it exists in hard evidence, or even as ephemera, traveling through our lives in bits and pieces, a jigsaw puzzle waiting to be assembled. There is Mrs. Mulder's memory, which is at war with the need of her son (in fact, Mrs. Mulder, the woman with no first name, is so afraid of her own memories in the fourth season's "Talitha Cumi" that they drive her into a coma.) There is Scully's suppressed memory and the hard evidence of her implant. There is the lost truth Bill Mulder was about to utter. Finally, there is the aggregated memory of the Navajo men who hold the key to our agents' survival. All these come together to form one of the more sophisticated sub-texts in this show, which is that no one is able to own their present without owning the past.

3.03 D.P.O.

ORIGINAL AIR DATE: October 6, 1995
WRITTEN BY: Howard Gordon
DIRECTED BY: Kim Manners
GUEST CAST: Mar Andersons as Jack Hammond
Giovanni Ribisi as Darren Oswald
Jack Black as Bart Liquori ("Zero")
Peter Anderson as Stan Buxton
Ernie Lively as Sherrif Teller
Karen Witter as Sharon Kiveat
Steve Makaj as Frank Kiveat
Kate Robbins as Darren's mom
Brent Chapman as the traffic cop
Jason Anthony Griffith as the first paramedic
Cavan Cunningham as the second paramedic
Bonnie Hay as the night nurse

Sleepy Connerville, Oklahoma, is the locus of a statistically implausible number of deaths by lightning: five people have died, the latest victim of weird weather blasted to death in a video arcade parking lot, just after an altercation with another teen, Darren Peter Oswald. Scully and Mulder discover that all the victims were connected to the angry and disaffected teen, himself the only living survivor of the recent lightning strikes, which leads Mulder to suspect that statistics have nothing to do with this case and that, in fact, Darren has become a kind of human lightning-rod, capable of directing the punishing power of Mother Nature at whomever he wishes.

Teenage frustration (and lust) finds a literal expression in the form of a greasy little lightning-rod called Darren. His dim-witted pal Zero, as well as his tyrannical hogging of arcade games, signal overtly that Darren is a loser who has loser friends — but did we have to get the back story on his awful home life to give us a *reason* for his angst? Wouldn't it have been better if they'd been like the Cleavers? Nice and clean and infuriatingly dull? But this is a minor problem. Darren, as a package, is scary — a deadly weapon wielded by an immature heart — and it is a tense showdown at the end because of this.

Coming as it does after the shocking revelations of the three-part extravaganza, "Anasazi," "The Blessing Way," and "Paperclip," this episode is oddly business-as-usual. Chris Carter has always maintained that stand-alone episodes are important and that they provide the fertile ground from which the "myth arc" episodes spring. But our agents seem a little too calm for people whose careers, families, and very lives have recently been under attack. The problem, however, is one of timing, and D.P.O. would look like the interesting, well-acted episode it is if it had appeared several episodes later in the season.

3.04 Clyde Bruckman's Final Repose

ORIGINAL AIR DATE: October 13, 1995
WRITTEN BY: Darin Morgan
DIRECTED BY: David Nutter
GUEST CAST: Peter Boyle as Clyde Bruckman
           Ken Roberts as the clerk
           Stu Charno as Puppet
           Karin Konoval as Zelma
           Frank Cassini as Cline
           Dwight McFee as Havez
           Jaap Broeker as the Stupendous Yappi
           David MacKay as the young husband
           Doris Rands as Mrs. Lowe
           Alex Diakun as the tarot dealer
           Greg Anderson as the photographer

"Why am I committing these terrible murders?": this is the burning question for a harmless-looking little man in Minneapolis / St. Paul who visits fortune tellers and, when they cannot answer his question, kills them. Local law enforcement is hanging on the every word of The Stupendous Yappi, a [SIC]tv psychic, while Mulder harries a witness who he thinks may be genuinely psychic, but the depressed Clyde Bruckman finally proves that he is, indeed, psychic, but only in one way: he can foretell the manner of anyone's death.

A profound, depthful, miserable script with the brilliant Darin Morgan's patented charm all over it, "Clyde Bruckman's Final Repose" is a beauty right down to the title. Peter Boyle seemed put on earth to play this character — but then it seems that way no matter what the character. It's just a good actor at work. The leads, too, seem to cohere and find a more subtle approach with such good writing and good company. Anderson's "pillow talk" scene with Bruckman is a moment of sweetness we rarely see (because Scully is rarely near a sweet person, frankly). Of his two apparently impossible "prophesies," (one about love, the other about death) one comes true, leaving us desperate

to know the validity of the other — especially in light of the revelations in the fourth season.

As usual, Morgan takes our expectations and reverses them. When we expect Mulder, we get The Stupendous Yappi, an absurd, posturing little television psychic, who sweeps dramatically into the room and spews useless clues as to the killer's motivation and appearance. In fact, Yappi's ridiculous behaviour is a kind of Vaudeville send-up of Mulder and his intuitive method. When we expect Scully to be a sourpuss, it is Mulder who is the biggest impediment to Yappi's radar. But the best creation here is Clyde himself. Named after a comedy writer/director who worked with Buster Keaton, and who committed suicide in 1955, Bruckman is a true pessimist. Whether this "gift" has made him a fatalist or not, Clyde Bruckman cannot see the future, as Mulder does, as a changeable thing; to him there is no point in trying to stop the unstoppable. This is a beautiful episode and, like most tragedies, it is all about the inevitable arrival of death.

3.05 The List

ORIGINAL AIR DATE: October 20, 1995
WRITTEN BY: Chris Carter
DIRECTED BY: Chris Carter
GUEST CAST: J.T. Walsh as Warden Brodeur
Denny Arnold as the key guard
Bruce Pinard as the executioner
Bokeem Woodbine as Sammom Roque
John Toles-Bey as John Speranza
Badja Djola as "Neech" Manley
April Grace as Danielle Manley
Greg Rogers as Daniel Charez
Don MacKay as Oates
Ken Foree as Parmelly
Mitch Kosterman as Fornier
Michael Andaluz as the tattooed prisoner
Paul Raskin as Ullrich
Craig Brunanski as the guard

Neech Manley is a formidable death-row inmate who with his last breath vows his revenge on the five people responsible for his suffering, and it appears he is true to his word when the maggot-ridden bodies begin to surface. The warden believes the killings are being carried out by prisoners, Scully believes there may be a conspiracy amongst the guards themselves, while Mulder theorizes Manley has indeed returned from the grave.

This is Chris Carter's return to directing. With "Duane Barry" as such a powerful debut, it's not too surprising "The List" does not measure up. Visually, it is one of the better episodes with its beautifully lit sequences and its conveyance of claustrophobia and powerlessness in the airless prison. Adding to the visual power of the episode, Anderson nicely conveys Scully's unease in the threatening setting of the prison after a disturbing encounter with a guard in the cell block. Her performance is more subtle but just as powerful as it was in "Beyond the Sea" as she impatiently waited to be released from the block. Anderson even makes a wry line about women getting lonely work.

Sadly, the story is lacking in suspense, in drama, and in resolution. Trite elements such as the corrupt warden who metes out justice in a series of beatings straight out of the prison-movies handbook only undermine the potential power of the story. Manley is killed off too early in the action for him to provide the menace required (despite a powerful cameo by Badja Djola). In fact, the entire exercise is frustrating rather than entertaining as the killings continue predictably but the agents never even come close to proving what has been happening. They even leave town before the last man on the list is dead. Apart from a moment of humor and another of warmth between the two agents, there is little here that compels the viewer to be engaged by any of the human tragedies played out in this rather cliché-ridden episode.

3.06 2Shy

ORIGINAL AIR DATE: November 3, 1995
WRITTEN BY: Jeffery Vlaming
DIRECTED BY: David Nutter
GUEST CAST: Randi Lynne as Lauren
Brad Wattum as the patrolman
James Hardy as Detective Cross
Catherine Paolone as Ellen
Glynis Davies as Monica
Suzy Joachim as Jennifer
Kerry Sandomirsky as Joanne
Beverly Elliot as Raven
Aloka McLean as Jesse
Dean McKensie as Lt. Blaine
William MacDonald as Agent Kazanjian
P. J. Prinsloo as Tagger
Jan Baily Mattia as the hooker
Lindsay Bourne as the hooker's john.

2Shy, we learn, is the online chat name of one Virgil Incanto — a seemingly reticent scholar and translator of classic Italian poetry (a predator and monster in the tradition of first season's Eugene Tooms), who feeds on the fatty tissues of his victims. The "gross-out factor" is high in this episode as Incanto (in a chilling performance by Timothy Carhart) regurgitates an acidic substance into the mouths of his victims in order to pre-digest the evening's repast. But he feeds on more than their bodies; he preys on their hearts and minds as he lures his overweight and insecure female victims with promises of romance and obscure 16th century love poetry.

This episode is Scully's for the most part, despite Mulder's usual leaps of intuition that not only connect this series of killings to a set in Aberdeen (which linked the victims to a Lonely Hearts column) but that also lead him to suppose the killer to be a "fat-sucking vampire." To flesh out the episode's theme, Scully finds herself exposed to the patronizing sexism of a local detective who questions, not only the suitability of a woman's involvement in such a case, but Scully's impartiality and even her medical credentials. The "boys club" in tedious gear. Despite Scully's "kick-ass" scene with Incanto (unfortunately telegraphed by a shot of Scully's abandoned gun) it is Ellen (Incanto's last "victim") who saves the agent's life in spite of her own injuries.

It's a suspenseful episode with not many light moments, although, in retrospect, Incanto's lack of interest in his skinny landlady does make one smile. Anderson's scene with Jesse, the landlady's blind daughter, is touching and personal and she illuminates Scully's burning hatred for the killer in the final scene where she demands an explanation from Incanto for his actions. His remorseless contempt for these women is patent even in his retort to the departing Scully.

3.07 The Walk

ORIGINAL AIR DATE: November 10, 1995
WRITTEN BY: John Shiban
DIRECTED BY: Rob Bowman
GUEST CAST: Deryl Hayes as Army Doctor
Don Thompson as Lt. Col. Stans
Beatrice Zeilinger as the burly nurse
Nancy Sorel as Capt. Draper
Thomas Kopache as Gen. Callahan
Williw Garson as Quinton "Roach" Freely
Ian Tracey as Sgt. "Rappo" Trimble
Rob Lee as the amputee
Pat Bermel as the therapist
Brennan Kotowich as Trevor Callahan
Andrea Barclay as Mrs. Callahan
Paul Dickson as the uniformed guard
Paula Shaw as the ward nurse
D. Harlan Cutshall as the guard

When Lt. Col. Victor Stans tries to commit suicide by immersing himself in nearly boiling water, he is thwarted by what he later claims is an invisible soldier, one who is the source of his misery and who will not let him escape the suffering of his life. Incredibly, Stans identifies Leonard "Rappo" Trimble, a man without arms or legs, as his tormentor — and Mulder agrees; Trimble is angry, at war with his own immobility, yearning so urgently for revenge that Mulder believes he has accomplished all of it through astral travel.

Here we see Scully's comfort with military personnel and her ability to summon a stern turn of phrase when needed. Once again, her theories are far more plausible than his, but who's counting? At least her character's consistency goes both ways: it is Scully, the doctor, who struggles to save the evil Trimble from his richly deserved fate, the horror of every moment played beautifully by Anderson as she watches, helpless to stop it.

The special effects in this episode have the unnerving quality of being just good enough to pass, so that you feel the scare despite yourself. The drowning of Captain Draper in the staff pool is at first clichéd and finally ferocious, while Trimble's bleeding stumps coupled with his barked demands for attention to them are just plain horrid. Centering on issues of military accountability, this tale of revenge does little to change Scully's or Mulder's life, apart from being yet another triumph of Mulder's world view over Scully's. It's a blip on the sophistication meter and could easily have been an episode of *The Outer Limits*.

3.08 Oubliette

ORIGINAL AIR DATE: November 17, 1995
WRITTEN BY: Charles Grant Craig
DIRECTED BY: Kim Manners
GUEST CAST: Michael Chieffo as John Wade
  Jewel Staite as Amy
  Tracey Ellis as Lucy Householder
  Ken Ryan as Banks
  Sidonie Boll as Mrs. Jacobs
  David Fredericks as the photographer

Alexa Mardon as Sadie
Dollie Scarr as the supervisor
Dean Wray as the tow truck driver
Jaques LaLonde as Henry

During the night shift at a Seattle diner, a burnt-out young waitress named Lucy Householder collapses on the floor behind the counter; simultaneously, across town, a teenage girl, Amy Jacobs, is kidnapped from her bedroom by a lone man. Scully and Mulder are called in when it is learned that Lucy was kidnapped as a teen and kept in a basement dungeon for years, possibly by the same man, and when Lucy begins to manifest the physical and emotional signs of Amy's experiences, Mulder suspects that they have found a true empath — and a way to find Amy.

This is a scary depiction of a ruined life. Tracy Ellis is perfect as the bombed-out Lucy. And could there be a more horrifying story of psychological sadism than what is depicted here? Charles Grant Craig, in his debut with *The X-Files*, outdid himself. Too bad he overlooked Scully in the process. In an otherwise solid plot, Scully's motivations are oddly lacking, as if someone forgot they were necessary. Her resistance to Mulder's theory is to be expected, but she is given no plausible alternative to stand behind. Anderson does her best, but Scully's suspicion of Lucy is kind of arbitrary. The blood evidence is simply baffling, nothing more, and, coupled with the presence of witnesses, would hardly lead the usually cautious Scully to any firm conclusion. Most perplexingly, when the two agents are administering CPR to the recently drowned Amy, Scully gives up after about 30 seconds and badgers Mulder to do the same, as if there weren't any point. However, there is good material in the two agents' debate over Mulder's interest in Lucy being based on his lost sister. For once, Mulder refuses to lean on his past in order to find a reason to care about his present. For a show that has based nearly *everything* on the past of its lead characters, it is refreshing to see this idea dismissed when it really isn't needed. The material is compelling enough on its own and is actually watered down by overtly tying it to a dimly remembered trauma.

Despite these difficulties for Scully's character, Oubliette continues the rich *X-Files* debate over the nature of human connection and the responsibility that comes with memory.

3.09 Nisei

ORIGINAL AIR DATE: November 24, 1995
WRITTEN BY: Chris Carter, Howard Gordon, Frank Spotnitz
DIRECTED BY: Rob Bowman
GUEST CAST: Yasuo Sakurai as Kazeo Takeo
Bruce Harwood as Byers
Dean Haglund as Langly
Tom Braidwood as Frohike
Corrine Koslo as Lottie Holloway
Gillian Barber as as Penny Northern
Roger Allford as the Harbourmaster
Paul McLean as the Coast Guard Officer
Lori Triolo as Diane
Raymond J. Barry as Senator Matheson

Brendan Beiser as Agent Comox
Robert Ito as Dr. Ishimaru
Warren Takeuchi as the Japanese Escort
Carrie Cain Sparks as the Train Station Clerk
Steven Williams as X
Bob Wilde as the limo driver

A videotaped "alien autopsy" is interrupted by the arrival of a military assault team and when the agents apprehend the video maker's Japanese murderer they come into possession of a briefcase containing satellite photos of a ship, the Talapus, and a list of Mutual UFO Network (MUFON) members. While Scully learns some shocking news about her abduction from the MUFON group, Mulder traces a train car that is being used by scientists who were once members of the Japanese Army's Unit 731, a group who, like their Nazi counterparts, performed deadly experiments on humans during World War II, and who are now, Mulder theorizes, trying to create an alien-human hybrid.

Mulder's purchase of an alien autopsy tape leads the agents into the labyrinth of another two-part "mythology" episode. But it is Scully that gets more than she bargained for when MUFON members claim to know her from her ab-duction. Carter's great gift is his ability to create an atmosphere of fear and paranoia against the backdrop of the ordinary. Here the Scully "arc" is propelled forward as the women show Scully they share not only the same neck implants as Scully found under her skin but, more ominously, an incurable cancer. It is just this juxtaposition of an unremarkable group of women in their suburban setting against their tales of abductions, experiments, and implants that works so well. Anderson's scene with the MUFON women is another example of the great work she and director David Nutter create together. Scully is uncharacteristically thrown off balance for the entire encounter as she is confronted by buried secrets of her "missing" days.

Mulder's apparent disinterest as Scully relates the tale of her encounter and the possibility that she, too, may share the medical fate of the MUFON women seems out of character but it fuels the perception of a growing distance between himself and Scully. The audience will have to wait a year before this seed of alienation between the agents fully bears fruit in "Never Again." The scene also plays out the debate between Scully's skepticism and need for proof. Scully's belief in science and in human conspiracies rather than alien ones, which was so beleaguered in the first two seasons, gets a boost in this episode when she recognizes one of the supposedly deceased scientists (Ishimaru) as one of her abductors. But this is nicely undercut in the next scene when she asks Agent Pendrell (whose obvious crush on Scully is delightful) if the implanted chip is "man-made."

3.10 731

ORIGINAL AIR DATE: December 1, 1995
WRITTEN BY: Frank Spotnitz
DIRECTED BY: Rob Bowman
GUEST CAST: Robert Ito as Dr. Zama
Steven Williams as X
Stephen McHattie as the Red-Haired Man

Brenden Beiser as Pendrell
Colin Cunningham as Escalante
Mike Puttonen as the Conductor
Don S. Williams as the Elder
Victoria Maxwell as Mother
Sean Campbell as the soldier

This episode opens with the shocking mass execution of what appear to be alien grays or, at least, badly deformed human beings at a seemingly abandoned leper colony in West Virginia. Mulder and Scully continue to work apart: Scully follows up on Pendrell's discovery that the chip implant has the ability to record and mimic (and perhaps monitor) the memory functions of the brain while Mulder is on the train tracking down Ishimaru / Zama and subsequently his killer, the Red-Haired Man who dispatched Sakurai in "Nisei."

The action on the train is tense but there are a few oddities in the plotting of this episode. Mulder enlists the help of a conductor who seems only there to facilitate a rescue of Mulder from the hands of the Red-Haired Man (well played by Stephen McHattie) and the entrapment the assassin and Mulder in the train car which is, inexplicably, wired with explosives. X mysteriously shows up in time to execute the Red-haired Man and rescue an unconscious Mulder, but *why*? We never discover what or who dies in the train explosion, but what's new, eh?

There are some great moments: Mulder may have solved the problem of losing his gun but how did he think he was going to jump onto a moving train and hold onto a cell phone? The ever cell-phone-dependent Mulder even gets a call on Red-Haired Man's phone! Pendrell's "doof!" line is a scream. Scully's frantic trip to Mulder's apartment where she pulls out all the stops in an effort to save Mulder's life contrasts sharply with Mulder's near-disregard for Scully's life in "Nisei."

The conclusion to this two-part episode leaves the audience, as always, with more questions than answers. But the questions are themselves intriguing. Who, if anyone, has told the truth, or even a half-truth? Scully's willingness to accept the Elder's explanation of events is not uncharacteristic, given her respect for "authority." One might wonder if she is being misled by a truth hidden between two lies. Whatever the case, there is an overwhelming sense that the agents are being pitted against one another by turning their own biases against themselves. Neither Scully's theories of experimentation on human subjects, nor Mulder's of alien-human hybridization, seem all-encompassing. But Scully seems to be left with the proof she needs of the human origin of her abduction.

3.11 Revelations

ORIGINAL AIR DATE: December 15, 1995
WRITTEN BY: Kim Newton
DIRECTED BY: David Nutter
GUEST CAST: R. Lee Ermey as Reverend Findley
Kenneth Welsh as Simon Gates
Nicole Robert as Mrs. Tynes
Kevin Zegers as Kevin Kryder

Michael Berryman as Owen Jarvis
Selina Williams as School Nurse
Hayley Tyson as Susan Kryder

Mulder and Scully protect a boy from a killer who has murdered 11 others, all of whom fraudulently claimed to be stigmatics. After the boy exhibits bleeding wounds from both his palms, Scully begins to see other signs that lead her to doubt the rational explanations that Mulder, for a change, is offering of events.

The episode is ripe for nit-picking, with some of its sharp plot turns based on the lamest of intuitive leaps by Scully, but there are some fun moments for Duchovny as the children in the shelter describe the kidnapper to Mulder and he teases Scully about her drawing Kevin's bath. Actor Kevin Zegers never quite convinces as a boy who witnesses his mother's death and is pursued by the fanatical Simon Gates. As a consequence, the killer, Gates, never really develops into the menace he ought to be. But there is some good work from the supporting cast, particularly the saintly Owen Jarvis (a name echoing that of Scully's guide Nurse Owens of "One Breath") played beautifully by Michael Berryman. There is something terribly affecting in the shot of Owens in his attic with the light streaming through his pink translucent ears as if there were a halo illuminating him from behind.

Anderson offers a moving performance throughout this episode as Scully, fresh from the revelations in "Nisei" and "731" of the all-too-human forces behind her abduction, now faces a test of her religious convictions. Her partnership with Mulder is also tested as she is met with his incredulous challenges, his obvious disdain for organized religion and his virtual dismissal of what she has seen. There is even a hint that he is suspicious of her motives when he questions whether or not she believes herself to have been "chosen" to protect the boy, Kevin. Anderson also does a lovely job as Scully exposes herself to Mulder's ridicule and suspicions when she makes the first outright statement of religious faith we've heard from her. Writer Kim Newton, director David Nutter and the actress create a rare moment of insight into Scully in the closing scene, as she confides in a priest, and not in her partner, her doubts in what she saw, in what she believes, and her fear that God may be speaking but, perhaps no one is listening. The scene could have been trite but with Anderson's skill it is poignant and heart-felt and serves to develop an aspect of Scully's character we have only glimpsed in past episodes.

3.12 War of the Coprophages

ORIGINAL AIR DATE: January 5, 1996
WRITTEN BY: Darin Morgan
DIRECTED BY: Kim Manners
GUEST CAST: Alex Bruhanski as Dr. Bugger
Raye Birk as Dr. Eckerle
Dion Anderson as Sheriff Frass
Bill Dow as Dr. Newton
Alan Buckley as the "Dude"
Tyler Labine as the "Stoner"
Nicole Parker as the "Chick"
Wren Robertz as the orderly

Bobbie Phillips as Bambi
Tony Marr as the motel manager
Norma Wick as the reporter
Tom Heaton as Resident #1
Bobby Stewart as Resident #2
Ken Kramer as Dr. Inanov

It is the weekend: while Scully relaxes and watches TV, eats ice cream, washes her dog with "Die Flea, Die" shampoo, or cleans her gun, Mulder visits Miller's Grove, a known UFO hot spot where victim after victim falls to killer roaches — but all is not as exotic as it seems — even to the audience. Mulder calls his partner each time the death toll rises and she calmly de-mystifies each case, predicting he will find evidence (and he does) of a natural death — that is, until Mulder hitches up with the brainy and pneumatic Dr. Bambi Berenbaum, and then even Scully begins to suspect an invasion.

Perhaps one of the most truly comic of all, this episode uses the tired "Scully squashes Mulder's theory" gambit against itself. For once, the action is firmly from Scully's world perspective, with each of Mulder's wild experiences bursting like a bubble on nothing. The king of inter-textual reference, Darin Morgan, has tipped his hat to Orson Welles here — the town's name is a reversal of *War of the World*'s Grover's Mill. It seems this Morgan makes a career out of reversing expectation. The idea of probes from space is a crock, and then it isn't. Mulder and Bambi look like a sure thing, and then they're not. Scully arrives in full macho stride, and then she's covered with dung. There is the moment when a hysterical crowd momentarily pauses to consider Scully's FBI badge and her call-to-order, and then they go right on freaking. Morgan plays it for laughs, whether you get the references or not.

A couple of worthy repeats here: the appearance of stoned teens (see "Deep Throat" and the later "Quagmire" for more close encounters with teen spirit) and Scully, disgusted with her fellow man and alone in an abandoned store, reaching down and pensively crunching a chocolate ball that looks like a bug, recalling her famous scene in "Humbug" where she really does pop a beetle in her mouth.

This episode also gives us another peek into the most bizarrely complex relationship on TV. It's a good touch to show the two agents' personal lives as dull and grounded in the ordinary, where the only entertainment may be sudden bursts of paranoia (Mulder's being bug-related and Scully's being Mulder-related). On top of suggesting these folks are dull like the rest of us, the writers here suggest they are babies, too, with Mulder's disappointment finding expression in telling Scully she smells (they are both covered with dung after a massive methane explosion), and Scully rubbing his nose in his own failure to get a date. They both look like angry five-year-olds.

3.13 Syzygy

ORIGINAL AIR DATE: January 26, 1996
WRITTEN BY: Chris Carter
DIRECTED BY: Kim Manners
GUEST CAST: Ryan Reynolds as Jay "Boom" DeBoom
Lisa Robin Kelly as Terri Roberts
Wendy Benson as Margi Kleinjan

Dana Wheeler-Nicholson as Det. Angela White
Richard Brown as the minister
Garry Davey as Bob Spitz
Denalda Williams as Zirinka
Russell Porter as Scott Williams
Gabrielle Miller as Brenda J. Summerfield
Tim Dixon as Dr. Richard Godfrey

The good people of Comity, a town whose very name means "mutual courtesy" are in a froth of paranoia over the possibility of satanic cults because three young men have died in as many months, the most recent hanged in the presence of two gum-chewing teens named Margi and Terri. Scully and Mulder must try to calm the situation, but no one is immune to the astrological mosh-pit they are in and the two agents begin to act in a way that makes Margi and Terri look like sober citizens.

Scully and Mulder literally enter the action here bitching at each other, Scully disgusted at chasing a load of poop and Mulder baiting her all the way, going for the jugular and suggesting that she is a boring FBI mouthpiece. Once again, the writers give us a rival for Scully in the person of Detective Angela White (get it, white angel?) Only this time Scully reacts the way the rhetoric of the situation demands, with fury, which is such a refreshing change from her usual tack. Even as Margi and Terri begin to look like brides of Dracula, the locals are marching around with weapons, and Scully is ominously irritable. The only one here who doesn't seem over-faced by his own temper (or libido) is Mulder. Instead, he merely lets his subconscious wander a bit farther out on the leash. What is so different here? He teases Scully endlessly? He embarrasses himself in public? He is a seriously twisted guy (see him make a highball without a glass in this one and you'll vow never to try it yourself!) The surprise here is Scully. It is a wink to fans who constantly bemoan the fact that Mulder always drives the car when the two agents rip into each other during their hilarious spat over who drives whom, who is a macho jerk, and who's too diminutive to take seriously. And look who's in the driver's seat in the last shot, practically airborne on the way out of town.

3.14 Grotesque

ORIGINAL AIR DATE: February 2, 1996
WRITTEN BY: Howard Gordon
DIRECTED BY: Kim Manners
GUEST CAST: Mitch Pileggi as Assistant Director Walter Skinner
Levani Outchaneichvili as John Mostow
Kurtwood Smith as Agent Bill Patterson
Greg Thirloway as Agent Nemhauser
Susan Bain as Agent Sheherlis
Zoran Vukelic as the model
John Milton Brandon as Aguirre
James McDonnell as the glass blower
Paul J. Anderson as the paramedic
Amanda O'Leary as the Doctor
Kasper Michaels as the young Agent

Agent Bill Patterson, head of Quantico's Investigative Support Unit and Mulder's former boss, and his partner Greg Nemhauser have spent the last three years getting inside the head of a serial killer who grotesquely mutilates his young male victims. When John Mostow is arrested in his studio filled with drawings of gargoyles and demons the hard work seems to have paid off, that is, until new a series of new murders begin, all bearing Mostow's signature mutilations.

Duchovny makes the most of this Mulder-centered story, showing us Mulder's gradual decline and growing exhaustion, and a peek into what could have been had he remained a profiler with the ISU. This story gives us a startling but not unexpected peek into the depth of Mulder's compulsive pursuit of truth. The intensity with which he pursues an extraterrestrial "truth" now, to an extent which frequently puts his and his partner's lives at risk, we see turned inward here as he follows Mostow into madness. Goaded by Patterson, despite the enmity between them, he soon adopts the very methods he first decried finding himself deep inside the violent mind and nightmares of the killer. The theme of demon possession serves only as a red herring to the theme of the greater demons we can summon from our own psyches. As with the best of *The X-Files* episodes, it is the human monster which is the most threatening.

Scully, for the most part, plays wet-nurse in this episode, worrying as Mulder moves closer to the edge of madness and confronting Patterson as to his motives for taunting Mulder into this investigative method. Her "casting" as sidekick in this episode rings false and is further reinforced by several shots of her with Nemhauser, Patterson's lackey.

"Grotesque," despite some cheesy tricks (Scully startled by a cat in Mostow's studio, and gargoyle make-up on the fleeing Patterson), is a rich visual treat with its blue lighting, labyrinthine chase scenes, evocative soundtrack and its claustrophobic and horrifying images of mutilation and madness.

3.15 Piper Maru

ORIGINAL AIR DATE: February 9, 1996
WRITTEN BY: Chris Carter, Frank Spotnitz
DIRECTED BY: Rob Bowman
GUEST CAST: Mitch Pileggi as Assistant Director Walter Skinner
Nicholas Lea as Alex Krycek
Lenno Britos as Hispanic Man
Joel Silverstone as the 1st Engineer
Ari Solomon as Gauthier
Darcy Laurie as the 2nd Engineer
Robbie Maieri as the WWII Pilot
Paul Batten as Dr. Seizer
Stephen L. Miller as Wayne Morgan
Kimberly Unger as Joan Gauthier
Robert Clothier as Commander Chris Johansen
Russell Ferrier as the medic
Richard Hersley as Capt. Kyle Sanford
Peter Scoular as the sick crewman
Jo Bates as Jeraldine Kallenchuk
Rochelle Greenwood as the waitress

Morris Panych as the Gray-haired Man
Tom Scholte as young Johansen
David Neale as the guard
Tegan Moss as young Dana
Christine Viner as young Melissa

In this two-part chapter of the "conspiracy arc" Mulder and Scully work separately to uncover the alien life-form that caused the severe radiation burns killing a ship full of French sailors who have limped into port from a spot in the Pacific Ocean (where the Talapus ["Nisei"] raised UFO wreckage). Scully learns from Skinner that the official investigation into her sister Melissa's death has been dropped but when Skinner makes good his promise to go over the facts again he is threatened and later shot.

We are treated to a new addition to *The X-Files* catalogue of aliens in this episode. This is not one of the grays nor one of the shape-shifters; it is a new life-form and it moves through a black, oily medium to produce an inky, cloudy look in the eyes of its host. It's an ingenious invention on the part of the special effects team. There are other visual treats particularly when Mulder travels to Hong Kong (in a thrilling sequence shot in exotic reds and blues) where he finds Krycek (can anyone kill this man?) selling off secrets from the lost DAT tape from "Paper Clip."

It is Scully's emotional journey that is the core of this episode. Scully's outrage is clear despite Skinner's assurances that he will personally go over the case. Pileggi and Anderson's scenes together are usually very satisfying and this scene is outstanding. Scully's anger is mixed with guilt but even more so with pain. The circumstances of her work and her relationship with Mulder have led to her sister's death and have now been the cause of its cover-up (this theme will be played out more fully in season four). When she visits one of her father's old navy friends, Commander Johansen, childhood memories return and Anderson gives us a poignant performance as she lets her mind drift back from the sight of two young girls playing to her own days of hopscotch with her sister. It's one of those rare personal moments for the character, prized by any Scully fan. Most importantly, Scully is finally given the opportunity to mourn the loss of Melissa.

3.16 Apocrypha

ORIGINAL AIR DATE: February 16, 1996
WRITTEN BY: Frank Spotnitz, Chris Carter
DIRECTED BY: Kim Manners
GUEST CAST: Mitch Pileggi as Assistant Director Walter Skinner
Nicholas Lea as Alex Krycek
Lenno Britos as Hispanic Man
Peter Scoular as the sick crewman
Craig Warkentoin as Young Cigarette-Smoking Man
Harrison R. Coe as 3rd Government Man
Richard Hersley as Capt. Kyle Sanford
Kevin McNulty as Agent Fuller
Sue Mathew as Agent Caleca
David Kaye as the Doctor

Brendan Beiser as Agent Pendrell
Francis Flanagan as the nurse
William B. Davis as Cigarette-Smoking Man
Bruce Harwood as Byers
Tom Braidwood as Frohike
Dean Haglund as Langly
Brian Levy as the Navy Doctor
John Neville as Well-Manicured Man
Don Williams as the 1st Elder
Stanley Walsh as the 2nd Elder
Martin Evans as Major Domo
Eric Breker as the ambulance driver
Jeff Chivers as armed man #1

Skinner, in the hospital, tells Scully that he knows the man who shot him is the same man who, along with Krycek, beat him and stole the DAT tape and Scully further determines that this man is also the man who shot her sister Melissa, one Luis Cardinal. Mulder tracks the escaped Alien-Krycek to an abandoned North Dakota missile silo too late to see the UFO stored there by Cigarette-Smoking Man, and too late to witness Krycek buried alive, screaming unheard in silo 1013.

"Apocrypha" opens with one of the best teasers of the series. Set in 1953, it's a glimpse into how far back the conspiracy reaches both in terms of time and personalities. It's apparently early days for Cigarette-Smoking Man and Bill Mulder, at least, is still an innocent. The Lone Gunmen return in an oddly charming sequence at an ice rink (apparently inspired by Bruce Harwood's real-life skating skills).

The bad guys seem to be winning many rounds here. Mulder, foolishly, is tricked by Well-Manicured Man. But Scully is the real hero here and Anderson is great as she tears off down the street after Skinner's would-be assassin, catches and confronts him shouting and repeatedly demanding he identify himself. She is by-the-book but right on the edge.

The episode closes with one of the most gruesome scenes of the series as Krycek vomits up the homesick alien (some broadcasters even cut parts of this scene believing that the sight of the black alien oozing from Krycek's eyes might be a bit harsh for some of its viewers). But never fear, the weasel who will never die will be back in season four!

3.17 Pusher

ORIGINAL AIR DATE: February 23, 1996
WRITTEN BY: Vince Gilligan
DIRECTED BY: Rob Bowman
GUEST CAST: Mitch Pileggi as Assistant Director Walter Skinner
Robert Wisden as Pusher (Robert Modell)
Vic Polizos as Agent Frank Burst
Steve Bacic as Agent Collins
D. Neil Mark as Deputy Scott Kerber
Julia Arkos as Holly
Don MacKay as the Judge

Meredith Bain-Woodward as Defense Attorney Brent
J.D. Sheppard as the Prosecutor
Darren Lucas as Lead SWAT Cop
Roger R. Cross as SWAT Lieutenant
Janyse Jaud as the nurse
Ernie Foot as the lobby guard
Henry Watson as the baliff

Mulder and Scully are called in by Agent Frank Burst to assist in the apprehension of the self-confessed killer of 14 people whose deaths had been thought to be suicides. The killer, one Robert Patrick Modell, who calls himself Pusher, uses the suggestive power of his voice to command his victims to kill themselves and has begun a deadly cat-and-mouse game with the FBI.

This episode contains some of the best writing and acting of the series. Mulder's taunting of Modell in the courthouse is witty and fun, and it is the natural invitation to Modell who soon becomes intrigued with Mulder as a "worthy adversary." The scene at the firing range is a luxuriously long opportunity for characterization as Mulder and Scully, agreeing on the who, debate the how of Modell's power. It's a rare and welcome chance to witness the sophistication of this pairing at its prime.

The episode is rich with details for the observant: Pusher (not immune himself to the suggestive power of Musak) ironically hums "Misty" in the teaser, the supermarket tabloid with its inside joke headlines is a favorite ploy of the production team, even the placement of three bullets and two spent shells on the floor of the MRI room heralds the game of Russian roulette. The final confrontation is a *tour de force* sequence of close-ups and sparse dialogue. Robert Wisden, another strong Canadian actor, is mesmerizing as the angry and determined Modell, Duchovny's helpless Mulder is heartbreaking as he turns the gun on Scully, and Anderson shines as Scully's courage and horror vibrate in a taut balance.

3.18 Teso Dos Bichos

ORIGINAL AIR DATE: March 8, 1996
WRITTEN BY: John Shiban
DIRECTED BY: Kim Manners
GUEST CAST: Gordon Tootoosis as Shaman
Vic Trevino as Bilac
Alan Robertson as Roosevelt
Ron Sauve as Mr. Decker
Tom McBeath as Dr. Lewton
Janne Mortil as Mona Wustner
Garrison Chrisjohn as Dr. Winters

When the ceremonial remains of an Ecuadorian woman shaman are transported to a Boston museum, archeologists and museum staff begin to get picked off, leaving nothing but bloody drag marks leading to museum air vents — naturally Mulder speculates that the shaman's curse is being fulfilled. The much-less-easily stupefied Scully suspects Antonio Bilac, overseer of the archeological expedition and a drug-addled, anti-cultural appropriation activist, but, sadly, Bilac turns out to be a ruse (and dinner!) and the agents must follow those big bloody arrows into the air vents and down into the museum basement.

As if to remind us that even intellect must rest once in a while, this wretched and disappointing episode takes a seat at the bottom of the ladder alongside other losers like "Space" and "The Jersey Devil." Riddled with clichés and skirting a serious problem with cultural stereotyping (those South Americans are soooo primitive, huh?), this show is also shot so dark it is periodically pointless to watch.

The notion that anyone without a weird phobia could be scared by a bunch of cats is perplexing. Similarly, the idea that these yowling vermin could take out a human (maddened by some ghostie into a vengeful hunt for humans or not) is *preposterous.* Ever seen cats do anything but ignore each other? But all of it seems like a good idea when compared to the final shot featuring Gordon Tootoosis (the versatile and busy Canadian actor) getting all-too-feline. You might care when Scully's face is lacerated by a seemingly levitating cat, if you couldn't basically see the arm attached to the puppet. Anderson and Duchovny escape from this episode with their dignity clawed to bits, but intact, and this is probably due to the solemn acting style the two have developed. Sadly, the cynical use of serious subjects, like the theft of cultural artifacts from poor countries powerless to stop it, transforms this episode from one that is merely silly, to one sporting a really ugly blemish.

3.19 Hell Money

ORIGINAL AIR DATE: March 29, 1996
WRITTEN BY: Jeff Vlaming
DIRECTED BY: Tucker Gates
GUEST CAST: B.D. Wong as Detective Chao
Michael Yama as Hsin
Graham Shiels as the Night Watchman
Doug Abrahams as Lt. Neary
Lucy Liu as Kim
Stephen Chang as the Large Man
Donald Fong as the Vase Man
Paul Wong as the Wiry Man
Dina Ha as Dr. Wu
James Hong as the Hard-Faced Man
Ed Hong-Louie as the Money Man

In San Francisco's bustling Chinatown, recent immigrants are playing a high stakes lottery: to the winners, a huge cash prize, to the losers, surgical removal of an organ; so far, nobody has won. As the investigation progresses, Scully begins to wonder if the detective in charge is telling them everything, and when they meet Hsin Shuyang (a man with a desperately sick daughter and recently missing an eye) the detective's cover story begins to disintegrate.

Yet another xenophobic episode centering on the scary superstitions of other cultures (see: "Shapes," "Fresh Bones," "The Calusari," "Teso Dos Bichos," "Teliko," "El Mundo Gira," or "Kaddish" for more delving into fear of the "other"). But then, *The X-Files* are multiply phobic, so why leave the *xenos* out of it — especially when the word translates from the Greek as "alien," "strange," or "guest." In this case, Chinatown stands as the urban equivalent of Mars, with the two FBI agents virtually lost without Detective Chow as their guide. It manages to be genuinely unnerving, too. The frightful effect of seeing a man burned alive in a crematorium, or a frog struggle from the body cavity of Scully's most recent autopsy subject, go a long way to balancing out the silliness of a bunch of guys in "ghost" masks scurrying into a dark graveyard.

And the caliber of the acting in this one helps, too. B.D. Wong is perfect as the dreamy Detective Glen Chao, a young American caught between two worlds, and the famous James Hong lends a forceful presence here as the Asian version of Cigarette-Smoking Man. (Another example of referential casting here: Hong is known for, among other things, his role as the genetic engineer of *Blade Runner* fame; "I only do eyes!") But the most moving element here (as a sub-plot to Scully and Mulder's investigation) is Hsin as the worried, literally self-sacrificing father, convinced there is only one way to help his daughter in this new world. Despite the horror, this is one of the only positive images of parenting you will see in *The X-Files*.

3.20 Jose Chung's "From Outer Space"

ORIGINAL AIR DATE: April 12, 1996
WRITTEN BY: Darin Morgan
DIRECTED BY: Rob Bowman
GUEST CAST: Charles Nelson Reilly as Jose Chung
William Lucking as Roky
Jason Gaffney as Harold
Sarah Sawatsky as Chrissy
Jesse Venture as 1st Man in Black
Larry Musser as Detective Manners
Alex Diakun as Dr. Fingers
Terry Arrowsmith as Air Force Man
Andrew Turner as CIA Man
Mina Mina as Dr. Hand
Allan Zinyk as Blaine
Michael Dobson as Lt. Schaeffer
Jaap Broeker as Yappi

At its core this story seems to be about two Air Force pilots, dressed as grey aliens, who kidnap a young couple (who have witnessed the flight of an experimental plane) and take them back to base to be hypnotized into believing they've been abducted by aliens. The story is complicated by the abduction of the pilots and their captives by Lord Kinbote, ruler of the inner earth, and by the recurring appearance of the mysterious Men in Black. The telling of the tale, by a bemused Scully to writer Jose Chung, is further complicated by the levels of narrative and narrators each with their own agendas and recollections of events.

Writer Darin Morgan's fourth offering is a delightful maze of tales within tales. This send-up of UFO abduction lore is hilarious, filled with inside jokes, references to sci-fi films and pop culture as well as references to Morgan's own interests in Harold Lloyd, Ray Harryhausen and Vladimir Nabokov. The appearance of game-show host Alex Trebek is a wink to the audience members who saw Duchovny's appearance on *Celebrity Jeopardy*. The appearance of Charles Nelson Reilly as Jose Chung is an example of genius casting rivaling Peter Boyle's appearance in "Clyde Bruckman's Final Repose."

Anderson and Duchovny are priceless in self-parody from Scully's appearance in her own "Alien Autopsy" styled video (her own worst dream come true!) to, easily one of the best scenes, Mulder's pie-eating interrogation of a disinterested diner cook (a nod to *Twin Peaks'* Agent Dale Cooper). The editing is brilliant in this episode as stories move seamlessly between storytellers. Finally, the episode is really an examination of the untrustworthy and subjective nature of truth, memory and recollection and, as with "Clyde Bruckman's Final Repose," the episode ends with Chung's final thoughts on human loneliness.

3.21 Avatar

ORIGINAL AIR DATE: April 26, 1996
STORY BY: David Duchovny, Howard Gordon
TELEPLAY BY: Howard Gordon
DIRECTED BY: James Charleston
GUEST CAST: Mitch Pileggi as Assistant Director Walter Skinner
Tasha Simms as Jay Cassal
Amanda Tapping as Carina Sayles
Bethoe Shirkoff as Old Woman
Tom Mason as Detective Waltos
Cal Traversy as the Young Detective
Stacy Grant as Judy Fairly
Janie Woods-Morris as Lorraine Kelleher
Jennifer Hetrick as Sharon Skinner
Malcolm Stewart as Agent Bonnecaze
Brendan Beiser as Dr. Rick Newton
William B. Davis as Cigarette-Smoking Man
Michael David Simms as Senior Agent
Morris Paynch as the Gray-Haired Man

In order to drown his sorrows over an impending divorce, Walter Skinner goes to a hotel bar, where he meets a beautiful young woman and, after a few drinks, they go up to a room together. But when Skinner awakes (after dreadful dreams featuring an old woman) he finds the young woman beside him in bed, very dead.

Our first glimpse into the life of Assistant Director Walter Skinner, the beefy enigma who acts as Scully's and Mulder's boss, is a surprisingly bleak one. He's a tough guy with some big problems.

This is a poor vehicle for the versatile Mitch Pileggi and only deepens the enigma surrounding Skinner. Although the spirit being that visits Skinner seems at first to be a succubus (a highly sexualized monster of the dream world) her role is to protect, and so she most closely resembles the Irish "banshee" — hence the ear-piercing shriek she makes when Skinner is in danger of being caught napping. The conspiracy seems to loom over Skinner, especially when he is on unstable personal ground, suggesting that he is a good guy, deep in enemy territory. This recalls one to earlier cryptic comments (in "F. Emasculata") that he straddles an invisible boundary his two agents barely seem to know exists. But somehow, we come out of a knowledge of Skinner's personal life, his professional dangers, and even his dreams, with only more questions. One gets the feeling that this is because the writers haven't quite worked out who this guy is or where he stands in relation to the overlying conspiracy (all of which is used to advantage later in "Zero Sum.")

3.22 Quagmire

ORIGINAL AIR DATE: May 3, 1996
WRITTEN BY: Kim Newton
DIRECTED BY: Kim Manners
GUEST CAST: Timothy Webber as Dr. Farraday
Peter Hanlon as Dr. Bailey
Murray Lowry as the fisherman
R. Nelson Brown as Ansel Bray
Mark Acheson as Ted
Chris Ellis as the Sheriff
Nicole Parker as the chick
Terrance Leigh as the Snorkel Dude

Something in vacationland, Georgia, is eating people, picking them off the beaches and docks, leaving the occasional bloodied boot or severed torso as a calling card, and Mulder immediately assumes it is "Big Blue," a mythical (and very lucrative) creature supposed to be living in the lake. Big Blue, says Mulder, has run out of frogs and has turned to hunting bigger game; Big Blue, says Scully, is a crock — instead, there is a serial killer out there.

They had to do it, a Loch Ness Monster episode. Not surprisingly, Mulder had to literally drag Scully and her little pooch, Queequeg, into this one. For a pure study of the relationship between Scully and Mulder, this episode is packed, from his tyrannical demands on her free time to her fatigued disinterest in his theories. The friction between them is on a par with the bitch-fest in "Syzygy," with Scully disgusted at how low Mulder will stoop to find something paranormal in a case. But when Scully's beloved Queequeg gets snapped up, right under her nose during evening walkies, we see Scully, faced with the biggest load of hooey in the world, begin to wonder what the heck. (Note, too, that the re-appearance of the little man-eating dog from "Clyde Bruckman's Final Repose" is no mistake.) Finally, there is Scully's funny, unflinching dissection of Mulder's personality as they sit stranded on a rock in the middle of the lake. She likens him to the brutish Captain Ahab of *Moby Dick* fame, and seems indifferent to his squirming and his wounded pride. It's like she is just starting to realize how irritating Mulder can be, and she enumerates his perversions in a bemused, almost awed manner. This scene was rumored to be, in large part, the work of Darin Morgan and must be a reference to Buster Keaton's "The Boat" which has a similar punch-line.

The creepy, boggy atmosphere of this episode sets off an intriguing mystery which, in the end, resolves in a cornball way (the last shot should have been flicked off the film like the schmutz it is), but overall there is a charming humor here. It is as if *The X-Files* team have reached a place of comfortable strength, where they know they can tackle horrible clichés and get away with it.

3.23 Wetwired

ORIGINAL AIR DATE: May 10, 1996
WRITTEN BY: Mat Beck
DIRECTED BY: Rob Bowman
GUEST CAST: Mitch Pileggi as Assistant Director Walter Skinner
William B. Davis as Cigarette-Smoking Man
Bruce Harwood as Byers
Tom Braidwood as Frohike
Dean Haglund as Langly
Steven Williams as X
Sheila Larken as Margaret Scully
Linden Banks as Joseph Patnik
Zinaid Memisevic as the Cruel-Faced Man
Sandy Tucker as Mrs. Riddick
Colin Cunningham as Dr. Stroman

A late-night meeting with an anonymous tipster leads Mulder and Scully to Braddock Heights, Maryland, where Joseph Patnik's murder of his wife and four others is the latest case in a series of seemingly unmotivated homicides. Scully theorizes that violent television images are a factor in the murders when she and Mulder find a huge collection of video tapes at Patnik's house and, although Mulder is initially unconvinced of the connection, he soon discovers that someone has been brain-washing victims with a video trapping device located in the outside cable box.

Scully's secret fear of betrayal by Mulder strikes something of a false note especially after their intimate and quirky conversation in "Quagmire." But we do see that once again Mulder's focus has blinded him to his partner's increasingly odd behaviour. Anderson does a great job depicting Scully's rapid disintegration from sullen suspicion to animal self-protection and her final confrontation with Mulder at gun-point ending with her tearful collapse in her mother's arms. We are also treated to nice work from Duchovny when he has to identify a body he fears may be Scully's.

Written by special-effects producer Mat Beck, this episode features the original and clever visual effect of having the brain-washed victim see the world as a poorly broadcast TV signal. An equally inventive auditory effect will be put to use in the fourth season's "Demons" to track the course of Mulder's downward spiral. The final scene is a beautifully crafted piece of symmetry as Mulder falsely reports to Skinner that the assassin's identity remains unknown, and X reports to Cigarette-Smoking Man (a neat surprise for fans) that Mulder's source also remains unknown. A parallel is also drawn between Cigarette-Smoking Man and Skinner as men who hold a line they are certain their subordinates disregard.

3.24 Talitha Cumi

ORIGINAL AIR DATE: May 17, 1996
TELEPLAY BY: Chris Carter
STORY BY: David Duchovny, Chris Carter
DIRECTED BY: R.W. Goodwin
GUEST CAST: Hrothgar Mathews as Galen
Roy Thinnes as Jeremiah Smith
Angelo Vacco as the door man
Stephen Dimopoulos as the detective
Mitch Pileggi as Assistant Director Walter Skinner
William B. Davis as Cigarette-Smoking Man
Steven Williams as X
Bonnie Hay as the Night Nurse
Brian Barry as the Last Man
Ross Clarke as Pleasant Man

Scully and Mulder are called in to investigate a fast-food restaurant shooting and are surprised to find no wounded and only tales, from the victims and the shooter, of a man (played by Roy Thinnes in a neat piece of casting) who healed them with the touch of his hand. The man, who inexplicably disappears from the scene, turns out to be Jeremiah Smith, a shape-shifting alien, no longer loyal to the goals of "The Project," whose healing skills are needed by Mrs. Mulder who has had a stroke after a confrontation with Cigarette-Smoking Man.

"Talitha Cumi," despite Mulder's race against time to save his mother's life and despite the PALM/LAMP puzzle is not a particularly tense season-ender. Duchovny does get some juicy scenes to play and he's up to the challenge. His breakdown at his mother's bedside is affecting. His chance to rough up the ever-smug Cigarette-Smoking Man is gratifying even though he doesn't give Mulder the satisfaction of a good fight. But a good fight is *exactly* what he gets from a clearly terrified X who is desperate to get his hands on the stiletto weapon — this is another in a series of wonderful scenes between Duchovny and Steven Williams. Williams has a knack for presenting a good street fight and the two actors get down and dirty in a brawl that they, for the most part, choreographed themselves.

There are plenty of references in this episode for the observant: both obscure and pop. The captive Smith (restrained as Lechter was in *Silence of the Lambs*) and Cigarette-Smoking Man square off in a debate on good and evil, in a scene inspired by Dostoevsky's *Grand Inquisitor*. All the Jeremiah Smiths, working for the Social Security Administration, could be a reference to the film *Buckaroo Banzai*, in which all the aliens work for the government and are called John: John Smallberries, John Yaya, John Bigbouteille. Roy Thinnes (neatly cast as Jeremiah Smith after a chance meeting with Duchovny aboard a plane) was the star of a 60s TV show called *The Invaders*, in which his character was ridiculed for his warnings that aliens were already here trying to take over the Earth.

In "Talitha Cumi" we get a familiar theme: we must look to the past for the secrets that reveal the truths of today. There are shocking implications to the confrontation between Cigarette-Smoking Man and Mrs. Mulder, at the old Mulder family summer house on Rhode Island. Cigarette-Smoking Man's assertion that he was better than her husband at many things besides water skiing (a reference to Davis's real-life championship level prowess in the sport) suggests a deeper relationship than friendship once existed and perhaps, by extension, one of her children's parentage may be in question.

Scully has little to do in this episode and will have even less to do in the follow-up episode "Herrenvolk." Yet one cannot fail to observe the irony that Cigarette-Smoking Man is dying of lung cancer (at least for a short time) in light of the revelations of the season to come.

SEASON FOUR (1996–1997)

4.01 Herrenvolk

ORIGINAL AIR DATE: October 4, 1996
WRITTEN BY: Chris Carter
DIRECTED BY: R.W. Goodwin
GUEST CAST: Roy Thinnes as Jeremiah Smith
　　　　　　Mitch Pileggi as Assistant Director Walter Skinner
　　　　　　William B. Davis as Cigarette-Smoking Man
　　　　　　Steven Williams as X
　　　　　　Brian Thompson as the Bounty Hunter
　　　　　　Garvin Cross as the repairman
　　　　　　Don Williams as The Elder
　　　　　　Morris Panych as Grey-Haired Man
　　　　　　Rebecca Toolan as Mrs. Mulder
　　　　　　Brendan Beiser as Agent Pendrell

On the run from the shape-shifting Bounty Hunter/Pilot, Jeremiah Smith (eager to expose and undermine "The Project") takes Mulder to an Alberta farm whose flowers and lethal bees are tended by drone-like cloned children (the girls are identical to Samantha at the age she was abducted). Scully, with the help of Agent Pendrell, uncovers definitive proof, in Smith's computer files, of a government conspiracy to inventory the population with a protein molecule "marker" using the small pox eradication project (SEP) as a cover. X is executed by the Consortium after he is exposed as a traitor and Cigarette-Smoking Man lives up to his tender feelings, and convinces the Pilot to heal Mulder's mother.

The fourth season begins as it means to go on, with Mulder in singular pursuit of his own truth. For the most part it is a fairly satisfying beginning to the season despite the incomprehensible significance of the bees story-line. What the bees are meant to do, and why, we never discover. Scully, who is literally abandoned by Mulder, finds a renewed faith in science as she deciphers the coding in Jeremiah Smith's records from the Social Insurance Administration.

In fact, she sounds a little like her paranoid partner as she explains to Skinner the breadth and depth of a conspiracy needed to pull off the kind of inventory she is describing.

The true surprise of this two part story is played out by Cigarette-Smoking Man, who we see tenderly holding the hand of the comatose Mrs. Mulder (who still has no first name — wouldn't it have been a shocker to hear it from Cigarette-Smoking Man's lips). William B. Davis has come a long way from his silent, but nonetheless powerful, presence in the series' pilot. He exposes a compassion never before suspected in Cigarette-Smoking Man and Davis looks like a kid (nearly) caught with his hand in the cookie jar when the Elder walks in on him at Mrs. Mulder's bedside.

If Cigarette-Smoking Man's humanity is a surprise, then X's execution is a shock. His is one of the many losses mourned by the audience. But one must hand it to Carter and Co., they are not afraid to break the rules. Unfortunately Williams' departure ushers in the arrival of Marita Covarrubius, the Assistant to the Special Representative to the Secretary General, and Mulder's new mole. Not much of a trade, to be sure. But the episode ends with a lovely piece of emoting from Duchovny, the master of the small moment and the small gesture, as he gives us a forlorn Mulder, nearly hopeless after a month of strain, sorrow, and searching.

4.02 Unruhe

ORIGINAL AIR DATE: October 27, 1996
WRITTEN BY: Vince Gilligan
DIRECTED BY: Rob Bowman
GUEST CAST: Pruitt Taylor Vince as Gerry Schnauz
Scott Heindl as the boyfriend
Sharon Alexander as Mary LeFante
Walter Marsh as the druggist
William MacDonald as Officer Trott
Ron Chartier as Inspector Puett
Michele Melland as the doctor
Angela Donahue as Alice

Scully and Mulder's mutual skills lead them to a killer, Gerry Schnauz, who not only gives his victims a powerful sedative and a home-lobotomy, but who seems to have the ability to impress his nightmarish thoughts on any photographic paper nearby — something that Mulder calls "psychic photography." But Schnauz believes he is doing his victims a favor by removing their "unruhe" (German for unrest), and the next person he intends to help is Scully.

A perfect balance of reason and intuition, this scary episode reasserts Scully and Mulder's very different abilities. We have seen Scully use her wits and courage to deal with a threat, but this is the first time in a while that Mulder's original vaunted "spookiness" has been in evidence. He sees "long legs" which brings Scully to focus on Schnauz (who at that moment is standing on stilts), and he sees headstones, which leads him to the cemetery where Scully is being held captive. Though the images themselves are a little Halloweenish, the salient visual clues seem to peek out at the viewer, so we recognize them just at the moment Mulder does. It is news (and very convenient) that Scully can speak German, but somehow we believe it. Her desperate attempt to communicate with the demented Gerry (played by the almost lovable Pruitt Taylor Vince in another inspired piece of casting) shows her versatility and courage. Despite Scully's final voice-over, where she muses about getting inside the head of a monster in order to survive, she could not have survived Schnauz's dementia alone. In the end, the writers seem to say, she needs Mulder's more ephemeral abilities to survive — reason, without intuition, can only postpone the inevitable.

4.03 Home

ORIGINAL AIR DATE: October 11, 1996
WRITTEN BY: Glen Morgan, James Wong
DIRECTED BY: Kim Manners
GUEST CAST: Tucker Smallwood as Sheriff Andy Taylor
Sebastian Spence as Deputy Barney Paster
Judith Maxie as Mrs. Barbara Taylor
Chris Norris as Edmund Peacock
John Trottier as George Peacock
Adrian Hughes as Sherman Peacock
Karin Konoval as the Peacock mother
Cory Frye as the batter
Neil Denis as the catcher
Douglas Smith as the pitcher

Home, Pennsylvania, a sleepy Mayberryish town where no one locks their doors and kids play baseball in a sunny sand lot — a wonderful place, except for the discovery of a hideously misshapen infant found buried under home plate. The Peacock clan are immediate suspects; hideously misshapen inbred boys who are still sore about the Civil War (in a grossly unfair but not uncommon attack on rural Southerners) and who have somehow produced a baby — but who is the mother?

An uproarious gross-out with broad strokes of horror-genre humour. There is even a tip of the hat to future issues of reproduction, motherhood, and filial duty thrown in, and all of it is focused on Scully. In particular, motherhood is the obsession here, with Mulder teasing his partner about her maternal instincts, suggesting she work on producing "UberScullys," and even speaking highly of his own pedigree (in his most coquettish scene this season). Even the ghastly Mrs. Peacock gives Scully a piece of her mind, though the implications of her rousing "anything for Mom" speech couldn't be more disgusting. (In fact, all this maternal foreshadowing must be deliberate and Scully may someday know the pride of producing good sons — look for the revelations in "Memento Mori" and all those boys called Kurt.)

Besides the solid additions to the "myth arc," good writing, and broad humor, this one is scary! The violence is almost over the top. The scene where the sheriff and his wife are killed would make Stephen King skip for joy, especially with Johnny Mathis' ironically optimistic "Wonderful" wailing in the background. When the camera dips low during the baseball game, we *know* there's something down there the kids haven't seen yet, and when Scully inspects the hideous child, the camera swings up high, as if in revulsion. But when the action gets too gross, the writers pull a joke out of the bag, like Scully's "Baa-ram-ewe" nonsense, or Mulder's recital of the *Wild Kingdom* hyena voice-over while the deputy gets shredded. It looks like a horror film — which tells you something about *The X-Files*. A strange mixed-bag that somehow works despite its prurience and full-tilt violence.

4.04 Teliko

ORIGINAL AIR DATE: October 18, 1996
WRITTEN BY: Howard Gordon
DIRECTED BY: James Charleston
GUEST CAST: Mitch Pileggi as Assistant Director Walter Skinner
Don Stewart as the businessman
Maxine Guess as the flight attendant
Willie Amakye as Samuel Aboah
Geoffrey Ayi-Bonte as Seat Mate
Bob Morrisey as Dr. Simon Bruin
Carl Lumbly as Marcus Duff
Brendan Beiser as Agent Pendrell
Dexter Bell as Alfred Kittel
Laurie Holden as Marita Covarrubias
Zakes Mokae as Diabria
Sean Campbell as Lt. Madsen

The Centers for Disease Control contact Scully to help them understand the recent death of an African-American male, the cause of death somehow related to a complete lack of pigmentation due to a draining of the pituitary gland. Four other missing persons cases have the same elements, all of which suggests an epidemic in the making.

Another in a series of "alien" (i.e. foreign) paranoia stories where the subtext is obvious: immigration allows horrid monsters into the country — luckily, and by necessity, they only victimize each other. Well, now we can all sleep, huh? What could be more terrifying, the writers seem to be suggesting, than a Black man with no pigment? Even Mr. Diabria, Minister for the African republic of Burkina Fasso (formerly Upper Volta) seems scared to death of the idea. Played with the usual grace and authority by Zakes Mokae, Diabria's ghost story is reminiscent of the stupid Wendigo story in "Shapes," a young boy somehow spared by a formerly human monster. The tale is told by a silky voice, in a shadowy room, within a shadowy episode. Light seems barely to enter. So, what are we to take from that? Light good: Dark bad?

You'd be justified in finding the premise of this story prurient and xenophobic, and the depiction of Africans as superstitious shadow-dwellers lazy and cheap. In all, Scully has little to do except save Mulder at the last second from a ravenous monster. One wonders what the monster wants with Mulder, anyway? Could the man *be* any whiter?

ORIGINAL AIR DATE: November 3, 1996
WRITTEN BY: Glen Morgan, James Wong
DIRECTED BY: Rob Bowman
GUEST CAST: Mitch Pileggi as Assistant Director Walter Skinner
Kristen Cloke as Melissa Riedal-Ephesian
Michael Dobson as BATF Agent
Michael Massee as Vernon Ephesian
Les Gallagher as the attorney
Doug Abrahams as Harbaugh
Donna White as the therapist
Anthony Harrison as Agent Riggins
Douglas Roy Dack as Mighty Man

The members of The Temple of the Seven Stars are arming for a confrontation with the "devil's army" and based on a phone tip, from a fellow named Sidney, Mulder and Scully are assisting in a joint FBI-ATF raid on the compound run by the charismatic Vernon Ephesian. Ostensibly there to follow up Ephesian's claims of "channeling" and "astral projection," Mulder finds himself strangely drawn to a field outside the compound where he discovers an old Civil War bunker in which Ephesian and his six wives are hiding and praying and preparing to commit suicide. When Melissa Ephesian (played with real depth by Kristen Cloke) is questioned, "Sidney" emerges and Scully's diagnosis of "multiple personalities" is countered by Mulder's assertion that Melissa is regressing to a "past life" — one which he will soon discover he shares.

This is the most sentimental of *The X-Files* stories to date and, for the most part, it is handled feelingly and shot beautifully. As a tragic love story the episode succeeds only to a point by evoking the memory of Sullivan Ballou, who wrote one of the best-known love letters of the Civil War to his wife Sarah. (Mulder learns from Melissa/Sarah that he was her lover, Sullivan Biddle, and a soldier who died in her arms.) But there are some rocky moments as well when he himself goes under and confirms that he was indeed Biddle, that Scully was his sergeant and that he, Scully, and Samantha have shared lives through the centuries. With Duchovny, less is always more and after Cloke's multicolored performance as Melissa/Sarah/Sidney/Lily, his own past-life regression to a Jewish mother in Nazi-occupied Poland and the soldier Sullivan Biddle falls a little flat. It is not only Duchovny who is trying too hard, though. The writers' heavy-handed personification of Cigarette-Smoking Man as a Gestapo officer and the simplistic assertion that evil will always return as evil undercuts the fragile connection between the two lovers, Biddle and Kavanaugh.

Morgan and Wong's scripts have always offered new possibilities for Mulder and Scully. In this tale Mulder plumbs new depths of single-mindedness. Scully doesn't miss a beat and calls him on it right from the outset, challenging him to admit to his selfish and wholly irresponsible quest for the truth of Sarah's story even at the expense of Melissa's life. Yet it is the ever-professional Scully who, searching for a Civil War period map that might show the location of more hidden bunkers, uncovers a county register and photographs that bear out Sarah's tale. Like the character, Paracelsus, in the Browning poem that frames this episode, Mulder, in his singular pursuit of truth, may fail in his quest, unable to recognize his connection to, or his responsibility for, others.

4.06 Sanguinarium

ORIGINAL AIR DATE: November 10, 1996
WRITTEN BY: Vivian Mayhew, Valerie Mayhew
DIRECTED BY: Kim Manners
GUEST CAST: O-Lan Jones as Nurse Rebecca Waite
Nancy J. Lilley as the liposuction patient
John Juliani as Dr. Harrison Lloyd
Andrew Arlie as Attorney
Arlene Mazerolle as Dr. Theresa Shannon
Celine Lockhart as the skin peel patient
Richard Beymer as Dr. Jack Franklin
Paul Raskin as Dr. Prabu Amanpour
Gregory Thirloway as Dr. Mitchell Kaplan
Nina Roman as Jill Holwagerm
Martin Evans as Dr. Hartman
Marie Stillin as Dr. Sally Sanford

A series of murders all committed by different doctors at the Aesthetic Surgery Unit in the Greenwood Hospital in Chicago wouldn't have come to the attention of our agents if not for the fact that the most recent killer claims "demonic possession" as his defense. Scully sensibly points to this man's drug addiction and high work load, but Mulder, as usual, pursues the outrageous claim and, as usual, he's right.

Beyond gross! There's a cross-hatching here of distrust of the almighty physician with a broad cynicism about plastic surgery — the wicked Dr. Franklyn standing in as the ultimate plastic-surgery junkie. The images of violence here (an unconscious man being literally stabbed to death with a liposuction probe; a woman's head bored clean through by a laser technician) are so over the top it's actually impressive. But Franklin levitating off his bed, or Nurse Waite rising out of a bathtub filled with some rude substance, just barely duck under the line of hilarity — perhaps in the tradition of slasher movies. Scully's better judgment is bypassed as per usual, and the two agents stumble two steps behind as the death toll rises like clockwork and images of witchcraft and Satanism jumble and mix together. In the end, this episode is the picture of a well-built wall falling on its face.

4.07 Musings of a Cigarette-Smoking Man

ORIGINAL AIR DATE: November 17, 1996
WRITTEN BY: Glen Morgan
DIRECTED BY: James Wong
GUEST CAST: William B. Davis as Cigarette-Smoking Man
Chris Owens as Young Cigarette-Smoking Man
Colin Lawrence as the troop leader
Dean Aylesworth as young Bill Mulder
Morgan Weisser as Lee Harvey Oswald
Anthony Ashbee as the Corporal
Donnelly Rhodes as General Francis
Peter Mele as the Mob Man

Dan Zukovic as Agent Man
Gonzalo Canton as Cuban Man
Steve Oatway as the Supervisor
David Fredericks as the Director
Peter Hanlon as the aid
Michael St. John Smith as the Major-General
Paul Jarrett as James Earl Ray
Laurie Murdoch as Lydon
Marc Baur as Matlock
Jude Zachary as Jones
Jerry Hardin as Deep Throat
Tom Braidwood as Frohike
Bruce Harwood as Byers

Hang on to your seats, folks, there's news. Most of the tragedies of the last 50 years can be attributed to one person: Cigarette-Smoking Man. In a pastiche of new footage and old episodes, with Frohike's voice-over, The X-Files team regale us with stories of the evil guy assassinating the Kennedys, Martin Luther King, orchestrating things for Nixon, and even (gasp) fixing the World Series.

Perhaps Cigarette-Smoking Man was behind the Oklahoma bombings, too. Because of the narrative peek-a-boo the writers play here, nothing is for sure. It could all be no more than the paranoid ravings of our favorite Lone Gunman (rumor has it that Morgan and Wong wanted to kill Frohike off, but Carter nixed the idea!). In fact, the episode is basically an ill-conceived joke. The only thing that is certain here, is that the writers of *The X-Files* believe that a character can be utterly evil and still have a wizened heart of sorts. And yet this mean-spirited episode doesn't accomplish much beyond applying a battering ram to Cigarette-Smoking Man mythos; his writing hopes are pegged on a hackneyed genre piece, sold to a publishing slimeball, and his hilariously peevish soliloquy (a satire of Forrest Gump's insipid "box of choc-o-luts" speech) seems to identify him with the disheartened, disappointed, and humiliated of the world. Where is our anti-hero now? As a man he is hollow, as a writer he is a hack, and as an evil force he has suddenly lost his mystery.

Never mind. Close your eyes and take a deep breath. It was all a bad dream.

4.08 Paper Hearts

ORIGINAL AIR DATE: December 15, 1996
WRITTEN BY: Vince Gilligan
DIRECTED BY: Rob Bowman
GUEST CAST: Mitch Pileggi as Assistant Director Skinner
Tom Noonan as John Lee Roch
Rebecca Toolan as Mrs. Mulder
Byrne Piven as Robert Sparks
Vanessa Morely as Samantha Mulder
Sonia Norris as the young mother
Carly McKillip as Caitlin Ross
Paul Bittante as the local cop
John Dadey as the local agent

A dream leads Mulder to the shallow grave containing the remains of a girl, the fourteenth victim of serial killer John Lee Roch (Mulder's profile was instrumental in Roch's capture) imprisoned for the murders of thirteen girls. When further clues from Mulder's dreams lead Mulder and Scully to a copy of Alice in Wonderland *containing the "trophy" cloth hearts Roch collected from the night-clothes of his victims, the agents are horrified to discover there are sixteen hearts and that Roch is asserting that one of them belongs to Mulder's missing sister, Samantha.*

Vince Gilligan gives us the most powerful episode in the Samantha story arc to date and he does so by casting doubt on the very foundation of Mulder's belief system. Mulder challenges the audience and Scully when he asks if we believe that Samantha was abducted by aliens. Scully's faith in Mulder has never rested in such a belief but Mulder's *raison d'être* has. It's a daring move by Carter to throw the foundation of the series into serious doubt and it's an ingenious opportunity to inject new life into the very basis of Mulder's quest.

Roch, played brilliantly by Tom Noonan, is one of the most monstrous sociopaths in *The X-Files* canon. Noonan is an accomplished writer and actor who is no stranger to the role of psycho-killer (he starred in Michael Mann's *Manhunter*). Noonan plays Roch completely unsympathetically and unsentimentally — one can hardly imagine a more horrifying human predator. His merciless and intricate mind game with Mulder (particularly when he sadistically offers to tell Mulder where Samantha is only if Mulder can identify which of the hearts is Samantha's) makes the issue of their "connection" irrelevant. "Mulder's choice" is replayed in the final scene of the episode with fatal results in a cruel and perfect symmetry. Roch's manifestation in Mulder's psyche as the playful red sprite (accompanied by Mark Snow's equally playful and childlike score) is inspired and makes this episode one of the best to date.

4.09 Tunguska

ORIGINAL AIR DATE: November 24, 1996
WRITTEN BY: Frank Spotnitz, Chris Carter
DIRECTED BY: Rob Bowman
GUEST CAST: Mitch Pileggi as Assistant Director Skinner
William B. Davis as Cigarette-Smoking Man
Nicholas Lea as Krycek
Campbell Lane as Committee Chairman
Fritz Weaver as Senator Sorenson
John Hainsworth as Gaunt Man
Olesky Shostak as Bundled Man
Jan Rubes as Vassily Peskow
Stefan Arngrim as the prisoner
Robin Mossley as Dr. Kingsley Looker
Brendan Beiser as Agent Pendrell
John Neville as Well-Manicured Man
Malcolm Stewart as Dr. Sacks
Jessica Schreier as Dr. Bonita Sayre
Brent Stait as Terry Edward Mayhew
Eileen Pedde as Angie
David Bloom as Stress Man

The globe-hopping action in this two-parter is framed by Scully's testimony before a Senate Select Subcommittee on Intelligence and Terrorism whose single purpose inexplicably seems to be to determine Mulder's whereabouts. Krycek returns with information that has the duo tracking the black-oil alien ("Piper Maru") from a NASA research laboratory to a prison camp in Russia where prisoners are being used as test subjects in experiments with the "black cancer" (as the prisoners call the black oil).

This first installment of a densely plotted, two-part conspiracy episode picks up where "Piper Maru" and "Apocrypha" left off. This episode brings the unexpected return of Krycek. Nicholas Lea does some of his best work in this episode as Krycek, the ultimate survivor, nervous, trapped, filled with anger, and thirsty for revenge. Mark Snow's piano heartbeat underlines the weight of Krycek's assertions that he can help expose the men behind the conspiracy, the men who hide behind the law in the name of national security. There is a great running bit of business throughout the episode as Kycek is punched, slapped, and generally abused or abandoned by everyone he encounters. Mulder is not above a bit of petty revenge, it seems. Even Skinner (who really *does* owe Krycek one) greets him with a sucker punch. (His shirtless appearance does much to justify Pileggi's reputation as one of the sexiest men in TV.)

Scully's testimony, or more properly, her refusal to testify, brings her in conflict with the very figures of authority her idealism would lead her to trust. This episode will mark a significant maturation in her relationship with authority and her own ideals. As Mulder presses forward to Russia in his efforts to expose the sinister powers at work behind the cover-up, Scully, for her part, wonders how far Mulder will go and how far she can follow. By the end of the episode the two are in separate prisons: Scully wrestling with her conscience but not with her unconditional loyalty to her partner; Mulder immobilized by a chicken-wire body cage (in a nightmarish sequence of Kafkaesque proportions), as test subject and unwilling host to one of the black-oil aliens.

4.10 Terma

ORIGINAL AIR DATE: December 1, 1996
WRITTEN BY: Frank Spotnitz, Chris Carter
DIRECTED BY: Rob Bowman
GUEST CAST: Mitch Pileggi as Assistant Director Skinner
William B. Davis as Cigarette-Smoking Man
Nicholas Lea as Krycek
Campbell Lane as Committee Chairman
Fritz Weaver as Senator Sorenson
John Hainsworth as Gaunt Man
Olesky Shostak as Bundled Man
Jan Rubes as Vassily Peskow
Stefan Arngrim as the prisoner
Robin Mossley as Dr. Kingsley Looker
Brendan Beiser as Agent Pendrell

John Neville as Well-Manicured Man
Malcolm Stewart as Dr. Sacks
Jessica Schreier as Dr. Bonita Sayre
Brent Stait as Terry Edward Mayhew
Eileen Pedde as Angie

Experiments, involving the black-oil alien, are being conducted on elderly patients in a Baton Rouge convalescent hospital under the auspices of Dr. Bonita Charne-Sayre, a virologist, small pox specialist, and house guest of Well-Manicured Man. An ex-KGB agent, Vassily Peskow, is summoned from retirement by "Comrade Arntzen" (none other than the ubiquitous Krycek) to prevent further exposure (by the now free Mulder) of the American counterparts to the Russian "black cancer" experiments.

Revelation follows upon revelation in the conclusion to "Tunguska." Unfortunately, not all of it crystal clear, nor easy to follow on the first viewing. Having seen the black-oil alien in "Apocrypha" as a cognizant being with a definite mission, a powerful survival instinct and a built-in lethal weapon, it is difficult to accept the notion that it can be controlled by either Russian or American scientists. Further, the concept that some version of this parasitic entity was used in the Gulf War as a weapon does not seem to be fully developed. Leaving aside the being's ability to kill others with a burst of radiation, how does Mulder, as test subject, escape the fate of the Gulf soldiers?

While Mulder does make his escape from Russia intact, Krycek is less fortunate when locals amputate his arm in a truly horrifying scene. It's one of the most terrifying turn of events in the series but it is quickly eclipsed by the bombshell that Krycek is a highly placed Russian spy who seems to have been orchestrating much of the action from the beginning. It's another amazing revelation from *The X-Files* writers.

Anderson gets a real chance to shine in this episode. Not only has she given us a portrayal of Scully as nervous, respectful, fearful, and awed, then powerful, rebellious, and determined in the face of a Congressional Subcommittee through small changes in her voice and her body language, but she makes credible Scully's final self-exposure. Scully has come a long way to bring her to the point where she can publicly proclaim the existence of extraterrestrials. Her moment in the sun is cut short by Mulder's return and grandstanding before Congress, but the scene plays well, and the agents' reunion is given real warmth by Duchovny and Anderson. We are also treated to another of those wonderful scenes between Pileggi and Anderson, this time a pivotal scene as Scully weighs her natural inclinations against the growing realization of how far up the ladder the corruption and conspiracy reaches.

Like many of the two-parters, "Tunguska" and "Terma" leave us with more questions than answers. The mission of the black-oil alien still remains a mystery. The Cold War seems alive and well and we get another peek into the power struggles within the Shadowy Syndicate. It is great fun to see Neville and Davis bring to life the apparent personal distaste Well-Manicured Man and Cigarette-Smoking Man have for each other. Some of Cigarette-Smoking Man's mystery may have been diminished with his first words but the dramatic possibilities opened way up. In the end, "Terma" is less Scully's Inquisition than it is Mulder's opportunity to publicly, and for the record, assert his belief in the existence of extraterrestrials. His claims are only as outlandish in this context as Galileo's seemed in his.

4.11 El Mundo Gira

ORIGINAL AIR DATE: January 12, 1997
WRITTEN BY: John Shiban
DIRECTED BY: Tucker Gates
GUEST CAST: Mitch Pileggi as Assistant Director Skinner
Ruben Blades as Conrad Lozano
Raymond Cruz as Eladio Buente
Pamela Díaz as Maria Dorantes
Jose Yenque as Soledad Buente
Lillian Hurst as Flakita
Susan Bain as the County Coroner
Robert Thurston as Dr. Larry Steen
Simi as Gabrielle Buente
Tina Amayo as the older shanty woman
Mike Kopsa as Rick Culver

A young Mexican boy, Eladio, who is on the hook for a girl's murder, seems to carry something more than guilt because everyone who crosses his path ends up rotted to death by a gray-green furry mold. As the agents close in on him, he is mutating into the dreaded "chupacabra," a mythical creature that just happens to look like a "gray" type alien.

This whopper gives "Teso Dos Bichos" a run for its baloney. Also set south of the U.S. border, it makes one wonder if there isn't something about the area that stupefies *The X-Files* writers. But at least the special effects here are stunning, the condition of the corpses getting worse as the boy gets sicker until, finally, a convenience store clerk becomes a gray, putrescent carpet on the polished tile floor — yuck! Scully and Mulder's differing motives for following the case (Scully because he is the logical suspect in a murder case; Mulder because the boy was present at a rare meteorological event) should allow for interesting dialogue, but doesn't. In fact, Scully should be calling in the biohazard folks seen so often in other episodes — for instance, what happens if Eladio, exuding his poisonous enzymes, decides to go to a public pool or visit a mall? Instead, this virulent fungal peril from space is identified as an immigration problem. Sure, but only if you *really* stretch the definition of "immigration."

In the end, there is much here for the cliché seeker, from the suspicious village gossip, to the gun-waving Latin boy bent on vengeance, to the cynical don't-call-me-Mexican Immigration officer. (Ruben Blades' performance as Conrad Lozano is understated and effective, in any case.) Eladio himself seems locked in a maze, unable to escape his miserable circling without money or the magical Green Card. The story even has two contradictory endings as told by the village women — why? Perhaps a gesture to the Chris Carter Uncertainty Principle, or a tip of the hat to Central American literature and its fascination with multiple narration. You could stand it better if the episode didn't end with one of the worst alien costumes ever, coupled with a long, vaguely hateful musing on Mexico, as if it embodied the inner ring of Hell, where unfortunate people, who are reviled as "aliens" (get it?) up north, cross the border and sink without a trace.

4.12 Kaddish

ORIGINAL AIR DATE: February 16, 1997
WRITTEN BY: Howard Gordon
DIRECTED BY: Kim Manners
GUEST CAST: Justine Miceli as Ariel Luria
David Groh as Jacob Weiss
Harrison Coe as Isaac Luria
Channon Roe as Derek Banks
Jabin Litwiniec as Clinton Bascombe
Timur Karabilgin as Tony
Jonathan Whittaker as Curt Brunjes
David Wohl as Kenneth Ungar
George Gordon as the Detective
Murray Rabinovitch as 1st Hasidic man
David Freedman as Rabbi

A suspect in the hate-motivated murder of Hassidic Jew, Isaac Luria, is later found dead — with the murdered Luria's fingerprints all over him — and Scully's suspicion falls on the two most likely to want revenge: Ariel Luria, Isaac's bride-to-be, and her father, Jacob Weiss. But clues lead them to a Hebraic scholar who speaks of a mythical being called the golem, *a body with no soul, which a righteous man can fashion from the earth.*

We see, once again, Scully's discomfort at grave desecration, reminiscent of "Irresistible" and the horrific coffin-rolling scene in the pilot episode. Yet she hunkers down in the grave with Mulder and braves the stench. She bears down on the wretched printer Brunjes with cold determination, and her comfort with the outrageous ideas she is forced to support is a welcome change. It's as if, in this investigation, her methodology can deal with both the occult and scientific explanations, and she feels no need to pick sides. And Anderson's expression on seeing Luria on the security video is worth the whole episode.

4.13 Never Again

ORIGINAL AIR DATE: February 2, 1997
WRITTEN BY: Glen Morgan, James Wong
DIRECTED BY: Rob Bowman
GUEST CAST: Rodney Rowland as Ed Jerse
Carla Stewart as the Judge
Barry "Bear" Hortin as the Bartender
Igor Morozov as Vsevlod Pudovkin
Jan Bailey Mattia as Ms. Hadden
Rita Bozi as Ms. Vansen
Marilyn Chin as Mrs. Shima-Tsuno
Jillian Fargey as Kaye Schilling
B.J. Harrison as Hannah
Natasha Vasiluk as Russian Store Owner
Bill Croft as Comrade Svo
Peter Nadler as Ed's Lawyer

Jen Forgie as Ed's Ex-Wife
Jay Donahue as Detective Gouveia
Ian Robison as Detective Smith

Still struggling with the news of her cancer, Scully accepts a dinner invitation from recently divorced and recently tattooed Ed Jerse, while staking out a tattoo parlor in Philadelphia on the instructions of a vacationing Mulder. Unknown to Scully, Jerse has already murdered one woman, after receiving some highly misogynistic messages from his jealous tattoo, "Betty," who will brook no competition.

Scully's mortality weighs heavily on her in this dark and sad tale. Still keeping the truth from Mulder about her illness, Scully is examining her life and her work and her relationship with Mulder and she is finding them wanting. Her observation that she has no desk, no space, no room of her own bespeaks the blurring of her identity with Mulder's, the conflation of her world into his. Morgan and Wong fill this script with hidden humor, insightful observations, pained moments and loaded language. It is also the sexiest *X-Files* episode yet.

Unable to reveal herself to Mulder, Scully exposes herself completely to a stranger and the two have an immediate chemistry. We learn of the patterns of her life, the circles of repeated behaviour, and repeated rebellions against the authority figures she is (sadly) drawn to all her life. It's a sophisticated exploration of Scully's motivations and Anderson takes flight — particularly when she goes with Ed to get a tattoo (a snake eating its own tail). Anderson and Rowland turn the act of getting a tattoo into the mutual sexual exploration of first-time lovers. Rowland, as Ed, feels every sensation, every intake of breath along with Anderson's Scully. And Anderson charges the mixture of pain and pleasure with Scully's never before seen sexuality. Mark Snow's music and Jon Joffin's stunning photography all enhance the actress's best work to date.

When the morning after brings the truth about Jerse and the hallucinogenic toxins now in both their blood streams, we get a terrific fight sequence which fulfills the promise of violence hinted at in the previous evening's foreplay. Again the camerawork is stunning, just as with the first murder — where a traveling and panning camera moves down the hallway, down a staircase, and to the furnace.

A week apart hasn't warmed the chill in the air; Scully and Mulder are further apart than ever. Mulder is full of snide and sarcastic remarks even when faced with a bruised and battered Scully (wearing the outward scars of her inner battle). His pilgrimage to Graceland hasn't left him with much grace and he's no nearer to recognizing how patronizing he truly can be. As much as he believes it to be, she informs him that not everything is about *him*. He never finishes his reply but his unspoken words hang in the air, louder than the silence.

4.14 Leonard Betts

ORIGINAL AIR DATE: January 26, 1997
WRITTEN BY: Frank Spotnitz, John Shiban, Vince Gilligan
DIRECTED BY: Kim Manners
GUEST CAST: Jennifer Clement as Michele Wilkes
Paul McCrane as Leonard Betts

Lucia Walters as EMT
Marjorie Lovett as Elaine Tanner
Ken Jones as the Bearded Man
Sean Campbell as the Local Cop
Greg Newmeyer as the New Partner
Dave Hurtubise as the Pathologist
Bill Dow as Dr. Charles Burks
Brad Loree as the Security Guard
Peter Bryant as the Uniformed Cop
Don Ackerman as the Night Attendant
Laara Sadiq as the Female EMT
J. Douglas Stewart as the Male EMT

Leonard Betts, an emergency medical technician with amazing diagnostic skills is killed, decapitated actually, when a truck slams into the ambulance his partner is driving. His death will be a loss, to be sure. Well, maybe not . . . apparently Betts finds the loss of his head a mere inconvenience because when the coast is clear he's back on his feet again and out the door.

Just when you thought you were safe from ludicrous plotlines like killer pussycats and ghostly visitors from Mars, along comes "Leonard Betts." This one is a hard sell as Scully and Mulder bicker over Mulder's ludicrous but correct explanation of the events. The *only* way to sell Betts's escape from the morgue *had* to be shoot his reflection in the freezer door. But when a security camera reveals video "interference," obscuring the image of the headless man, even the most earnest suspension of disbelief takes a beating. The story is ludicrous and filled with ludicrous moments. When Scully concludes body-snatching-for-profit, Mulder heads for Betts' apartment and finds a bathtub full of povidone iodine; but why Mulder, in search of a torso, does not look in the torso-sized container is anyone's guess.

The are some fun moments — there would *have* to be! The ever-squeamish Agent Mulder is pressed into service to help Scully dig around in a medical waste container and the look on Duchovny's face is priceless. We get to see the generally unflappable Scully falter when she examines Betts' head and it opens and closes its eyes and mouth. And when Betts is determined to be an entirely cancerous being (and you thought there was only one Cancer Man), gags (literally) abound as the agents stumble across Betts' "snack pack" in the trunk of his Dodge *Dart*. The writers also throw in some classic *X-Files* "winks" to the audience: Betts' new EMT unit number is 208 and Scully is awoken by a nosebleed at 2:08 am.; 208 is also the episode number for "One Breath" — the episode in which Scully is returned (having survived the experiments that are the cause of her disease).

Betts, unlike *X-Files* predators Virgil Incanto and Eugene Tooms, who also kill to survive, is a strangely sympathetic character. It may be because he apologizes beforehand and it may be because he derives no joy from killing. It may be because, unless desperate to survive, Betts uses his unique powers for good and not for evil — helping save lives as an EMT. Adding to all this is the memorable scene of Betts' "rebirth" out of his own body and his cry as he sheds his torso as a snake might his skin. After nearly an hour of silliness the audience is offered the pay-off: a final and wholly shocking confrontation as Betts turns on a lone Scully and utters his, by now, familiar apologia. Scully composes herself long enough to dispose of Betts tidily but her world (and the viewer's) has just been turned upside down. And with this news, Scully's 'arc' is redefined and the horrors begun in "One Breath" and promised in "Nisei" begin to emerge.

4.15 Memento Mori

ORIGINAL AIR DATE: February 9, 1997
WRITTEN BY: Chris Carter, Frank Spotnitz, John Shiban, Vince Gilligan
DIRECTED BY: Rob Bowman
GUEST CAST: David Lovgren as Kurt Crawford
Gillian Barber as Penny Northern
Shiela Larken as Mrs. Scully
Tom Braidwood as Frohike
Dean Haglund as Langly
Bruce Harwood as Byers
William B. Davis as Cigarette-Smoking Man
Mitch Pileggi as Assistant Director Skinner
Julie Bond as The Woman
Morris Panych as The Grey-Haired Man
Sean Allen as Dr. Kevin Scanlon

Scully discovers that she's fatally ill with cancer — just as Leonard Betts prophesied and, ever the rationalist, she accepts her diagnosis with courage, but decides to investigate the possible cause: her abduction. Clues lead back to the MUFON women, all dead now but one, and while Scully decides to take treatment alongside this woman, Mulder follows clues to find a group of hybrid clones who are the "sons" of the MUFON women (including Scully) whose work, it seems, is to find a cure for the cancer that is killing their "mothers" — an answer which lies with the very doctor now helping Scully to die.

This is a terribly dark turn in the myth arc. Issues of motherhood and control rise again, and again they are unnatural (see "Home" for a lighter touch on motherhood). One of the many Kurts pointing blankly at Scully's drawer full of ova would be a sufficiently potent image of a woman's loss of control, but this is nothing compared to Mulder who, in a misplaced gesture of protection (or ownership?), takes a vial of it and puts it in his pocket, glancing at it later with a kind of awe. It ties in with Scully's insistence (in "Never Again") that she owns her life and Mulder's unfinished refutation of that idea.

Scully's "family" enacts three of the five stages of dealing with death: Scully's acceptance is matched by Mrs. Scully's impotent rage and Mulder's frantic bargaining with fate. Skinner's involvement is another step in the eventful role this man plays as buffer for his two agents. (After all, he has been shot, beaten up, and in "Zero Sum" he will be blackmailed because he cares for his agents — or is it *just* Scully?) We get some great acting here, a somber plot development, and a strange tension between Scully's yearning, rambling soliloquy and Mulder's high-tech espionage. Anderson's depiction of an inward-looking Scully is affecting, as is the early warning that Scanlon is evil, when her first sight of him with a brilliant light behind him is distinctly alien.

4.16 Unrequited

ORIGINAL AIR DATE: February 23, 1997
WRITTEN BY: Howard Gordon, Chris Carter
DIRECTED BY: Michael Lange
GUEST CAST: Mitch Pileggi as Assistant Director Skinner
Scott Hylands as General Benjamin Bloch
Peter Lacroix as Nathaniel Teager
Ryan Michael as Agent Cameron Hill
Don McWilliams as P.F.C. Gus Burkholder
Bill Agnew as Lt. General Peter MacDougal
Mark Holden as Agent Eugene Chandler
Larry Musser as Denny Markham
Lesley Ewen as Renee Davenport
Allan Franz as Dr. Ben Keyser
William Nunn as General Jon Steffan
William Taylor as General Leitch
Jen Jasey as Female Private

The murder of two other generals, McDougal and Stefan, by an apparently invisible soldier causes Mulder to theorize that the vet, a Nathaniel Teager, is a POW, who has learned how to use a naturally occurring "blind spot" in everyone's vision as a place to hide and can enter rooms unnoticed and kill at will. The generals he is targeting are a three-man team who orchestrated a cover-up of the fact that the government knew, all along, that American soldiers were still being held captive in Vietnam.

A clunky essay on "looking and not seeing," this is a leisurely hour's worth of our favorite agents (and their boss) flailing around in a crowd while flags wave and marching bands clang. The way Teager pops in and out would seem cheap, if not for Lacroix's unnerving gaze, and the scene where he intones the soldier's mantra (name, rank, serial number, date of birth) is another interesting fragmentation of "Good Old America" into far more interesting shards of moral complexity. This is something *The X-Files* does particularly well. Overall, the viewer's eye is barraged here, the screen busy with color and activity, sometimes zeroing in so tight on someone's eye that this, too, seems "noisy." Perhaps the best element is the plot twist where the "who" doesn't change, while the "why" is turned on its head. But the final scene where Mulder must remind Skinner that he, too, was in Vietnam seems tacked on, as if the writers had only just remembered, too.

4.17 Tempus Fugit

ORIGINAL AIR DATE: March 16, 1997
WRITTEN BY: Chris Carter, Frank Spotnitz
DIRECTED BY: Rob Bowman
GUEST CAST: Mitch Pileggi as Assistant Director Skinner
Joe Spano as Mike Millar
Tom O'Brien as Corporal Frish
Scott Bellis as Max Fenig
Chilton Crane as Sharon Graffia

Brendan Beiser as Agent Pendrell
Greg Michaels as Scott Garrett
Robert Moloney as Bruce Bearfeld
Felicia Shulman as Motel Manager
Rick Dobran as Sargeant Armondo Gonzales
Jerry Schram as Larold Rebhun
David Palffy as Dark Man
Mark Wilson as the Pilot
Marek Wiedman as the Investigator
Jon Raitt as the Father

In this jam-packed two-parter, our agents learn that Max Fenig has died two hours earlier in a plane crash, that a woman claiming to be his sister also claims he was carrying something important (for which the plane was shot down), and that, at the crash site itself, there is a nine-minute difference between the time of the crash and the time on all the victims' watches. When military air-traffic controller, Corporal Frisch, approaches them and admits that he was ordered to lie about the presence of a military jet shadowing the plane, the agents are led to a second crash site in which Mulder finds a body that is definitely not human.

They brought back Max Fenig, the adorable ufologist from "Fallen Angel," only to kill him off again! Still carrying Mulder's business card, and appearing only in flashback, imagination, and home video, our Max has a strange story to tell. In fact, much of the truth is unveiled to the audience but not to Scully and Mulder (especially in the marine retrieval scene in Part *II*, which unfolds with Max's voice-over as a kind of awkward but effective narration). Despite his open demeanor and his life literally ripped apart by his death (his trailer, his little knapsack containing his signature NICAP hat, his mail, even his destroyed body are now up for grabs), Max is still an enigma to us. His "sister" is merely a partner in crime, a fellow sufferer. The object he was carrying (which was simultaneously his reason for living and the cause of his death) is gone.

There are some nice stylistic elements to this piece, not least of which is the stunning crash site itself. The camera starts high, surveying the horror, then descends to mud and puddle level as Scully bends over a body (or a part of a body). Beginning with a birthday celebration (Scully's, as if to make us ask how many more she's got) this episode is beautifully circular, and is filled with a kind of fated violence — against Max, Pendrell, Frisch. Finally, there is the scene where Pendrell goes into shock and the screen dissolves to Mulder, floating in dark water at the second crash site, which links the two "crossings" with each other.

4.18 Max

ORIGINAL AIR DATE: March 23, 1997
WRITTEN BY: Chris Carter, Frank Spotnitz
DIRECTED BY: Kim Manners
GUEST CAST: Mitch Pileggi as Assistant Director Skinner
Joe Spano as Mike Millar
Tom O'Brien as Corporal Frish

Scott Bellis as Max Fenig
Chilton Crane as Sharon Graffia
Brendan Beiser as Agent Pendrell
Greg Michaels as Scott Garrett
Robert Moloney as Bruce Bearfeld
Felicia Shulman as Motel Manager
Rick Dobran as Sargeant Armondo Gonzales
Jerry Schram as Larold Rebhun
David Palffy as Dark Man
Mark Wilson as the Pilot

When the agents search Max's trailer, they find a video tape in which he claims to have stolen proof the government has been studying and using alien technology, but the truth comes when Scully interviews Max's "sister," now institutionalized, who says she stole a piece of alien technology from the military contractor where she worked, an object made of three interlocking parts of which only one remains. Aboard a plane bound for Washington, Mulder and Pendrell's assassin vie for the last piece of the puzzle; but a bright light fills the cabin and . . . when the plane lands the man and the device are gone.

Littered with clues, theories, and extreme events, this compelling two-parter is almost too much. By the time Mulder posits the existence of a second and *third* aircraft we are in danger of losing him. It is too much info, too fast. And yet this episode is nonetheless a wild success, almost because of the piling on of information. The cruel trick of bringing Max back two hours after he's died makes one want to imagine, throughout the first part, that this is a clone, a dream, a lie — Max must be alive. The linking of Max to Mulder, and Pendrell to Scully is deliberate, Mulder's blood-spattered business card serving as a visual reminder of the kind of bad luck that seems to dog those close to him. Finally, the "mythology" content, while considerable, is dwarfed by the more realistic elements of this story: the crash site, the twisted debris filling a dark hangar, the destruction of innocents, both known and anonymous. Perhaps the highlight of both episodes comes when Mulder describes his guess at the chain of events in an imagined scene right out of *Fearless*. There is a leisure to the way the scene is shot, the long silent moments as Max's body hangs in the air, hammering home the cruelty of "minutes to live." There is a movie's worth of material in these two parts and the level of acting is far above the usual TV show. Joe Spano as Mike Millar is as close to being a real person as possible on *The X-Files*, and the fact that his resistance to Mulder is *not* a factor of his being part of the conspiracy is beyond refreshing.

4.19 Synchrony

ORIGINAL AIR DATE: April 13, 1997
WRITTEN BY: Howard Gordon, David Greenwalt
DIRECTED BY: Jim Charleston
GUEST CAST: Jed Rees as Lucas Menand
Joseph Fuqua as Jason Nichols
Michael Fairman as Lisa Ianelli
Hiro Kanagwa as Dr. Yonechi

Jonathan Walker as Chuck Lukerman
Brent Chapman as Security Cop
Eric Buermeyer as the Bus Driver
Patricia Idlette as the Desk Clerk
Austin Basile as Bellman
Alison Matthews as the Doctor

Scully and Mulder pursue an old man who seems bent on destroying the best and brightest grad students working on ultra-powerful freezing agents. Back from the future, armed with the very technology these young people will eventually invent, he turns out to be one of them — very aged — come back to save the world from the implications of his own work.

If you could go back and knock off J. Robert Oppenheimer (the grandfather of nuclear technology), would you? This is the thesis at hand in this confused story. Vaguely plausible extrapolations from quantum theory aside, this initially suspenseful piece begins to wade through its own detritus about halfway through. Never mind the logical snarls inherent in "time travel" stories, what about the narrative missteps? Why didn't Old Nichols end up like Yonechi, if by implication his body has been through the same process? What was a grad student doing supervising the team of doctors? Does aging 30 years make you unrecognizable, even to yourself? And finally, the idea that "the same matter from different time periods cannot co-exist" is a statement proceeding from a model of logic, not pyrotechnics. However, there is something *chilling* about the final shot and its implications.

4.20 Small Potatoes

ORIGINAL AIR DATE: April 20, 1997
WRITTEN BY: Vince Gilligan
DIRECTED BY: Clifford Bole
GUEST CAST: Mitch Pileggi as Assistant Director Skinner
Christine Cavanaugh as Amanda Nelligan
Constance Barnes as O.R. Nurse
Carrie Cain Sparks as Duty Nurse
Monica Gemmer as Second Nurse
Darin Morgan as Eddie Van Blundht
P. Lynn Johnson as Health Department Doctor
David Cameron as the Deputy

When five babies are born with tails in the sleepy town of Martinsburg, West Virginia, all sharing the same genetic father, things look pretty hot for the local fertility doctor, until Mulder spots a janitor with sagging trousers and an oddly tail-like scar on his backside. Eddie Van Blundht has the ability to alter his appearance (which is how he duped all those women) and, needing to get out of town, he takes on Mulder's appearance — with hilarious and telling results.

This is a charming episode with an excellent performance by Darin Morgan as nice-guy loser Eddie Van Blundht — with an H please! (Look for the shot of the H falling off the front of Eddie's house.) The fact that the "monster," Eddie, is nicer, warmer, and more human than anyone else on screen is a welcome surprise, and his reactions (to the way Mulder lives, to Skinner's gruff authority, to Scully's loneliness) work as a wry comment on what oddballs the fans have become attached to.

This is also an eye-opener for those who claim Duchovny's range is limited. His face is an open book as the inner Eddie listens to a former girlfriend laugh about him, as he takes guff from Skinner for spelling errors, or as he mocks for the mirror, checking out his gorgeous new look in minute detail. This recalls some other teasing Mulder has taken (most notably in "Humbug") for being just *too GQ*. Interesting to see Mulder literally kick Scully's door down, eyes ablaze, when something he really values (her attachment to him) is threatened. For her part, Anderson is hilarious in her pursuit of more idiocy from the poor girl who thinks the father of her child is Luke Skywalker, silkily asking if he brought his light saber, while Mulder squirms with embarrassment in the background. Her girlish happiness as Mulder/Eddie laps up her dull tales of college hijinks is as comic as her amazement when Mulder swoops in for a kiss and seems to hover in an ecstasy of waiting. But there's a tinge of sadness here, too. Scully's slow warming to the 'new' Mulder, her obvious gladness for the change, is a little heartbreaking. Virtually a sleight-of-hand aimed at relationship-driven fans, this episode nonetheless rocks the world of both our agents, leaving each a little different and, sadly, a little more alone.

4.21 Zero Sum

ORIGINAL AIR DATE: April 27, 1997
WRITTEN BY: Howard Gordon, Frank Spotnitz
DIRECTED BY: Kim Manners
GUEST CAST: Mitch Pileggi as Assistant Director Skinner
William B. Davis as Cigarette-Smoking Man
Don S. Williams as 1st Elder
Morris Panych as Gray-Haired Man
Lisa Stewart as Jane Brody
Nicolle Nattrass as Misty
Fred Keating as Detective Hugel
Allan Gray as Dr. Peter Valedespino
Theresa Puskar as Mrs. Kemper
Barry Creene as Dr. Emile Linzer
Paul McLean as Special Agent Kautz
John Moore as 2nd Elder
Laurie Holden as Marita Covarrubias

We are treated to the incredible sight of Skinner 'sanitizing' a crime scene where a postal worker has been unaccountably stung to death by bees; he steals and incinerates the victim's body, tampers with evidence at the FBI lab under the assumed name of Fox Mulder, and erases all evidence of the case from Mulder's computer — all of it stemming from a deal he has made with Cigarette-Smoking Man in the balance of which hangs Scully's life. But when Mulder turns out to be more tenacious than he thought, and a witness turns up dead, Skinner finds himself cornered, double-crossed by Cigarette-Smoking Man, with Mulder closing in, and he must find a way out before an incriminating photograph is revealed.

Skinner shows both his stratospheric tolerance for pressure and, apparently, his training in the dark science of covering up in this episode. Along the way, Carter seems to resuscitate, weave together, and confuse many earlier themes. Again we meet the bees, this time carrying cholera (remember the bees from "Colony" and the flies from "Blood"?). Again we suffer Marita Covarrubias as she lets negligible morsels of info slip from her apparently numb lips. Again, we see Cigarette-Smoking Man show no fear of would-be assassins. But, in general, this is Skinner's show, from the cool first sight of him "sanitizing" a crime scene, to the revelation of his "deal with the devil," to his veiled surprise that Mulder is good at his job, as Mulder unknowingly helps tighten the vise.

Incorporating references to films like *Pulp Fiction* and *No Way Out*, this episode has its local origins in Skinner's warning to Mulder in "Memento Mori." Breathless and claustrophobic in its intensity, this plot presses Skinner hard enough to force an amazing character into the light. The initial shots are meant to shock the audience into assuming Skinner is, and always has been, one of "them." But this is quickly turned around. His urgency to "save" Scully, his willing self-sacrifice, speak to an undercurrent of something approaching yearning in Skinner, and one wonders, once again, what motivates the man.

4.22 Elegy

ORIGINAL AIR DATE: May 4, 1997
WRITTEN BY: John Shiban
DIRECTED BY: Jim Charleston
GUEST CAST: Steven M. Porter as Harold Spuller
Alex Bruhanski as Angelo Pintero
Sydney Lassick as Chuck Forsch
Nancy Fish as Nurse Innes
Daniel Kamin as Detective Hudak
Lorena Gale as The Attorney
Mike Puttonen as Martin Alpert
Christine Willes as Karen Kosseff
Ken Tremblett as Uniformed Officer
Gerry Naim as Sergeant Conneff

Investigating what looks like another of Mulder's nutbar stories, Scully has what amounts to her first real "sighting": a blonde coed, bleeding from the neck, trying to say the words "she is me." This links her to an autistic man, a series of brutal murders, and a number of ordinary people who have nothing in common except that they, too, have seen similar apparitions — and they are all about to die.

A scary ride for Scully fans, this eerily beautiful episode seems to put the final nail in any hope for her survival. The sighting is undeniable and, rhetorically, it seals her doom. Carter takes us on a slow descent into a world driven by the disastrous logic of nightmares. Even senseless things come to make sense, like bowling alley employee Harold Spuller's manic repetition of numbers turning out to be a full recital of each victim's bowling scores, as if by repeating the numbers he keeps the girls in the world with him.

Except perhaps for the slightly campy back story for Nurse Innes, played by (Joan Rivers look-alike) Nancy Fish, this is a solid story. It is also a very well-acted episode, with at least one stunning piece of work from Anderson as she follows the unearthly murmuring to see its horrifying source. Of course, this is a first for Scully: an impossibility that she nonetheless *believes*. She gives herself the usual outs, stress, suggestibility, but for once she and Mulder are in synch and these rational excuses mean as little to her as they have always meant to him. And there are other firsts: she openly talks about her reliance on Mulder's work with the FBI psychiatrist and she actually *admits* to Mulder what she has seen. Interestingly, he reacts angrily at not being told sooner, just as Mrs. Scully did in "Memento Mori" and as he himself did in "Beyond the Sea" when she, similarly, followed her intuition into a dangerous situation. In this episode, her illness, her life and death, are connected in an overt way to Mulder's quest. It's as though, in submitting to the wild logic of her experiences, she will die.

4.23 Demons

ORIGINAL AIR DATE: May 11, 1997
WRITTEN BY: R.W. Goodwin
DIRECTED BY: Kim Manners
GUEST CAST: Jay Acovone as Detective Joe Curtis
Mike Nussbaum as Dr. Charles Goldstein
Chris Owens as Young Cigarette-Smoking Man
Rebecca Toolan as Mrs. Mulder
Andrew Johnston as Medical Examiner
Terry Jang Barclay as Imhof
Vanessa Morley as Young Samantha
Eric Breker as Admitting Officer
Rebecca Harker as Housekeeper
Shelley Adam as Young Mrs. Mulder
Dean Aylesworth as Young Bill Mulder
Alex Haythorne as Young Mulder

Mulder awakes on a Rhode Island motel-room floor in a blood-soaked shirt after experiencing a highly charged flashback to his childhood, but he has "lost" several days and is clearly the prime suspect in the death of two locals (his gun is missing two rounds). Scully's investigation reveals that Mulder, like the victims, has been undergoing a dangerous and unreliable "therapy" to unearth long-buried childhood memories.

Mulder's childhood and the mystery of Mrs. Mulder's "choice" are revisited in this stylish, fast-paced episode. There are two mysteries, actually. There is the straightforward unraveling of Mulder's missing days and there is the more intriguing question of what lies in Mulder's buried memories. With the single-mindedness we've come to know so well, Mulder travels inward to confront repressed childhood events and Duchovny doesn't flinch at exposing that obsession. When Mulder confronts his mother about the night in question and about the role of Cigarette-Smoking Man in the Mulder family history, Duchovny presents his character as a shuffling, angry twelve-year-old.

It is to Scully that Mulder turns in a crisis and she makes it to his side at breakneck speed after getting a call from him at 5:00 a.m. Scully is a picture of efficiency as she moves through a personal, then medical, then professional checklist of what might be wrong and what is known. Despite Scully's protests (what's new?) and Mulder's repeated seizures, each bringing more details of that fateful night, Mulder pushes forward to solve the mystery of the missing days. Scully's loyalty to her partner gets a real workout in this episode, especially after he ditches her in pursuit of more drugs and more memories. But Scully sets aside her concerns for her own health and safety, travels to the Mulder summer house, and walks in unprotected to face a suicidal-homicidal partner.

This episode is as sad a Mulder story as "Never Again" is for Scully. And it is another in a series of *X-Files* stories about the unreliable nature of memory. While Mulder continues to plumb new depths of self-involvement and obsession, it is Scully, dying of cancer, who can see the difficulty of his re-living and retrieving his past in order to discover the present. Hers is a loving act when she repeats her entreaty of "Nisei" and asks Mulder to let go of the past.

4.24 Gethsemane

ORIGINAL AIR DATE: May 18, 1997
WRITTEN BY: Chris Carter
DIRECTED BY: R.W. Goodwin
GUEST CAST: John Finn as Michael Kritschgau
Matthew Walker as Arlinsky
James Sutorius as Babcock
Sheila Larken as Mrs. Scully
Pat Skipper as Bill Scully Jr.
John Oliver as Rolston
Charles Cioffi as Scott Blevins
Steve Makha as Ostelhoff
Nancy Kerr as Agent Hedin
Barry W. Levy as Vitagliano
Arnie Walters as Father McCue
Rob Freeman as Detective Rempulski
Craig Burnanski as Saw Operator

The shock of the opening scene wherein Scully makes her way through a crowd of detectives and police officers to a body on the floor of Mulder's apartment and identifies it with a nod as "him" is quickly eclipsed by her appearance before a boardroom filled with FBI department heads (including Scott Blevins, the man who originally assigned her to the X-files). She states she has come (in an apparent betrayal of the highest order) to report on the illegitimacy of Mulder's work, to show how he became a victim of his own misguided quest and belief in the existence of extraterrestrials, and to report that Mulder has died of an apparent self-inflicted gunshot wound to the head.

Scully, having been pulled from a family dinner, is drawn into what appears to be another one of Mulder's wild "gray-chases." But Scully has had enough. The weight of her mortality is pressing in on her and Scully finally voices some of what has remained unspoken between herself and Mulder since "Never Again." What she doesn't tell him (as usual) is that the cancer has begun to spread. She is dying.

We soon see the agents engaged in a familiar argument. Mulder wants to believe and Scully cannot. This time the stakes are at their highest. Scully believes she has "proof" of Mulder's misguided belief in the authenticity of an alien corpse in the person of (the all-too-conveniently identified) Michael Kritschgau. When Mulder pushes Scully to defend her belief in Kritschgau's assertions of manipulation, the final blow upon the many bruises of this season is dealt. Scully was given her cancer to make Mulder believe.

Scully's life and death are connected in an overt way to Mulder's quest — a literalization of the cost of faith. The revelation that her cancer was given to her to convince him of "truth" of extraterrestrial life occasions the first time she has confronted him with his own unwitting complicity. Samantha may be the "holy grail" of Mulder's quest but Scully is clearly the "sacrificial lamb." If it is a lie, it is a profoundly cruel one and more effective than any other tactic could have been. After all, Scully abandons Mulder, and Mulder (apparently) dies by his own hand.

Anderson is terrific, as she pounds through a car park in pursuit of Kritschgau and as she listens to his revelations. Even in this darkest of tales the writers have some fun: Michael Kritschgau is the name of a former classmate of Gillian Anderson who was quoted in a recent issue of *People* magazine that featured Anderson's high school punk look in a school photo.

Anderson is perfectly marvelous as she ranges from calm denial to her family and Mulder of the seriousness of her illness, to weariness at the pursuit of Mulder's vision, to her shattering report that Mulder is dead. Duchovny proves again that less is more in his subtle portrayal of Mulder's despair as he fails to cocoon himself against the pain of the truth with old tapes of a 1972 NASA symposium on the possibility of life on other planets. His performance is heartbreaking (possibly his best to date) and the view of Mulder alone in the cold blue of the television screen is in sharp contrast to the candlelit warmth of the Scully household that opened the hour. Carter has offered a perfect puzzle in this show and cashed in all the chips built up over this season.

In this shocking fourth-season cliffhanger Chris Carter demands more than mere suspension of disbelief. He demands that we, like our heroes, forget everything we've seen in four years and that we, like them, are about to be used. We *want* to believe that it's all a lie. The question, as always, is which lies to accept and which to reject. Mulder has been left for dead before in season cliffhangers and two-parters, and though we know the actors have signed to return for a fifth season it does appear that Carter has painted himself into a corner this time. We can only hope that the it-was-all-a-dream cheat of "who shot J.R.?" is not being repeated with the variation "it-was-all-a-lie." While modems across the nation light up as fans get onto the Internet and swap theories, we'll just have to wait and see.

APPENDIX

LIST OF DIRECTORS

DIRECTOR	EPISODE	NO.	AIR DATE
Bole, Cliff	Small Potatoes	4.20	4/20/97
Bowman, Rob	731	3.10	12/1/95
	Aubrey	2.12	1/6/95
	Dod Kalm	2.19	3/10/95
	End Game	2.17	2/17/95
	F. Emasculata	2.22	4/28/95
	Field Where I Died	4.05	11/3/96
	Fresh Bones	2.15	2/3/95
	GenderBender	1.13	1/21/94
	Jose Chung's "From Outer Space"	3.20	4/12/96
	Memento Mori	4.15	2/9/97
	Never Again	4.13	2/2/97
	Our Town	2.24	5/12/95
	Paper Clip	3.02	9/29/95
	Paper Hearts	4.08	12/15/96
	Piper Maru	3.15	2/9/96
	Pusher	3.17	2/23/96
	Sleepless	2.04	10/7/94
	Syzygy	3.13	1/26/96
	Tempus Fugit pt. 1 of 2	4.17	3/16/97
	Terma	4.10	12/1/96
	Unruhe	4.02	10/27/96
	Walk, The	3.07	11/10/95
	Wetwired	3.23	5/10/96
Carter, Chris	Duane Barry	2.05	10/14/94
	List, The	3.05	10/20/95
Charleston, James	Avatar	3.21	4/26/96
	Elegy	4.22	5/4/97
	Synchrony	4.19	4/13/97
	Teliko	4.04	10/18/96
Contner, James	Soft Light	2.23	5/5/95
Freedman, Jerrold	Ghost in the Machine	1.06	10/29/93

Gates, Tucker	El Mundo Gira	4.11	1/12/97
	Hell Money	3.19	3/29/96
Gerber, Fred	Eve	1.10	12/10/93
Goodwin, R.W.	Anasazi	2.25	5/19/95
	Blessing Way, The	3.01	9/22/95
	Erlenmeyer Flask, The	1.23	5/13/94
	Gethsemane	4.24	5/18/97
	Herrenvolk	4.01	10/4/96
	One Breath	2.08	11/11/94
	Talitha Cumi	3.24	5/17/96
Gordon, Howard & Alex Gansa	Born Again	1.21	4/29/94
Graham, William	E.B.E.	1.16	2/18/94
	Space	1.08	11/12/93
Katleman, Michael	Shadows	1.05	10/22/93
Lange, Michael	Ascension	2.06	10/21/94
	Miracle Man	1.17	3/18/94
	Unrequited	4.16	2/23/97
	Young at Heart	1.15	2/11/94
Longstreet, Harry	Squeeze	1.02	9/24/93
Mandel, Robert	Pilot: "The X-Files"	1.00	9/10/93
Manners, Kim	Apocrypha	3.16	2/16/96
	D.P.O.	3.03	10/6/95
	Demons	4.23	5/11/97
	Die Hand Die Verletzt	2.14	1/27/95
	Grotesque	3.14	2/2/96
	Home	4.03	10/11/96
	Humbug	2.20	3/31/95
	Kaddish	4.12	2/16/97
	Leonard Betts	4.14	1/26/97
	Max pt 2 of 2	4.18	3/23/97
	Oubliette	3.08	11/17/95
	Quagmire	3.22	5/3/96
	Sanguinarium	4.06	11/10/96
	Teso Dos Bichos	3.18	3/8/96
	Tunguska	4.09	11/24/96
	War of the Coprophages	3.12	1/5/96
	Zero Sum	4.21	4/27/97
Marck, Nick	Colony	2.16	2/10/95
Napolitano, Joe	Darkness Falls	1.19	4/15/94
	The Jersey Devil	1.04	10/8/93
Nutter, David	2 Shy	3.06	11/3/95
	3	2.07	11/4/94
	Beyond the Sea	1.12	1/7/94
	Blood	2.03	9/30/94
	Clyde Bruckman's Final Repose	3.04	10/13/95
	Firewalker	209	11/18/94
	Ice	1.07	11/5/93
	Irresistible	2.13	1/13/95

	Lazarus	1.14	2/4/94
	Little Green Men	2.01	9/16/94
	Nisei	3.09	11/24/95
	Revelations	3.11	12/15/95
	Roland	1.22	5/6/94
	Shapes	1.18	4/1/94
	Tooms	1.20	4/22/94
Phelps, Win	Red Museum	2.10	12/9/94
Sackheim, Daniel	Conduit	1.03	10/1/93
	Deep Throat	1.01	9/17/93
	Host, The	2.02	9/23/94
Shaw, Larry	Fallen Angel	1.09	11/19/93
	Fire	1.11	12/17/93
Surjik, Stephen	Excelsis Dei	2.11	12/16/94
Vejar, Michael	Calusari, The	2.21	4/14/95
Whitmore, Jr., James	Fearful Symmetry	2.18	2/24/95
Wong, James	Musings of a Cigarette		
	Smoking Man	4.07	11/17/96

LIST OF WRITERS

WRITER(S)	EPISODE	NO.	AIR DATE
Barber, Larry & Paul Barber			
	GenderBender	1.13	1/21/94
Beck, Mat			
	Wetwired	3.23	5/10/96
Biller, Kenneth & Chris Brancato			
	Eve	1.10	12/10/93
Brown, Paul			
	Ascension	2.06	10/21/94
	Excelsis Dei	2.11	12/16/94
Carter, Chris			
	Anasazi	2.25	5/19/95
	story by: David Duchovny & Chris Carter		
	Blessing Way, The	3.01	9/22/95
	Colony	2.16	2/10/95
	story by: Chris Carter & David Duchovny		
	Darkness Falls	1.19	4/15/94
	Deep Throat	1.01	9/17/93
	Duane Barry	2.05	10/14/94
	Erlenmeyer Flask, The	1.23	5/13/94

Pusher	3.17	2/23/96	
Small Potatoes	4.20	4/20/97	
Soft Light	2.23	5/5/95	
Unruhe	4.02	10/27/96	

Gilligan, Vince &
  John Shiban &
  Frank Spotnitz

Leonard Betts	4.14	1/26/97

Goodwin, R.W.

Demons	4.23	5/11/97

Gordon, Howard

Avatar	3.21	4/26/96

  story by: David Duchovny &
  Howard Gordon

D.P.O.	3.03	10/6/95
Firewalker	2.09	11/18/94
Fresh Bones	2.15	2/3/95
Grotesque	3.14	2/2/96
Kaddish	4.12	2/16/97
Sleepless	2.04	10/7/94
Teliko	4.04	10/18/96

Gordon, Howard &
  Alex Gansa

Born Again	1.21	4/29/94
Dod Kalm	2.19	3/10/95
Fallen Angel	1.09	11/19/93

Gordon, Howard &
  Chris Carter

Miracle Man	1.17	3/18/94
Unrequited	4.16	2/23/97

  story by Howard Gordon

Gordon, Howard &
  David Greenwalt

Synchrony	4.19	4/13/97

Gordon, Howard &
  Frank Spotnitz

Zero Sum	4.21	4/27/97

Kaufer, Scott &
  Chris Carter

Young at Heart	1.15	2/11/94

Mayhew, Valerie &
  Vivian Mayhew

Sanguinarium	4.06	11/10/96

Morgan, Darin

Clyde Bruckman's Final Repose	3.04	10/13/95
Humbug	2.20	3/31/95
Jose Chung's "From Outer Space"	3.20	4/12/96
War of the Coprophages	3.12	1/5/96

Morgan, Glen			
	Musings of a Cigarette Smoking Man	4.07	11/17/96
Morgan, Glen & James Wong			
	3	2.07	11/4/94
	Beyond the Sea	1.12	1/7/94
	Blood	2.03	9/30/94
	Die Hand Die Verletzt	2.14	1/27/95
	E.B.E.	1.16	2/18/94
	Field Where I Died	4.05	11/3/96
	Home	4.03	10/11/96
	Ice	1.07	11/5/93
	Little Green Men	2.01	9/16/94
	Never Again	4.13	2/2/97
	One Breath	2.08	11/11/94
	Shadows	1.05	10/22/93
	Squeeze	1.02	9/24/93
	Tooms	1.20	4/22/94
Newton, Kim			
	Quagmire	3.22	5/3/96
	Revelations	3.11	12/15/95
Osborn, Marilyn			
	Shapes	1.18	4/1/94
Shiban, John			
	El Mundo Gira	4.11	1/12/97
	Elegy	4.22	5/4/97
	Teso Dos Bichos	3.18	3/8/96
	Walk, The	3.07	11/10/95
Spotnitz, Frank			
	731	3.10	12/1/95
	End Game	2.17	2/17/95
	Our Town	2.24	5/12/95
Spotnitz, Frank & Chris Carter			
	Apocrypha	3.16	2/16/96
	Piper Maru	3.15	2/9/96
	Terma	4.10	12/1/96
	Tunguska	4.09	11/24/96
Vlaming, Jeff			
	2Shy	3.06	11/3/95
	Hell Money	3.19	3/29/96

Sure. Fine. Whatever.